LINERS, TANKERS
& MERCHANT SHIPS

LINERS, TANKERS
& MERCHANT SHIPS

ROBERT JACKSON

Grange BOOKS

This edition first published in 2002 for Grange Books
An imprint of Grange Books plc
The Grange
Kingsnorth Industrial Estate
Hoo, Nr Rochester
Kent ME3 9ND
www.grangebooks.co.uk

Reprinted in 2003

ISBN: 1-84013-477-1

Editorial and design:
Amber Books Ltd.
Bradley's Close
74–77 White Lion Street
London N1 9PF

Project Editor: Naomi Waters
Design: Floyd Sayers

Printed in Singapore

PICTURE CREDITS
TRH Pictures

ARTWORK CREDITS
All artworks supplied by De Agostini, Tony Gibbons and
Mainline Design (Guy Smith)

CONTENTS

Introduction

This book is a pictorial record of the most interesting, innovative and important merchant ships that have sailed the oceans of the world, or plied its lakes and rivers, since the earliest times, from the river barges of ancient Egypt to the huge container ships and cruise liners of today. As such, it provides a comprehensive guide to merchant vessels from every historical period, and also gives an insight into the factors that have influenced ship design and operation over the centuries.

Changes in the nature of ships comes about thanks to progress in developing new materials and methods. Until the start of the industrial revolution, the state of the shipbuilder's art, and his technology, changed very slowly. Then, quite suddenly, the whole world was transformed, and a definite divide in maritime history opened up. Although we may not be able to pin the watershed between ancient and modern down to any one year, or

Above: A group of Arabian 'dhows' at the beginning of the twentieth century. Their basic form has not changed for centuries, and they can still be seen today.

even decade, it definitely lies at some point just this side of the introduction of the all-iron hull, the screw propeller, the vertical compound steam engine and the water-tube boiler – in other words, near the mid-point of the second half of the nineteenth century. Looking back, it seems clear that the ship, more than any other single entity, benefited from the technological advances of that period.

Yet the ships of the age of steam may best be described as ugly and functional, displaying none of the grace that characterized, say, the ships of the Pharaohs and the Phoenicians, which were sophisticated and quite beautiful objects, their hulls carefully formed to a shape which cut cleanly through the water. As far as we know, these peoples knew nothing at all about streamlining or theoretical hydrodynamics, but they certainly knew what fish and aquatic mammals looked like, and sought to copy their attributes. Not all ships in ancient times were so shapely, though, for seafarers had already begun to make the distinction between the hull form of merchant ships and that of warships. Even in the earliest times, cargo ships tended to be deep, beamy craft, well adapted to the carriage of barrels, bales and other bulky cargo, and designed with an eye towards capacity rather than speed.

THE TRANSITION FROM SAIL TO STEAM

By the later years of the seventeenth century, the European merchant ship had developed to a point where it was fully capable of making long ocean passages in comparative safety, if not comfort. The great age of exploration was at its zenith; much of the earth's surface had been mapped, and trade followed in the wake of these intrepid explorers. As far as shipbuilding was concerned, the pace of change was to slacken over the next century and a half, as the wooden sailing ship reached the limits of its materials and technology. The hardwood forests of Europe were becoming exhausted, and shipbuilders were turning to India and North America for the raw material they needed. But the change that would sweep the 'wooden walls' from the seas was on the horizon. By the end of the second decade of the 19th century steam engines were regularly (if not commonly) to be found in small

Right: The Sedov, *a four-masted barque was built at Kiel in Germany in 1921 as the* Magdalene Vinnen. *At the end of World War II she was handed over to the Soviet authorities. Now named* Sedov, *she is the world's biggest wind-jammer in commission, and is a very popular sail training ship.*

ships, at first on inland waterways, but soon on short sea passages too. Iron had already made its appearance as a construction medium, first of all in the form of the towed barge, but shortly afterwards in self-propelled ships also.

The transition from wooden sailing ships to iron and steel steamers took a surprisingly short time. Despite an excursion down a dead-end road – the paddlewheel – it was completed in under half a century. The change came fastest, and was almost complete, in the world's navies. Steam-powered merchant ships were rather slower to catch on, except on certain specific routes – the North Atlantic route from Liverpool to New York, for example, and on short crossings like the English Channel – chiefly because the space their fuel bunkers occupied consumed too much of the available cargo capacity. It was not until significant refinements in steam engine technology reduced their fuel consumption dramatically that merchant steamships finally

Above: Nedloyd Africa *is typical of the container ships that ply the world's ocean's today. Containerization has completely transformed the handling of cargo in port, and the types of cargoes that can be carried over vast distances.*

took over from sailing ships. In essence, even if a steamer could make three voyages to a sailing ship's one, it was still only worthwhile in economic terms on high-traffic routes for the carriage of passengers and perishable cargo. Ironically, the introduction of iron and steel as shipbuilding materials gave the sailing ship a new lease of life, albeit for a short period. In the last half of the nineteenth century, the composite wood-on-iron tea clippers enjoyed a brief heyday. They, in turn, were succeeded by all-metal barques and barquentines with four, five and even six masts, which continued to serve well into the twentieth century, particularly in the nitrate fertilizer trade from Chile to North America and Europe.

INCREASING DIVERSIFICATION IN MERCHANT SHIPS

The last third of the nineteenth century saw a drastic reduction in the size of powerplants, together with huge increases in their efficiency, thanks to the development of new types of boiler and compound multi-cylinder engines operating at previously impossible temperatures and pressures. These engines found application in warships and merchantmen alike, bringing unheard-of speed to the former and fuel economy to the latter. Then, a young engineer named Charles Parsons startled the Royal Navy with an unofficial demonstration of what was a truly revolutionary new powerplant, the steam turbine, at the Diamond Jubilee Naval Review at Spithead in 1897. With new, much more powerful engines available to them, naval architects began to increase the size of their designs, and maritime legends like the ill-fated *Titanic* were born. The primary purpose of such vessels was to carry both passengers and mail at high speed across the Atlantic, and by the time the *Titanic* had her unfortunate encounter with the iceberg in 1912 ship design had followed a number of specialist paths. By 1900 oil tankers, refrigerated carriers and bulk carriers had all been built in considerable numbers to sail alongside general cargo vessels and passenger liners.

World War I saw an enormous increase in mercantile marine traffic, and an even greater diversification of the number and type of ships. The emergency shipbuilding programmes of 1914-18 meant that large numbers of merchant vessels were available as cheap surplus after the end of hostilities, leading to the foundation of new merchant fleets across the world. After 1945, too, a huge influx of shipping to the world's merchant fleets coincided with a vast increase in manufacturing capacity, first of all in the West, then in Asia, and this led to further developments in maritime operations, particularly in the way cargo was handled.

The post-war years saw a gradual change in design, in passenger liners as well as merchant vessels, with a growing tendency to place the engines either right aft or three-quarters aft. This meant that most of the cargo space was located forward of the engine room and the navigation bridge incorporated in the poop superstructure, the resulting much higher bridge structure compensating in some measure for the attendant loss of forward visibility. A further development was the introduction of a navigation tower to replace the usual bridge, forward visibility being assisted by a TV monitor installed in the vessel's stem. Funnels also went into redesign, the twin 'stove-pipe' arrangement becoming a common feature of passenger liners, cargo vessels, tankers and tugs alike.

Two main areas of seaborne trade suffered during this period. The first was the decline, followed by the virtual disappearance of the carriage of passengers on long routes, the jet airliner providing a comfortable and speedy alternative, and the few remaining ocean liners survived for a time as cruise ships. In the last two years of the twentieth century, it was the cruise industry that gave impetus to the design of new and graceful ships; vessels like the purpose-built sail-assisted cruise liner Club Med 1, a remarkable marriage of modern technology and traditional grace. She can operate under sail alone, with a computer monitoring her progress and automatically switching to engine power if required.

The second area was the reduction of coastal general cargo traffic, as road haulage became increasingly popular. On the other hand, the change from coal to oil fuel ashore led to an increase in coastal and estuarine tanker traffic. In this context, the second half of the twentieth century witnessed a revolution in the transportation of oil and natural gas. This was the age of the supertanker, which was developed in response to the maritime chaos caused by the closure of the Suez Canal by the Egyptian government in 1956, an event that led to an unfortunate intervention by Britain and France on the one hand, and Israel on the other.

The architects of the supertanker could not perhaps have forseen the catastrophic effects on the environment that might be generated by an accident. Today we have witnessed such effects on numerous occasions all around the world, from Alaska to Great Britain, and we have seen the development of specialist vessels to cope with such emergencies. Giant strides have also been made in the technology of rescue and recovery vessels – vessels purpose-made to deal with any emergency at sea.

Above: P&O's newest superliner, Aurora, *seen during trials in the North Sea. She sailed on her maiden cruise from Southampton, England, on 1 May 2000. At 77,219 tonnes (76,000 tons) and accommodating 1874 passengers plus 850 crew,* Aurora *is the largest vessel in P&O's fleet.*

NEW FIELDS OF DISCOVERY

The exploitation of the earth's natural resources has also led to a new age of exploration, and a new breed of ship. Just as the explorers of Captain Cook's era charted the surface of the earth, these vessels and their crews today chart its sub-surface, mapping the ocean floor and sounding its geological formation to detect further vast reservoirs of oil and gas which will be opened up in years to come. These hi-tech vessels and their crews are the modern-day equivalent of Captain Columbus who set sail to discover whole new worlds. Today, that new world lies below the ocean's surface.

In this book, divided into broad sections covering all aspects of merchant shipping, the reader will find a wealth of information on the diverse range of vessels, ancient and modern, that have enabled the world of maritime commerce to flourish over the centuries.

Early Ships

Brig

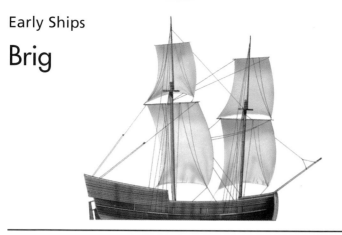

The word 'brig' is a shortened form of the earlier 'brigantine', a name possibly derived from 'brigand', signifying that vessels of this type were originally used as pirate ships. By 1695, however, the word brigantine was used to describe any two-masted ship with the foremast square-rigged and the mainmast fore-and-aft–rigged. The brig evolved from this design as being square-rigged on both masts, but with a fore-and-aft sail rigged on gaff, and boom abaft the mainmast. Both terms were later used to refer to vessels with differing kinds of two-masted rig. In the seventeenth and eighteenth centuries, the brig was the maid-of-all-work of the North Sea trade; it was small enough to be handled by the minimum crew, but had enough capacity to carry a worthwhile cargo. The Dutch example shown here evolved as both a merchant vessel and a 14-gun warship.

Country of origin:	The Netherlands
Date of origin:	1610
Length:	19.8m (65ft)
Beam:	6m (20ft)
Displacement:	162.5 tonnes (160 tons)
Rigging:	Two masts, square-rigged with course and topsail
Complement:	12
Main routes:	North Sea coastal routes
Cargo:	Timber, ore, general goods

Caravel

The caravel emerged from the basic form of a thirteenth-century Iberian fishing boat, enlarged, decked, and fitted with first two, and then later three, masts. The three-masted caravel was the finest sailing ship of its time, capable of oceanic voyages of unprecedented length. Its capacity, sailing qualities and weatherliness gave captains the confidence to take long voyages in unknown waters; it was in a caravel that Bartholomew Diaz rounded the Cape of Good Hope in 1487. With the encouragement of the Portuguese Prince Henry the Navigator, the type's progress was driven, rather than evolutionary. The caravel was originally lateen-rigged, but many were converted to square rigging on the foremast and mainmast, notably *Pinta* and *Niña*, the ships in which Christopher Columbus sailed to the New World. The caravel was later replaced on the routes it had pioneered by ships of greater capacity.

Country of origin:	Portugal
Date of origin:	1470
Length:	22.9m (75ft)
Beam:	7.6m (25ft)
Displacement:	61 tonnes (60 tons)
Rigging:	Three masts, lateen-rigged
Complement:	12–20
Main routes:	African coast
Cargo:	Tropical products, bulk goods

Early Ships

Carrack

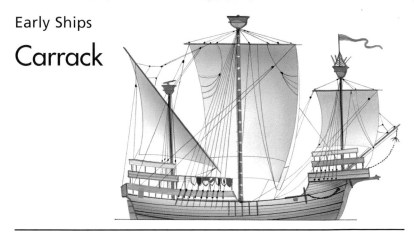

E uropean shipyards began building three-masted ships in the early years of the fifteenth century. The Italian port of Genoa has been suggested as the most likely point of origin, as it specialized in handling bulk cargoes such as timber, alum and ore. The name is something of a puzzle: although apparently derived from the Italian *caracca*, the Italians referred to this type of vessel simply as a *nave* (ship). The design differed radically from anything that had gone before and was the first step in a process of evolution that would see ship sizes double within a few years. One of the earliest detailed drawings of a *Kraek* (carrack) was made by a Flemish artist around 1470. The carrack was the workhorse of Europe's merchant fleets for a long time and did much to establish regular trade links between the major European ports.

Country of origin:	The Netherlands
Date of origin:	1470
Length:	34.1m (112ft)
Beam:	10m (33ft)
Displacement:	182.8 tonnes (180 tons)
Rigging:	Three masts; square sail on fore and main; lateen mizzen
Complement:	20
Main routes:	Long-distance trade routes
Cargo:	Hides, oil, ore, wine, iron

Cat

The North Country cat was essentially an enlarged version of the Dutch *fluyt*, many of which had been seized as English prizes in the wars between 1652 and 1674. These wars were the consequence of the so-called Navigation Act, passed by the English, which prohibited Dutch ships from trading with England. Sturdy and blunt-bowed, the cat was a bulk carrier with a flush deck and flat bottom, and was chiefly used for the coal trade. It was three-masted and could carry a considerable amount of sail. With the cat design, shipbuilders in the northeast of England seized the initiative from East Anglia, previously England's main shipbuilding region. The expression 'cat-built' referred to the blunt, unornamented stern and bow, and the boxy section of these hulls, many of which were re-rigged and remained in service for more than a century.

Country of origin:	England
Date of origin:	1680
Length:	36.6m (120ft)
Beam:	9.75m (32ft)
Displacement:	381 tonnes (375 tons)
Rigging:	Three masts; square-rigged on fore and main; lateen mizzen with square topsail
Complement:	12
Main routes:	English coast and short North Sea routes
Cargo:	Coal, wood, pig iron

Cheops Ship

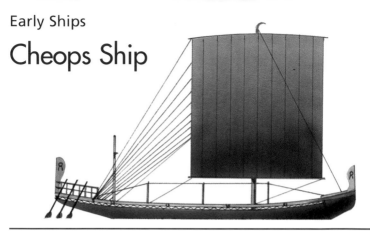

The Cheops ship, the oldest preserved ship from antiquity, was found in 1954, close to the Great Pyramid in Egypt. Built almost entirely of imported cedar, its 'shell-first' design shows that the hull was shaped before the internal members were added. It has no keel and the side planking is lashed with rope for security. Two cabins stand on the deck, the two-roomed main cabin covered by a canopy to provide extra coolness. The ship is equipped with oars, plus steering oars. The Cheops ship was clearly a ceremonial vessel and compression marks made by ropes show that it saw considerable service. A famous Egyptian pharoah of the fourth dynasty, Cheops reigned around 2800 BC; the building of the Great Pyramid at El Giza has been attributed to him, a supposition often disputed by historians. What is beyond dispute, however, is that ancient Egypt was at the height of its power during this period.

Country of origin:	Egypt
Date of origin:	2500 BC
Length:	43.6m (143ft)
Beam:	5.7m (18ft 7in)
Displacement:	95.5 tonnes (94 tons)
Rigging:	Single mast
Complement:	12, plus officers
Main routes:	River Nile, eastern Mediterranean
Cargo:	None

Chinese Junk

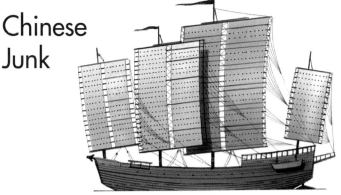

First described to westerners by Marco Polo in 1298, the junk, in its various guises, has enjoyed a long career. The thirteenth-century product seen by Polo was clearly the result of a Chinese shipbuilding tradition going back centuries. As in other sciences, China made many innovations in shipbuilding techniques that only came much later in the West. Notable features of the junk include a single stern rudder and pontoon-type hull divided into as many as 20 watertight compartments, with the deck built above its arched top. The planking was flush, with heavy rubbing strakes, and the vessel's bottom was flat, enabling it to sit level if beached. A series of hatches gave access to the watertight compartments. Up to four or even five masts were fitted, two of which could be dismounted. The sails were of fibre matting, woven in an interlocking pattern and strengthened by lateral bamboo battens.

Country of origin:	China
Date of origin:	Thirteenth century
Length:	54.9m (180ft)
Beam:	9.1m (30ft)
Displacement:	Not known
Rigging:	Four unstayed masts; lugsail-type rig, reefed from top downwards
Complement:	8–10
Main routes:	Coast and main rivers of China
Cargo:	Timber, rice, metals, cloth, foodstuffs

Curragh

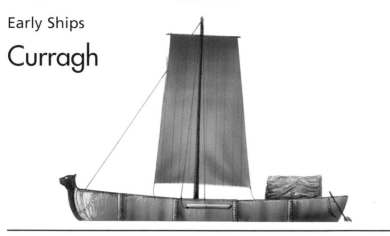

The Celtic peoples were not great sailors, despite some celebrated early voyages. Apart from the famous voyage of Brendan the Navigator, who is said to have sailed to Newfoundland, ancient Celtic texts record that Irish bishops sent men out into the Atlantic to seek the Land of Promise, 'where the pious might emigrate'. On the west coast of Celtic Ireland, boatbuilding techniques changed little from the fifth century to the nineteenth century. The basic boat used for fishing and for the transport of goods and people was the curragh. It consisted of a framework formed of thin, strong laths covered with stretched and sewn hides. By the nineteenth century, the hides had been replaced with tarred canvas. Curraghs were still in daily use on the Irish lakes in the 1930s. The boats that were used by the early explorers were coracles, capable of holding up to 40 people.

Country of origin:	Ireland
Date of origin:	Fifth century
Length:	9.1m (30ft)
Beam:	1.5m (5ft)
Displacement:	Not known
Rigging:	Dismountable mast with square sail
Complement:	4–8
Main routes:	West coast of Ireland, Irish loughs
Cargo:	Animals, fish, hides

Dutch Merchant Ship

A small galleon of the mid-sixteenth century, intended as a cargo vessel, this ship was in fact quite well armed, with gun ports along the main deck and quarter deck, as piracy was still widespread in the North Sea area. Up to 30 guns were carried for self-defence. The stern below the counter was rounded, suggesting that this Dutch-built ship may have represented a transitional phase between the galleon and the *fluyt*, which appeared at the end of the sixteenth century. The shallow draught enabled these vessels to operate along the comparatively shallow inshore waters in safety. All had excellent carrying capacity for their size. This period saw a rapid expansion in Holland's maritime commerce: while the British and Spanish concentrated on opening trade routes with the Americas, the Dutch turned to the eastern hemisphere, probing into the Indian and Pacific oceans.

Country of origin:	The Netherlands
Date of origin:	1564
Length:	27.7m (91ft)
Beam:	7.9m (26ft)
Displacement:	Not known
Rigging:	Three masts; square-rigged on fore and main; lateen mizzen, split sail
Complement:	30–40
Main routes:	North Sea, Indian and Pacific oceans
Cargo:	General

Egyptian Barge

The great temple obelisks for which the ancient Egyptians have become famous were hewn from granite at Aswan, and floated down the Nile to Luxor and Heliopolis. Designed to carry two obelisks lying side by side, this ship had a total weight of 700 tonnes (688 tons), and was 59.4m (195ft) long, and as such, was the largest ship yet built. The vessel was unpowered but fitted with a pair of steering oars at each side of the stern. It was prevented from hogging by a set of ropes that were secured at the bow, and wound round a windlass at the stern. The giant ship was towed by 27 small oared vessels, with a total manpower of 900. A massive obelisk barge like this example was constructed for Queen Hatshepsut who ruled ancient Egypt between 1478 and 1458 BC, and the vessel was depicted in the rock temple of Deir-el-Bahri.

Country of origin:	Egypt
Date of origin:	1550BC
Length:	59.4m (195ft)
Beam:	21.3m (70ft)
Displacement:	700 tonnes (688 tons); 1500 tonnes (1476 tons) loaded§
Rigging:	None
Complement:	900 including auxiliary crews
Main routes:	River Nile
Cargo:	Obelisks

Egyptian Reed Boat

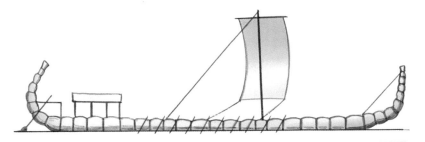

Evidence of reed boats from Egypt and South America has led us to assume that these were among the earliest boat types developed. Depictions of boats made from papyrus reeds go back to around 3200 BC. In the Nile delta, where timber was scarce and water was everywhere, papyrus made a natural material for boat building. Although the life of each vessel was only a few months, the supply of reeds was endless, and small reed boats are still constructed to this day for fishing purposes. Fishing techniques have remained unchanged over thousands of years, except that an ancient Egyptian fisherman would have a rather curious companion in his boat. The Egyptians trained cats to dive into the water to retrieve fish and other game. In the *Ra I* and *Ra II* expeditions, the explorer Thor Heyerdahl demonstrated that a reed vessel was capable of crossing the Atlantic.

Country of origin:	Egypt
Date of origin:	c. 2500 BC
Length:	16.5m (54ft)
Beam:	2.7m (9ft)
Displacement:	Not known
Rigging:	None
Complement:	Not known
Main routes:	Nile delta
Cargo:	Fish, reeds, grain

Fluyt

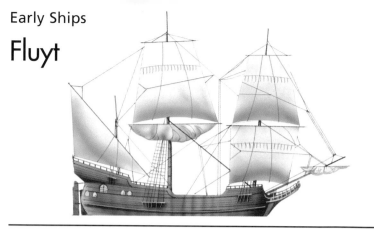

Accountancy and economics have always had an effect on merchant shipping. Greater capacity, simpler operation, fewer crew, faster sailing times – all were sought centuries ago, just as they are today. The Dutch *fluyt* was a seventeenth-century accountant's dream ship, its bulging sides and narrow deck minimizing the level of tax that was levied on a ship according to its dimensions and reducing the toll payable as a vessel passed through the sound between Denmark and Sweden. The first *fluyt*-type vessel was built in 1595, at Hoorn in Holland. Long in relation to beam, with a vast hold beneath a single deck, and almost vertical stem and stern, her low prow reduced exposure to the wind. The rounded stern was an innovation, as ships had been built with square sterns ever since the cog made its appearance. As it was intended for peaceful waters, the *fluyt* was unarmed.

Country of origin:	The Netherlands
Date of origin:	1595
Length:	32m (105ft)
Beam:	8.5m (28ft)
Displacement:	305 tonnes (300 tons)
Rigging:	Three masts; square-rigged on fore and main; lateen mizzen
Complement:	20–30
Main routes:	North Sea and Baltic trade routes
Cargo:	Timber, ore, baled and barrelled goods

Galeas

The Baltic *galeas* was a two-masted merchant vessel used in the North Sea and Baltic trades. A completely different type to the Mediterranean *galleass*, its original form was probably square-rigged; however, by the early 1700s, it was rigged fore and aft, with only a square topsail and sometimes a topgallant remaining – a precursor to the ketch. With square stern and greater sheer than the *galiot*, the *galeas* was more suited to the open sea. The square stern with raised bulwarks might suggest a raised quarterdeck under which crew accommodation could have been provided. By 1700, the jib boom had been greatly extended until it measured almost half the length of the vessel and accommodated a flying jib. Just as the brig was the most familiar sight on the British coast and along the ways of the North Sea, so the *galeas* made its mark on the commerce of the Baltic.

Country of origin:	The Netherlands
Date of origin:	1690
Length:	19.8m (65ft)
Beam:	5.5m (18ft)
Displacement:	86.4 tonnes (85 tons)
Rigging:	Two masts; fore-and-aft–rigged, with square topsail on main; staysail, jib and flying jib
Complement:	4–8
Main routes:	North European coast
Cargo:	Baled and barrelled goods

Galiot

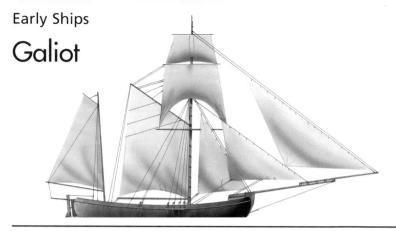

Similar in size to the *galeas*, and more typically Dutch with its rounded stem and stern, the *galiot* remained in use well into the nineteenth century. With a tall mast for its shallow draught, it usually carried a leeboard as a supplementary keel. The rig was basically fore-and-aft, but a square topsail and sometimes also a topgallant were fitted to the mainmast. The lengthy jib boom, usually formed of two spars fished together, could be hinged up when not in use. The *galeas* and *galiot* were splendid examples of the skill and ingenuity displayed by Dutch shipbuilders in the days of sail. Before the British Empire became firmly established in the eighteenth century, it was the Dutch who dominated maritime commerce, with explorers such as William Barentz and Abel Tasman paving the way in the late sixteenth and mid-seventeenth centuries, respectively.

Country of origin:	The Netherlands
Date of origin:	c. 1700
Length:	19.8m (65ft)
Beam:	5.5m (18ft)
Displacement:	86 tonnes (85 tons)
Rigging:	Two masts, fore-and-aft rigged, with topsail and possible topgallant on main; staysail, jib and flying jib
Complement:	4–8
Main routes:	North European coasts
Cargo:	Baled and barrelled goods

Greek Cargo Ship

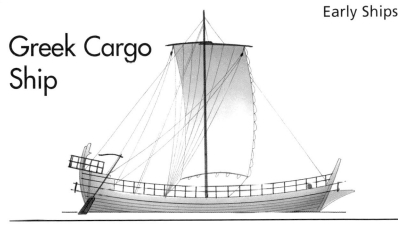

Some 2500 years ago, there was very little distinction between merchant ships and small warships in the waters of the Mediterranean and Aegean. With almost constant warfare between various city states, and pirates a perpetual menace, even a merchant vessel had to carry arms and might also be fitted with a ram at the prow. In emergencies, a city could commandeer its merchant fleet for use as warships. These pine-hulled vessels were light and manoeuvrable; sail technique was improving, and, while oars were still carried, they were used only in calm waters or confined spaces. Wine and oil were frequent cargoes, carried in clay jars (*amphorae*); numerous wrecks of wine-carrying vessels have been found. The Greeks became great sea traders during the Archaic period (800–500 BC), founding many coastal colonies from Asia Minor in the east to Spain in the west.

Country of origin:	Greek city states
Date of origin:	c. 500 BC
Length:	15.2m (50ft)
Beam:	4.3m (14ft)
Displacement:	Not known
Rigging:	Single mast stayed fore and aft; furlable square sail
Complement:	About 8
Main routes:	Black Sea, Aegean Sea and Ionian Sea
Cargo:	Wine, timber, grain, wool, hides

Early Ships

Hanseatic Cog

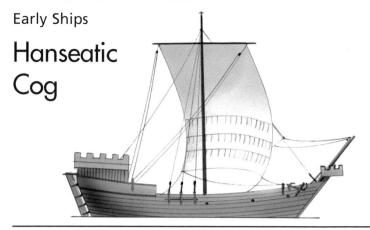

In 1962, a well-preserved ship was found in the River Weser at Bremen, Germany. It proved to be a fine example of the cog, mainstay of trade between the Hanseatic ports of the North Sea. The lowest part of the hull was flush-built, the upper parts clinker-built and the hull was rounded out between a pointed stem and stern to maximize carrying capacity. A rudder was fitted, with the tiller housed below the built-out stern platform. Cogs were often depicted on the seals of medieval seaport towns, and these provide a valuable source of detail for the design of the vessels. The ports were part of the Hanseatic League, a confederation of northern European trading cities that existed from the twelfth century to 1669. The basis of the league's power was its monopoly of the Baltic trade and its good relations with Flanders and England.

Country of origin:	Germany
Date of origin:	1240
Length:	24m (78ft 9in)
Beam:	8m (26ft 3in)
Displacement:	122 tonnes (120 tons)
Rigging:	Single mast; square sail, sometimes fitted with a bonnet, sometimes with reefpoints
Complement:	6
Main routes:	North Sea, southern Baltic
Cargo:	Wood, coal, hides, wine

Herring Buss

The herring *buss* was the typical larger Dutch fishing boat of North Sea waters. Its length to beam ratio of 4:1 was unusually great, giving it the strength in the water to hold a long drift net. Both foremast and mainmast were usually lowered while fishing, with the square mizzen keeping a slow headway on the taut net cable. The *buss* reached its maximum size in the mid-sixteenth century, after which smaller versions were built. By the mid-eighteenth century, the characteristic *buss* rig had been largely superseded by a version of the hooker rig. The herring was, and still is, a major staple of the northern European diet; the three species of the family (herring, sprat and pilchard) were present in huge quantities in the North Sea area until their stocks were virtually destroyed by intensive fishing in the latter part of the twentieth century.

Country of origin:	The Netherlands
Date of origin:	Early seventeenth century
Length:	19.8m (65ft)
Beam:	4.9m (16ft)
Displacement:	101.6 tonnes (100 tons)
Rigging:	Three masts, each with single square sail
Complement:	6–8
Main routes:	North Sea fishing grounds
Cargo:	Herring

Kon-Tiki

On 28 April 1947, Norwegian explorer Thor Heyerdahl and his crew set out from Callao, Peru, on a daring voyage that would take them 4300 nautical miles across the Pacific to the Marquesas Islands on a raft called *Kon-Tiki*. After 101 suspense-filled days on the open ocean, braving raging storms, whales and countless sharks, they made landfall on the Polynesian atoll of Raroia in the Tuamotu Archipelago, proving the point that ancient seafarers could have made similar journeys thousands of years ago. The balsawood *Kon-Tiki* was a replica of a prehistoric South American vessel, constructed of nine balsa logs collected from Ecuador. Heyerdahl went on to make more stirring voyages, including the *Ra II* expedition, which destroyed the accepted theory that Mediterranean vessels built prior to Columbus's time could not have crossed the Atlantic.

Country of origin:	Peru
Date of origin:	1947
Length:	13.7m (45ft)
Beam:	5.5m (18ft)
Displacement:	Not known
Rigging:	Single mast, square rig
Complement:	6
Route:	Peru–Polynesia
Role:	Exploration/scientific research

Mediterranean Cargo Ship

The salvaged remains of a wreck from Kyrenia, Cyprus, dating from the fourth century BC, give some guidance to the form and build of the typical 'round ship' that plied the Mediterranean trade routes at that time. Unlike a warship, it was built to stay at sea for days at a time and had a keel – probably a recent feature – and edge-joined planking. With one open deck, it was of 'shell-first' construction, with the frame members added once the hull was assembled. It was a seaworthy design as long as the vessel's head was kept to the wind; if she broached to, she could fill rapidly with water and go down. Vessels such as this would be used to serve the principal Greek colonies such as Taranto in southern Italy, founded by settlers from Sparta; Syracuse in Sicily, established by settlers from Corinth; Marseille in southern France; and Cyrenaica, North Africa.

Country of origin:	Cyprus or a Levant port
Date of origin:	c. 300 BC
Length:	12m (39ft 4in)
Beam:	5m (16ft 4in)
Displacement:	Not known
Rigging:	Single mast, square sail
Complement:	Not known
Main routes:	Mediterranean routes, Bay of Biscay and Cornwall
Cargo:	Grain, wine, wood, ores (tin from Cornwall)

Phoenician Cargo Ship

The Phoenicians were a great trading nation and practical seafarers. Our evidence for what a typical Phoenician vessel looked like comes from Egyptian tomb murals, now unfortunately destroyed, dating back to around 1500 BC. The murals showed such features as a masthead rope ladder and lookout point. The horsehead prow may have been a standard feature. There is no suggestion of rope bracing, implying that, even without a keel, the vessel had sufficient rigidity to withstand the sea. The wicker fencing was probably to separate deck cargo from the oarsmen. Timber was an important cargo, and one ancient relief, although from almost 700 years later, shows timber being towed. Ships at this time possessed no metallic fixings at all; the means of iron-making had not yet been discovered, and everything would be fashioned from wood, rope and cloth.

Country of origin:	Phoenicia
Date of origin:	1500 BC
Length:	16.8m (55ft)
Beam:	3.7m (12ft)
Displacement:	Not known
Rigging:	Single mast stayed fore and aft; square sail with upper and lower yards
Complement:	8–12
Main routes:	Eastern Mediterranean
Cargo:	Timber, grain, fish, metals

Roman Cargo Ship

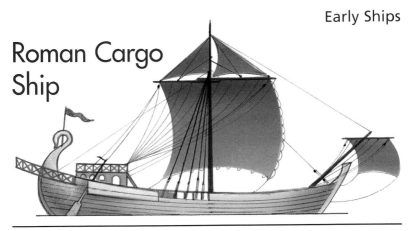

This is the ship that sustained Rome's far-flung empire. It was capacious, sturdy and featured a built-up stern; the steering oars were already more like rudders, partly housed within the built-out bulwarks. It was decked, with a hold below and relatively substantial crew and passenger space aft. The sternpost was formed into the shape of a swan's neck; the bow was businesslike, with a bowsprit (artemon) carrying a yard with a small square sail. The basic form of this vessel, although improved in some of its design detail, remained in existence from around AD 100–400. The Romans were not natural seafarers and often employed foreign personnel to man their ships; their favourite form of navigation was to hug the coastline, never leaving sight of land if at all possible. Pictures from the old port of Ostia show how a Roman merchant ship looked.

Country of origin:	Rome
Date of origin:	AD 100
Length:	24.4m (80ft)
Beam:	2.4m (8ft)
Displacement:	81–91 tonnes (80–90 tons)
Rigging:	Single mast stayed fore and aft; halyard blocks now in use; square mainsail could be brailed up
Complement:	8–10
Main routes:	Trans-Mediterranean, Black Sea, Atlantic coast of Europe
Cargo:	Grain, wine, military stores, firewood, mass-produced goods

Scandinavian Cargo Ship

In the eighth and ninth centuries, Scandinavian coast-dwellers developed shipbuilding skills of a high order, with the clinker-built hull as standard. Seagoing ships were the key to their territorial expansion, and vessels such as this one may have formed part of the Viking fleet that reached North America. Undecked and with a single mast stepped to the keel, its thwarts acted as both stiffeners to the hull and seats for oarsmen. Rounder and shorter than the famous Viking longships, the type was known as the *knorr*. Oars were used when plying harbours or rivers. Vessels such as these established a thriving trade between Scandinavia and Byzantium, which was reached via the great rivers of Russia and the Danube. The Byzantines avidly desired certain commodities, including flaxen-haired slave girls, which Viking raiders were able to provide.

Countries of origin:	Scandinavia
Date of origin:	Eighth century
Length:	16.8m (55ft)
Beam:	4.6m (15ft)
Displacement:	Not known
Rigging:	Single mast stayed fore and aft; square sail reinforced in a diaper pattern
Complement:	4–8
Main routes:	Western Scandinavian seaways, North Sea, Russian rivers
Cargo:	Sheep, grain, amber, hides, timber

Skuta

The name *skuta* goes back to the age of the Icelandic sagas, but is mainly identified with the clinker-built boats and homespun sails used for 200 years by the Aland islanders to carry firewood and lime on the 195-km (120-mile) route to Stockholm. Small *skutor* were single masted; the larger boats had two. It was in the nature of their work to carry deck cargo, and it seems to have been usual for them to be steered from the cabin roof. They went over to *galeas* rig in the nineteenth century. From the late eighteenth century on, three-masted *skutor* were also built. The dimensions given here are for a two-masted craft. Always competent seafarers and shipbuilders, the Swedes have maintained a long tradition of designing and building boats without being influenced by foreign ideas. Many of their innovations, such as the clinker-type hull, with its overlapping planks, remain standard features of boat building.

Country of origin:	Sweden
Date of origin:	1640
Length:	18.3m (60ft)
Beam:	7.3m (24ft)
Displacement:	c. 61 tonnes (60 tons)
Rigging:	Two masts, square-rigged with square topsail on mainmast
Complement:	2
Main routes:	Aland Islands – Stockholm
Cargo:	Firewood, lime, occasional passengers

Thames Sailing Barge

Navigation of the lower Thames was assisted by the tide. Ships lay below London Bridge and transferred their cargoes into flat-bottomed barges. Similar barges brought goods into the capital from rural areas, including baled straw and hay for the huge number of animals kept in the city. The seventeenth-century barge was little more than a lighter fitted with a single square sail, often set well forward; the cut-back stem was known as a 'swimhead'. The mast could be lowered in order for the barge to make the tricky passage under the old London Bridge, the many arches of which created a form of weir when the tide was running. For centuries, commerce on the Thames was bedevilled by the inefficiency of the City Corporation, the controlling authority, until control passed to the Crown in 1857. By this time, waterway traffic had begun to decline as more goods were shipped by rail.

Country of origin:	England
Date of origin:	1640
Length:	19.8m (65ft)
Beam:	5.2m (17ft)
Displacement:	50.8 tonnes (50 tons)
Rigging:	Single dismountable mast with square sail
Complement:	2–4
Main routes:	Thames river and estuary
Cargo:	General

Venetian Crusade Ship

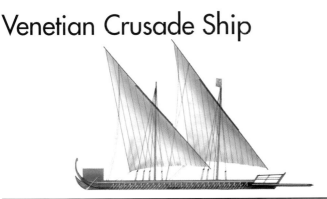

In 1268, Louis IX of France ordered ships for a crusade. Those built in Venice were substantial two-deckers; they were two-masted, with lateen rig, and their purpose was to carry both men and animals. The spars of the lateen rig were longer than the ship itself. Despite this, they could be handled adeptly by a small crew. The aftercastle was quite substantial, in order to provide accommodation for high-ranking officers. Although single rudders were in use in northern Europe, the Venetian ships retained paired side-rudders. Both masts had crow's nests fitted to the aftersides. The new fleet was ready by 1270, and Louis set out on his second and last crusade, intending to occupy Sicily, Malta and Tunis, and secure the central Mediterranean. In July 1270, Louis landed near Carthage with a strong army and besieged Tunis; however, disease broke out and, by the end of August, the crusading king was dead.

Country of origin:	Venice
Date of origin:	c. 1268
Length:	25.8m (84ft 6in)
Beam:	6.4m (21ft)
Displacement:	c. 122 tonnes (120 tons)
Rigging:	Two masts; lateen rig; rat-lined shrouds or rope ladders for access to tops
Complement:	Not known
Main routes:	Western Mediterranean to Sicily, Cyprus and Palestine
Cargo:	Soldiers, horses, military stores, foodstuffs

Cargo Ships

Alexander

Built in 1783, *Alexander* was the largest of the convict transports in the First Fleet that carried criminals to found the colony at Botany Bay, Australia (in fact, they eventually landed in what is now Sydney Harbour). There were five other transports, three store ships and two naval vessels that acted as escorts. Having left England on 12 May 1787, the fleet reached its destination on 20 January 1788. It had travelled a total of 24,140km (15,000 miles), having crossed and re-crossed the Atlantic to take advantage of favourable winds. Generally, the term of transportation was seven years; however, as there was no provision for a passage home and few could hope to raise the fare, being sent to Australia was effectively a life sentence. *Alexander* returned to England, picking up the crew of *Friendship* on the way. She was last heard of registered at Hull and disappeared from the record in 1808.

Country of origin:	Britain
Date of origin:	1785
Length:	34.7m (114ft)
Beam:	9.4m (31ft)
Tonnage:	457 tonnes (450 tons)
Rigging:	Three masts, ship rig
Complement:	Not known
Main routes:	England–Australia
Cargo:	Convicts

Archibald Russell

The four-masted barque *Archibald Russell* was the last square-rigger built on the Clyde and remained in commercial service until 1939. Built for John Hardie & Sons, she was intended to work in the Pacific nitrate and wheat trade, returning to Falmouth from Australia in 93 days on her maiden voyage. She was one of the very few square-rigged ships fitted with bilge keels to reduce roll. She was later sold to Gustaf Erikson of Mariehamn and continued to carry grain from Australia until the outbreak of World War II, when she was laid up. The *Archibald Russell* was broken up in 1939. The last comparable ship in British trade was the *Garthpool*, which ran aground in the Cape Verde Islands in 1929. She and others like her served out their last days carrying nitrates from Valparaiso, Chile, which was the base of the Anglo-Chilean Nitrates Company.

Country of origin:	Britain
Date of origin:	1905
Length:	88.8m (291ft 5in)
Beam:	13.2m (43ft 2in)
Tonnage:	2423 tonnes (2385 tons)
Rigging:	Four masts, three square-rigged
Complement:	70
Main routes:	England–Australia
Cargo:	Grain

Ariel

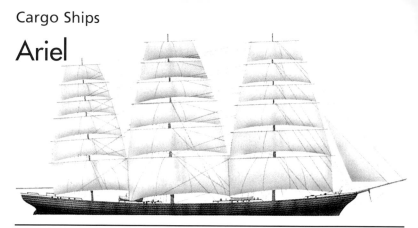

The 1860s saw the full-rigged, three-masted ship brought to the peak of its development in the shape of the composite wood plank on iron frame vessels, the China clippers, the majority of which were built in Scotland for the China tea trade. One of the best of them was the *Ariel*, built as part of a group of 16 ships by Robert Steele & Co of Greenock, at the mouth of the River Clyde. The composite building method was unknown before 1850 and, by 1885, it had ceased to be used, having given way to all-metal construction; however, in that short period, it was used to produce ships capable of almost incredible performances. They were expensive (*Ariel* cost £15,350, a huge sum in those days), but they lived up to their expectations. On her third voyage, *Ariel* sailed from Foochow, China, to London in 97 days. She was lost at sea on passage from London to Sydney in 1872.

Country of origin:	Britain
Date of origin:	1865
Length:	60.2m (197ft 5in)
Beam:	10.3m (33ft 10in)
Tonnage:	867 tonnes (853 tons)
Rigging:	Three masts, full rig
Complement:	62
Main routes:	England–China
Cargo:	Tea

Atland

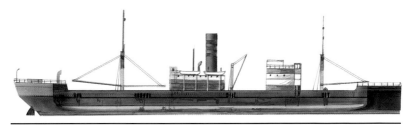

O f the various types of merchant ship built in the early part of the twentieth century, the turret steamer was amongst the most revolutionary. Below the waterline, the hull was of conventional shape, but above it it was only just over half the width. This design reduced the amount of steel used in construction, but still gave added strength. Costs were reduced, as fees paid in harbour dues on dead weight were lower, while the easy stowage of bulk cargoes saved much time. The *Atland* was designed for a Swedish firm by William Doxford & Sons of Sunderland, who built 178 of the type between 1890 and 1911. She was used in the iron ore trade with northern Europe; this traffic continued between neutral Sweden and Germany after the outbreak of World War II and became dangerous when Soviet submarines began to make their presence felt. *Atland* was lost in a collision in March 1943.

Country of origin:	Britain
Date of origin:	1910
Dimensions:	116m x 16m (388ft 9in x 52ft 4in)
Tonnage:	5109 tonnes (5029 tons)
Machinery:	Single shaft, triple-expansion; 2200hp
Service speed:	12.7 knots
Cargo:	Iron ore
Constructor:	William Doxford & Sons, Sunderland, England
Built for:	Tirfing SS Co., Sweden

Bideford Polacca Brigantine

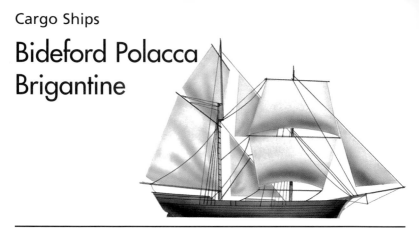

The Bideford Polacca (or poleacre, as it was sometimes known) was a variant of the standard brigantine, many of which were built in the North Devon town of Bideford, an important small shipbuilding centre. The genre had its origins in the Mediterranean, where a polacca was any vessel with one-piece masts, with no tops or crosstrees. The Bideford version (although the vessels were also built elsewhere) had a pole foremast, and it was instantly recognizable by it being noticeably shorter than the main mast, usually extending to only one topsail. Reducing the foremast to a single spar considerably simplified its rigging, and the shortened sail it carried was easier to handle. The Bideford-built ships were used extensively for the carriage of light cargo, but also carried some passenger traffic from point to point along the coast.

Country of origin:	Britain
Date of origin:	1860
Length:	25m (82ft)
Beam:	6.1m (20ft)
Tonnage:	81.2 tonnes (80 tons)
Rigging:	Two masts, square-rigged, shortened foremast
Complement:	10–12
Main routes:	Southwest coast of England
Cargo:	General

Boom

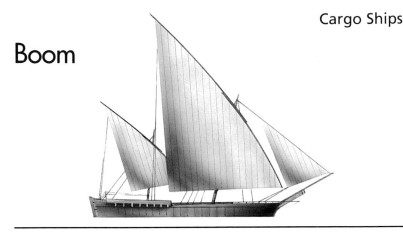

One of the largest types of Arab sailing vessel, the boom traded across the Indian Ocean and down the African coast as far as Zanzibar. Fitted with the traditional lateen rig on two masts, it also had a massively built-up bow with a long sprit on which a kind of staysail was fastened. There is something reminiscent of the galley's shape and ram here, but the boom was not oared. It is likely that ships of this form had been built in the Persian Gulf region since the sixteenth century. Some, assisted by auxiliary motors, were still in service in the late twentieth century. Although they transported orthodox cargoes such as animals, foodstuffs and bulk freight, the booms that sailed on to Zanzibar often took on a more sinister payload – slaves, taken from the tribes of central southern Africa and shipped to the east coast by Arab 'slavemasters'.

Country of origin:	Arabia
Date of origin:	1850
Length:	30.5m (100ft)
Beam:	6.1m (20ft)
Tonnage:	c. 193 tonnes (190 tons)
Rigging:	Two masts; lateen rig with fore staysail to bowsprit
Complement:	10
Main routes:	Persian Gulf, Indian Ocean
Cargo:	General

Cabotia

From 1917 onwards, small general-purpose British merchant ships were built to a set of standard designs, chosen largely for ease and speed of construction, in order to replace war losses. With German U-boats waging unrestricted warfare against the Allied merchant fleets in 1917, these losses were becoming very serious. In this one year alone, Britain lost 1197 merchant ships to enemy action, most of them victims of submarines. *Cabotia*, originally called *War Viper*, was an A Type, 120m (400ft) long between perpendiculars, with a single internal deck. A Types were essentially three-island vessels (although *Cabotia* had a shelter deck between the poop and the bridge deck), with two cargo hatches forward of the bridge and two aft. Ships of this type could carry about 8128 tonnes (8000 tons) of cargo. *Cabotia* went on to serve in World War II, but was sunk by a mine off the British coast in January 1940.

Country of origin:	Britain
Date of origin:	1917
Dimensions:	125.5m x 15.5m x 7.7m (411ft 7in x 50ft 8in x 25ft)
Tonnage:	5243 tonnes (5160 tons)
Machinery:	Single shaft, vertical triple-expansion; 1800hp
Service speed:	10 knots
Cargo:	General
Constructor:	Not known
Built for:	British merchant marine

Candiope

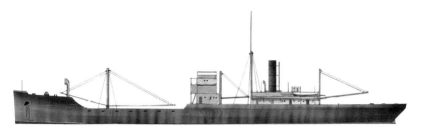

Like *Cabotia*, *Candiope* was built to a standard pattern which was intended to ensure ease and speed of construction. The difference was that, in order to preserve dwindling stocks of steel, she was built of wood. Although laid down for war service, she was not completed until after the Armistice of November 1918, and, in the following year, she was sold to an Italian bank, Credito Industriale di Venezia, and operated as a short-haul tramp steamer in the Mediterranean. She was broken up four years later. Originally named *War Mingan*, *Candiope* was built in Canada because British yards were full to capacity. In a sense, ships of *Cabotia*'s kind were the equivalent of the 'Liberty Ships' of World War II, and, like the latter, many were sold off after the war years and went on to give excellent service with various maritime companies around the world.

Country of origin:	Canada
Date of origin:	1918
Dimensions:	76.5m x 13.25m (251ft x 43ft 6in)
Tonnage:	3353 tonnes (3300 tons)
Machinery:	Single shaft, vertical triple-expansion; 1400hp
Service speed:	10 knots
Cargo:	General
Constructor:	Not known
Built for:	British merchant marine

Carelia

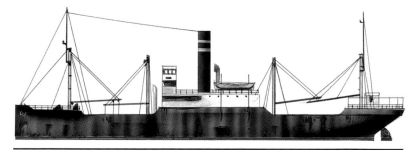

In the 1920s, the Baltic and North Sea timber trade provided employment for a large number of small steamers. By placing the masts and winches at the ends of the bridge deck and on the forecastle and poop, the well decks between these structures were left clear for the easy stowage of a deck cargo of timber. These ships were mainly built in Scandinavian shipyards. In 1925, *Carelia* and three near-sisters were absorbed into Finland's largest shipping concern, Finland SS Co. Although relatively small, *Carelia* could stow a large cargo of timber, thanks to the positioning of masts and winches at the extreme ends of the vessel and centre structure. *Carelia* was broken up in 1963. During World War II, she made many voyages to the north German ports; these ended abruptly when Finland signed an armistice with the Soviet Union in September 1944.

Country of origin:	Finland
Date of origin:	1921
Dimensions:	66m x 10.4m x 4.6m (217ft x 34ft 5in x 15ft)
Tonnage:	1141 tonnes (1123 tons)
Machinery:	Single shaft, triple-expansion
Service speed:	8 knots
Cargo:	Timber
Constructor:	Maskin & Brobygnade Aktiebolager, Helsinki
Built for:	Atlantic Rederi AB

Centennial State

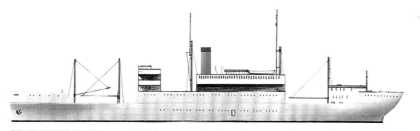

Centennial State made her maiden voyage in 1921. Although primarily a cargo vessel, she could also carry 80 passengers. In 1923, the *Centennial State* was sold and renamed *President Adams*. She underwent a refit in 1930, at which time her bridge, which had been situated forward, was repositioned and joined to the main superstructure. Renamed *President Grant* in 1938, she became a troop transporter at the end of 1941, following the Japanese attack on Pearl Harbor. In March 1942, she ferried troops and supplies to the Philippines, where United States forces were fighting a desperate rearguard action against the invading Japanese, and she subsequently assisted in the evacuation of personnel to Australia after the fall of the Bataan Peninsula on the island of Luzon. In 1944, after excellent service in the Pacific theatre, she ran aground off New Guinea and was abandoned.

Country of origin:	USA
Date of origin:	1920
Dimensions:	157m x 19m (516ft x 62ft 4in)
Tonnage:	10,727 tonnes (10,558 tons)
Machinery:	Two shafts, triple-expansion engines
Service speed:	14 knots
Cargo:	General cargo and personnel
Constructor:	Not known
Built for:	Not known

Cargo Ships

Cleopatra

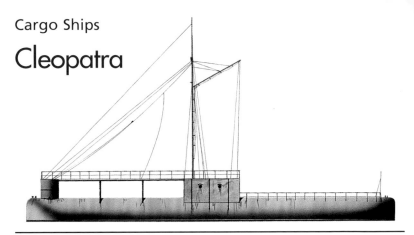

Cylindrical in form, with her bow and stern crudely brought together on the vertical axis, *Cleopatra* was designed by Benjamin Baker and John Fowler. She was purpose-built to transport the famous 'Cleopatra's Needle' from Alexandria to London. The iron hull had stout bulkheads inside at 3m (10ft) intervals to strengthen the sides and also to hold the 189-tonne (186-ton), 20m- (68ft 6in-) long obelisk in place. The crew were housed in a cabin on the upper deck. *Cleopatra*'s prefabricated plates were riveted around the obelisk and the entire ensemble rolled down to the sea. She set off for England, towed by the steamer *Olga*, but had to be cast adrift in a Biscay storm and her small crew taken off. Later, in calmer weather, she was towed to El Ferrol, Spain; a year later, in 1878, she finished her journey to Thames Embankment, where the obelisk was to be erected, behind the tug *Anglia*.

Country of origin:	Britain
Date of origin:	1877
Dimensions:	28m x 4.6m x 2.45m (92ft x 15ft 1in x 8ft)
Tonnage:	278 tonnes (274 tons)
Machinery:	None
Service speed:	Not known
Cargo:	Historic artefact
Constructor:	John & Wainman Dixon
Built for:	British government

Cockerill

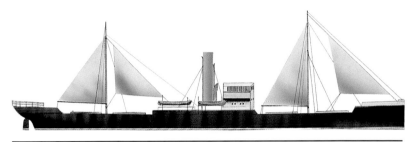

Until 1900, the vast majority of merchant vessels were still sailing ships. With the completion of the *Cockerill* in 1901, however, the age of commercial sail moved rapidly towards its end, for she was a new type of steam cargo boat, the concept of which was soon to be copied by all the maritime nations. Her two major cargo areas were separated by the boilers and engine room, and she also carried a light rig, more to act as steadying sails than to provide extra propulsive power. *Cockerill* bore the name of her constructor, John Cockerill & Co of Hoboken, Belgium, and carried perishables from Antwerp to London under the flag of that company. She was one of the earliest small steam liners on this short sea route and did much to set the standard for those which came after. Much to her builder's delight, she also proved very economical to operate.

Country of origin:	Belgium
Date of origin:	1901
Dimensions:	88m x 14m (288ft 8in x 45ft)
Tonnage:	2479 tonnes (2440 tons)
Machinery:	Single shaft, vertical compound; 1200hp
Service speed:	8 knots
Cargo:	Perishable foodstuffs
Constructor:	John Cockerill & Co, Hoboken, Belgium
Built for:	Constructor's private enterprise

Columbus

One of the most unusual vessels ever built, *Columbus* was one of two massive raft ships (rafts shaped like ships) built in Quebec in the 1820s. They were packed solid with timber, the idea being that they would cross the Atlantic to Europe, where they would be broken up and the timber with which they were laden and also constructed salvaged for industrial use. When she was launched in 1823, *Columbus* already had 4064 tonnes (4000 tons) of timber stowed, and a further 2338 tonnes (2300 tons) of timber was placed on board when the sailing rig was positioned. *Columbus*'s hull provided primitive accommodation for the crew of 60. By the time she reached the Thames, there was 5.5m (18ft) of water in the hold, and she was kept afloat only by her own cargo of timber. It was decided to make a second trip before dismantling her, but she sank on the return voyage to Canada.

Country of origin:	Canada
Date of origin:	1823
Length:	91.7m (301ft)
Beam:	15.6m (51ft 5in)
Tonnage:	10,160 tonnes (10,000 tons) including cargo
Rigging:	Not known
Complement:	60
Main routes:	North Atlantic
Cargo:	Timber

Commandant de Rose

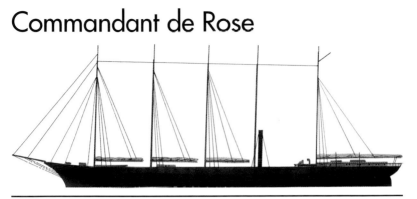

The *Commandant de Rose* and her sister vessels were basically steam-powered, with gaff courses to act as steadying sails, rather than true auxiliary schooners, even though they were classed as such. The *Commandant de Rose* was one of a score of wooden five-masted auxiliary vessels ordered during World War I by the French from US East Coast yards, where a building tradition still flourished. They were not delivered until late in 1917 and so never actually repaid the investment in them, despite the fact that freight charges had climbed to roughly ten times the 1914 levels by then. They were uneconomical to operate and were withdrawn from service as soon as the war was over, being scrapped in the early 1920s. The *Commandant de Rose* was named after a celebrated French fighter ace who rose to prominence in the early days of World War I.

Country of origin:	France
Date of origin:	1917
Dimensions:	85m x 14m x 7m (280ft x 45ft 6in x 23ft)
Tonnage:	4572 tonnes (4500 tons)
Machinery:	Two shafts, auxiliary vertical triple-expansion
Service speed:	10 knots
Cargo:	General
Constructor:	Not known
Built for:	French government

Connector

L aunched in 1852, this experimental steamship was conceived on a similar principle to the articulated truck, with detachable hull sections enabling the aft motor section to be separated and used on another hull. Designed for the bulk coal trade, the *Connector*'s hull was not rigid; its three self-contained sections, each with mast and sail, were hinged together, so that when the ship docked the three sections could be separated for ease of unloading. In practice, the concept proved almost unworkable and *Connector* was speedily scrapped. The siting of the engine in the afterpart of the ship, however, was a practice that would ultimately be adopted in the design of many bulk carriers. At this point in the nineteenth century, the height of the Industrial Revolution, there was a huge demand for bulk carriers to serve Britain's rapidly expanding coal trade.

Country of origin:	Britain
Date of origin:	1852
Dimensions:	51.8m x 9.1m (170ft x 30ft)
Tonnage:	2032 tonnes (2000 tons)
Machinery:	Single screw, compound
Service speed:	Not known
Cargo:	Coal
Constructor:	Not known
Built for:	Not known

Cornelis Vrolijk

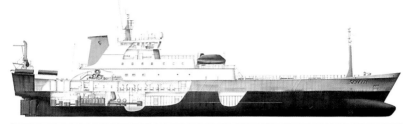

At the time of her inaugural voyage in June 1988, the Dutch factory ship *Cornelis Vrolijk* was the largest, most powerful and best-equipped factory ship in the world, with a capacity of 6500 cubic metres (229,500 cubic feet). Her on-board facilities are capable of processing 240 tonnes (236 tons) of fish every 24 hours, thanks to a system devised by Meyn Fish Processing of Oostzaan. The system is fully automated, so that no manual input is necessary. The ship was completed within a year of the order being placed. *Cornelis Vrolijk*'s main engine is a 10,000hp Deutz MWM marine diesel, auxiliary power being furnished by another Deutz motor developing 3311hp. The vessel is equipped with an advanced stabilization system, enabling her to continue efficient operations in very rough seas, and she also has the latest electronic equipment for navigation and sounding.

Country of origin:	The Netherlands
Date of origin:	1988
Dimensions:	114m x 17m x 7.5m (374ft x 55ft 9in x 24ft 7in)
Tonnage:	Not known
Machinery:	One Deutz MWM marine diesel, 10,000hp; one Deutz auxiliary motor; 3311hp
Service speed:	18 knots
Cargo:	Fish
Constructor:	Rederij C. Vrolijk, Scheveninge
Built for:	Ymuiden Stores of Holland

County of Peebles

The *County of Peebles* was the first four-masted ship built of iron and was destined to play an influential part in the story of maritime commerce. She was constructed for the jute trade between Dundee and India, and was later used in the North Atlantic trade until 1898. She was then bought by the Chilean government, renamed *Muñoz Gamero* and used as a coal hulk at Punta Arenas. She was sunk as a breakwater in the 1960s, but her living quarters, which remained above water, were preserved intact and furnished. Apart from barges, the first iron ship was probably the *Aaron Manby*, which was built in a Staffordshire ironworks in 1820, assembled in London and used on a direct run from London to Paris up the Seine. The largest iron ship was Isambard Kingdom Brunel's *Great Britain*, launched in July 1843 at Bristol.

Country of origin:	Britain
Date of origin:	1875
Length:	81.3m (266ft 7in)
Beam:	11.8m (38ft 8in)
Tonnage:	1718 tonnes (1691 tons)
Rigging:	Four masts, square-rigged
Complement:	70
Main routes:	Dundee–India, North Atlantic
Cargo:	Jute, general cargo, coal hulk

Cunene

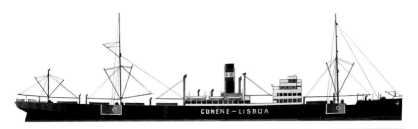

The *Cunene* was a typical cargo liner of the pre–World War I period, with accommodation for a dozen passengers. Her numerous derricks enabled her to handle her own cargo. Under the terms of the Treaty of Versailles, Germany was made to forfeit all merchant ships of over 1616 tonnes (1600 tons), and these were distributed among the Allied nations as reparation for war losses. As a member of the alliance, Portugal, whose troops had fought on the Western Front since the end of 1916, benefited from this distribution. The cargo liner *Adelaide* was handed over, renamed *Cunene* and put into service between Lisbon and the African colonies of Angola and Mozambique. She was laid up from 1925 to 1930, then reactivated, not being scrapped until 1955. Germany declared war on Portugal in March 1916, after the Portuguese seized 36 German ships in the River Tagus.

Country of origin:	Germany
Date of origin:	1911
Dimensions:	137m x 17.6m x 7.7m (450ft x 58ft x 25ft 3in)
Tonnage:	8966 tonnes (8825 tons)
Machinery:	Single shaft, triple-expansion, 4500hp
Service speed:	12 knots
Cargo:	General
Constructor:	AG Vulcan, Stettin
Built for:	Not known

Cutty Sark

The clipper *Cutty Sark*'s keel was laid at the Dumbarton yard of Scott, Linton & Coearly in 1869, and the ship was launched in November of that year. Her maiden voyage began on 15 February 1870, when she set sail for China, arriving at Shanghai on 31 May, just 104 days after leaving Britain. *Cutty Sark* spent eight years in the sea trade, making eight voyages; her best time was logged on her second voyage, when she made a home run in 107 days. With the decline of the clipper trade following the opening of the Suez Canal, Cutty Sark spent some years in general trade and was used to carry general cargo to Australia and raw wool on the return voyage, her fastest time being 69 days. In 1895, she was sold to a Portuguese owner and sailed under that country's flag for 27 years as the *Ferreira* and later the *Maria do Amparo*. She is now preserved at the National Maritime Museum, Greenwich.

Country of origin:	Britain
Date of origin:	1869
Length:	64.8m (212ft 6in)
Beam:	11m (36ft)
Tonnage:	978 tonnes (963 tons)
Rigging:	Three masts, square-rigged
Complement:	70
Main routes:	China–London, London–Australia–London
Cargo:	Tea, general goods, wool

Dos Amigos

The chief requirement of a slave ship was speed, both to reduce the deaths among its human cargo during the crossing of the Atlantic and to evade anti-slavery patrols. *Dos Amigos* was basically schooner-rigged, with very tall, raked masts; she set an upper topgallant on the mainmast, and a long boom protruded over the stern to accommodate the very large gaffsail on the aftermast. *Dos Amigos* was eventually captured by a British warship, commissioned into the Royal Navy as the *Fair Rosamond* and used to fight the vicious trade in which she had participated. It was the Royal Navy that put an end to the slave trade at sea, through years of patient and dangerous patrols off the coasts of Africa and in the Persian Gulf and the Caribbean. It also put an end to piracy, British gunboats hunting down the last pirate vessels in the 1860s.

Country of origin:	USA
Date of origin:	1830
Length:	27.4m (90ft)
Beam:	7m (23ft)
Tonnage:	Not known
Rigging:	Two masts; topsail schooner rig
Complement:	10
Main routes:	West Africa – West Indies – American Confederacy
Cargo:	Slaves

Dunkerque

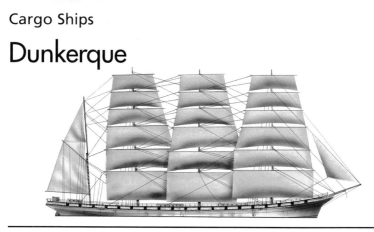

During the last two decades of the nineteenth century, the French government, intent on boosting domestic steel production, made a significant contribution (65 francs per ton) to the cost of building ships in this material, and French ship owners were quick to take advantage of the offer. One of the most important among them was AD Bordes et fils of Dunkerque. In February 1897, it took delivery of a new four-masted steel barque, the *Dunkerque*, from Laporte et Cie of Rouen. She was to replace a similar Scottish-built ship of the same name, lost in mysterious circumstances on a voyage from Cardiff to Rio de Janeiro with a cargo of coal in June 1891. The *Dunkerque* was intended for the Chilean nitrate trade and remained in that service until 1924, when she was broken up in Italy. In April 1906, she rescued the few survivors of a Belgian sail training ship which sank in the Atlantic.

Country of origin:	France
Date of origin:	1896
Length:	99.85m (327ft 8in)
Beam:	13.85m (45ft 6in)
Tonnage:	3392 tonnes (3338 tons)
Rigging:	Three masts, square-rigged; lateen mizzen
Complement:	100
Main routes:	France–Chile
Cargo:	Nitrates

Felucca

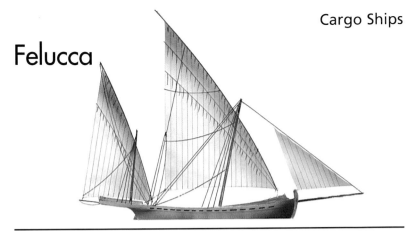

The racy lines of the felucca clearly display its Mediterranean descent from the galley, and variants of this craft were found everywhere between Gibraltar and the Levant. The forward-raked mainmast supports a lateen mainsail and a jib on a long boom; the raised afterdeck extends well out over the stern. Known from the early seventeenth century, its name suggests an Arab origin. With between eight and 20 oars to drive it along in calm conditions, it was capable of a fair turn of speed and was often used as a privateer or pirate ship. Few vessels of this type were built after the eighteenth century. In the late 1700s, the French used feluccas as blockade runners, and they were usually capable of outrunning the British warships that were blockading French ports during the long-running wars against Napoleon and republican France.

Country of origin:	Spain
Date of origin:	1800
Length:	17.8m (58ft 6in)
Beam:	5.1m (16ft 11in)
Tonnage:	50.8 tonnes (50 tons)
Rigging:	Two masts; forward-raked mainmast with lateeen mainsail and jib; lateen mizzen
Complement:	20
Main routes:	Mediterranean
Cargo:	Light general cargo

Cargo Ships

Flying Cloud

Designed by the Scots-Canadian Donald McKay and launched at East Boston, *Flying Cloud* was claimed to be the fastest American clipper, perhaps the fastest of all clippers. Her maiden voyage from New York to San Francisco was made in 98 days and 21 hours. In 1854, she shaved 13 hours from that time, a record broken only once before 1888 (by the *Andrew Jackson* in 1860) and then by only four hours. Her best day's run was a remarkable 647km (402 miles). From 1859, she sailed between England, China and Australia. She passed into British ownership in 1862, and for almost ten years she ran immigrant passengers from England to Australia, returning with wool. In her latter days, she carried pig iron between Newcastle, England, and St John's, New Brunswick, returning with timber. She ran aground in 1875, breaking her back, and her hulk was burned.

Country of origin:	USA
Date of origin:	1851
Length:	71.6m (235ft)
Beam:	12.4m (40ft 9in)
Tonnage:	1812 tonnes (1783 tons)
Rigging:	Three masts, full-rigged ship
Complement:	Not known
Main routes:	Main oceanic trading routes
Cargo:	Tea, wool, cotton, nitrates

Formby

Steel, with its much-superior strength, was a far more satisfactory material for the construction of large ships than iron or wood. With the widespread adoption of the Bessemer process (the first cheap method of making steel) from the mid-1850s, it also became much more realistically priced. In 1863, the shipbuilders Jones, Quiggin & Co. of Liverpool built their first ship in the material. The *Formby* was to be the first major steel ship – earlier efforts had been considerably less ambitious – and was an immediate success; Jones, Quiggin & Co. built at least three more ships to the same design. Though at £24,000 she cost perhaps 35 per cent more than an iron ship of similar size, the premium was considered reasonable, given that she could load over 15 per cent more cargo. Her crew was reduced, too, thanks to the adoption of labour-saving devices such as Emerson & Walker's patent windlass.

Country of origin:	Britain
Date of origin:	1863
Length:	63.85m (209ft 5in)
Beam:	10.95m (36ft)
Tonnage:	1291 tonnes (1271 tons)
Rigging:	Three masts, full-rigged ship
Complement:	40
Main routes:	Main ocean trading routes
Cargo:	General

France

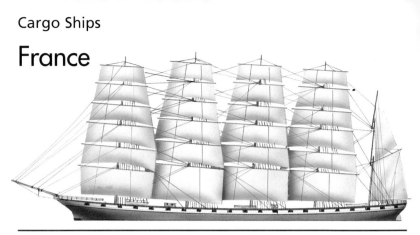

T he five-masted barque *France* was the biggest sailing ship in the world when she was launched – 110m (361ft) long and able to load up to 5582 tonnes (5500 tons) of bulk cargo. She was built for the Chilean nitrate trade; rainless northern Chile was rich in manganese ore, nitrate of soda, iodine and many other sought-after commodities. *France* also proved to be surprisingly fast, her best outward-bound passage being just 63 days. She was also comparatively easy to work, being equipped with steam winches used both for making sail and for cargo handling. In 1897, she suffered a freak accident when she was run down in the dark by the British cruiser HMS *Blenheim*, which saw lights at bow and stern and made to steer between them. She was repaired and returned to service, but foundered off Brazil in March 1901.

Country of origin:	France
Date of origin:	1890
Length:	110m (361ft)
Beam:	14.9m (48ft 9in)
Tonnage:	3844 tonnes (3784 tons)
Rigging:	Five masts, full-rigged ship
Complement:	80
Main routes:	France–Chile
Cargo:	Nitrates

Friendship

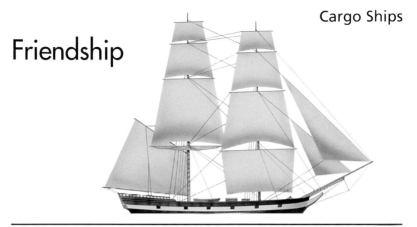

This ship, probably new in 1780, was chartered by the British government to transport convicts to Australia as part of the First Fleet of May 1787. She was intended to carry female convicts for the entire journey; however, when the fleet called at Cape Town, these were transferred to other vessels for the sake of good order and discipline, four members of *Friendship*'s crew having been flogged for 'excessive fraternization' with the women. *Friendship*'s new cargo was sheep, which supposedly would not lead the sailors into temptation. On the return journey, she was scuttled in Macassar Strait on 28 October 1788, and her remaining crew transferred to another ship, the *Alexander*. The First Fleet comprised a squadron of 11 ships under the command of Captain Arthur Phillip, carrying some 1500 convicts in addition to the crews.

Country of origin:	Britain
Date of origin:	1780
Length:	Not known
Beam:	Not known
Tonnage:	282.5 tonnes (278 tons)
Rigging:	Three masts, square rig
Complement:	Not known
Main routes:	England–Australia
Cargo:	Convicts

Great Republic

One of many notable ships designed by Donald McKay, *Great Republic*, built at East Boston, was the largest sailing vessel constructed in the United States and one of the largest wooden vessels ever built. Although her hull was drawn on clipper lines, she carried four masts – square-rigged on all but the mizzen, which was fore-and-aft rigged – and was in effect the first four-masted barque. She was loading at New York for a maiden voyage to Liverpool when a bakery adjacent to the quay caught fire. Sparks from the burning building rapidly set the rigging ablaze, and the upper works were severely burned. McKay sold her, and she was rebuilt in somewhat altered form internally, with three instead of four decks and reduced sail. Sold to an English company, she was renamed *Denmark*. She foundered off Bermuda on 5 March 1872 after springing a leak; all her crew were rescued.

Country of origin:	USA
Date of origin:	1853
Length:	92m (320ft)
Beam:	14.8m (48.4ft)
Tonnage:	4627 tonnes (4555 tons)
Rigging:	Four masts; fore-and-aft rigged on mizzen, square-rigged on remainder
Complement:	130 (later 70)
Main routes:	New York – San Francisco, transatlantic
Cargo:	Bulk freight

Hakuryu Maru

The *Hakuryu Maru* was built for a single purpose: to carry coiled sheet steel from the steelworks at Fukuyama either to deep-sea ports for trans-shipment or directly to consumer plants. She was built with almost 1400 tonnes (1378 tons) of permanent ballast to minimize her movement while loading and unloading, and cargo stowage always adhered to the same plan. Loading and unloading procedures are largely automated. The steel cable is transferred to a lift table suspended from four hydraulic cylinders. The table is then lowered to pallet carriers, each with a 90-tonne (88-ton) load capacity, and the steel coils are then stowed in the appropriate cargo spaces. To maximize cargo capacity, one load is left on the lift table while the ship is in transit. The ship's hull has a deep double bottom to accommodate the concrete ballast.

Country of origin:	Japan
Date of origin:	1991
Dimensions:	115m x 18m x 5m (377ft 4in x 59ft x 16ft 6in)
Tonnage:	5278 tonnes (5295 tons)
Machinery:	Single screw, diesel engines
Service speed:	11.5 knots
Cargo:	Sheet steel
Constructor:	Kawasaki Heavy Industries
Built for:	Japanese steel industry

Cargo Ships

Helena

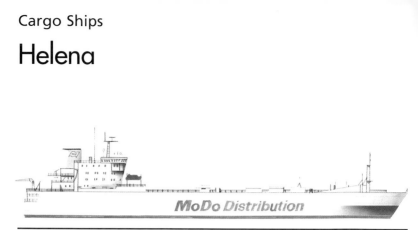

MoDo Distribution

The *Helena* is one of a new generation of roll-on, roll-off (ro-ro) freighters designed to carry a mixed cargo consisting of paper products, trailers, small cars and containers. She has a full-length double bottom, plus a double skin in the lower cargo areas and engine room. Traffic when loading is two-way, access to her three lower cargo decks being by gained by means of intermediate ramps from the level of the weather deck, which is itself accessed by a stern ramp. Containers can be stowed three deep on the weather deck. All cargo-handling operations are monitored by closed circuit television on display units in the wheelhouse and the engine room control centre. *Helena* entered service in August 1991 and operates between Sweden, the Baltic ports and other destinations in northern Europe.

Country of origin:	Sweden
Date of origin:	1990
Dimensions:	169m x 25.6m x 7m (554ft 6in x 84ft x 23ft)
Tonnage:	22,548 tonnes (22,193 tons)
Machinery:	Two shafts, diesel engines; 6250hp
Service speed:	14.5 knots
Cargo:	General
Constructor:	Daewoo
Built for:	MoDo Distribution

Herzogin Cecilie

In 1903, the Norddeutscher Lloyd Line took delivery of a purpose-built sail training ship, named after the *Herzogin Cecilie von Mecklenburg-Schwerin*. The *Herzogin Cecilie* was to be manned by a mixed crew of experienced seamen and the company's officer cadets (experience under sail was still a requirement, at the time, for an officer's 'ticket'). She was to trade between Bremerhaven, Australia and South America, carrying mixed cargo outward bound and grain, nitrates and other bulk cargo on the home run. From 1914 to 1920, she was interned in Chile and, on her return to Europe, was awarded in reparation to France, but then sold to Gustaf Erikson of Mariehamn in the Aland Islands. Homeward bound from Australia in April 1936, she ran aground near Bolt Head off England's south coast. Most of her cargo was offloaded and she was refloated, only to be wrecked off Salcombe harbour.

Country of origin:	Germany
Date of origin:	1902
Length:	94.5m (310ft)
Beam:	14m (46ft)
Tonnage:	3294 tonnes (3242 tons)
Rigging:	Three masts, square-rigged; lateen mizzen
Complement:	200, including cadets
Main routes:	Europe–Australia–South America
Cargo:	Bulk, mainly grain and nitrates

Hudson Rex

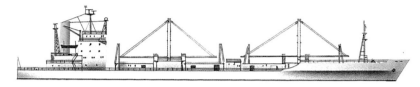

The design of *Hudson Rex* reflected a move away from modern, fully automated cargo-handling methods to the conventional derrick booms used previously in large cargo vessels. The vessel carries eight derrick booms, one for each cargo hold, and these are operated by electro-hydraulic winches. Fans supply cold air to the refrigerated area, and there is also a comprehensive insulation system. The refrigeration system is installed in the engine room. A composite boiler supplies steam, and three alternators supply power for all electrical requirements in the ship. Temperature control is monitored from the main control centre also located in the engine room. Like many other merchant vessels, *Hudson Rex* flies the Panamanian flag, a so-called 'flag of convenience'. Another such flag was that of Liberia.

Country of origin:	Panama
Date of origin:	1991
Dimensions:	148.5m x 20.6m x 9.4m (487ft 3in x 67ft 7in x 31ft)
Tonnage:	12,192 tonnes (12,000 tons)
Machinery:	Single shaft, diesel engines
Service speed:	19.2 knots
Cargo:	Refrigerated goods
Constructor:	Not known
Built for:	Not known

Huntsman

Despite having been constructed as late as 1921, the *Huntsman* was of somewhat antiquated appearance. She was one of the last vessels to be built with the classic four-masted rig popular during previous decades, although the masts served as anchor posts for derricks, rather than for setting sail. By this time, most merchant vessels were using the much handier king posts. *Huntsman* had two continuous decks, with a third deck partly covering number-one hold. The bridge was between the first and second mast, and a tall funnel was positioned amidships. It was this tall, unraked funnel, together with the straight stem and counter stern, which gave the impression of a ship from a bygone age. In October 1930, she became one of nine merchant ships that fell victim to the German commerce raider *Admiral Graf Spee*.

Country of origin:	Britain
Date of origin:	1921
Dimensions:	153m x 17.6m x 8.4m (502ft x 58ft x 27ft 6in)
Tonnage:	12,151 tonnes (11,960 tons)
Machinery:	Single shaft, single reduction turbine; 3200hp
Service speed:	13 knots
Cargo:	General
Constructor:	Not known
Built for:	Not known

Cargo Ships

Iris

The *Iris* was a French lugger successfully used in smuggling; she carried two lugsails for easy handling by a crew of four or five. The hold had false bulkheads plus an additional lining standing out from the hull, behind which was hidden contraband. More could be carried beneath a false bottom or beneath the ballast of stone or iron. Some luggers, including the *Iris*, were fast on a wind and could often leave a revenue cutter behind in a long chase, as they could change tack more easily. *Iris* was eventually captured in December 1819 after successfully landing a cargo earlier in the day on the south coast of England after a fast run from Boulogne. At one time during the 1800s, 20,000 people in England alone were engaged in smuggling, with ships such as the *Iris* playing a prime role in the 'trade'.

Country of origin:	France
Date of origin:	1818
Length:	18.3m (60ft)
Beam:	1.7m (5ft 6in)
Tonnage:	Not known
Rigging:	Two lugsails
Complement:	4–5
Main routes:	English Channel
Cargo:	Contraband goods

Isar

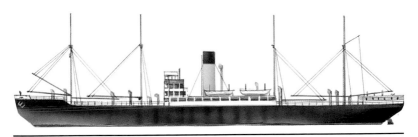

The *Isar* was one of the last in a group of successful cargo liners built for the German Norddeutscher Lloyd Line, all of which had a similar layout, with a short, raised forecastle, four tall masts and eight hatches. *Isar* differed from her sister ships by having a modified hull form, with a stem that sloped back sharply, joining the keel beneath the foremast. Isar was the first merchant vessel to feature this so-called 'Maierform' hull, which gave reduced skin friction and easier water flow, so producing better speed and fuel consumption. The design was used in many later passenger/cargo ships. A turbine could be coupled to *Isar*'s conventional reciprocating engine to provide economical steaming. Isar was sold on to other companies, being successively renamed *Stanroyal*, *Huron* and *Necip Ipar*.

Country of origin:	Germany
Date of origin:	1929
Dimensions:	166.6m x 19.4m x 8.5m (546ft 6in x 63ft 6in x 28ft)
Tonnage:	9170 tonnes (9026 tons)
Machinery:	Single shaft, triple-expansion/geared turbine; 6500hp
Service speed:	14 knots
Cargo:	General
Constructor:	AG Vulcan, Hamburg
Built for:	Norddeutscher Lloyd Line

Krasnograd

The *Krasnograd* was one of many modern ships built for the Russian merchant marine at a foreign yard following the glasnost era that came in the later years of the Soviet Union. She was a multi-role container ship/bulk cargo carrier – for grain, in particular – with four holds and general cargo in containers on two throughdecks. She was equipped with five electric cranes and two 24.6-tonne (25-ton) derricks to allow her crew to handle cargo themselves. After only a short time in Russian service, she was sold to Greek interests and sailed under Maltese registration as the *Nordana Surveyor*. The years following the end of World War II saw a massive increase in the number of vessels flying the Russian flag, as the Soviet Union expanded its overseas commitments. In recent years, however, the requirement has been for a reduced merchant fleet equipped with modern vessels.

Country of origin:	Russia
Date of origin:	1992
Dimensions:	164m x 20m x 8.5m (538ft x 66ft 3in x 27ft 10in)
Tonnage:	16,333 tonnes (16,075 tons)
Machinery:	Single shaft, diesel; 12,960hp
Service speed:	18 knots
Cargo:	Bulk and general
Constructor:	Neptun Industrie, Rostock
Built for:	Murmansk Shipping Co.

Kruzenstern

The four-masted barque *Kruzenstern* was originally constructed for one of Germany's great shipping concerns, Ferdinand Laeisz's Flying 'P' Line, as the *Padua* (all Laeisz's ships had names beginning with P). She was one of 16 similar vessels, most from the same yard, carrying nitrates from Chile and later wool from Australia, and was one of the last sailing ships in the commercial trade. She was acquired by the Soviet Union after World War II and was much modified below decks, being used as an oceanographic survey ship. Ownership passed to Estonia in the early 1990s. One other sailing vessel was acquired by the Soviet Union at the end of World War II; she was the sail training ship *Gorch Fock*. Scuttled at Stralsund in May 1945, she was raised and went to Russia as the *Tovarishch*. In the 1990s, she took part in the Tall Ships races.

Country of origin:	Germany
Date of origin:	1926
Dimensions:	114.6m x 14m x 6.9m (376ft x 46ft x 22ft 6in)
Tonnage:	3113 tonnes (3064 tons)
Machinery:	Two shafts, auxiliary diesels; 1600hp
Service speed:	Not applicable
Cargo:	Nitrates, wool
Constructor:	J. C. Tecklenborg, Bremerhaven
Built for:	Reederei Ferdinand Laeisz

Lakatoi

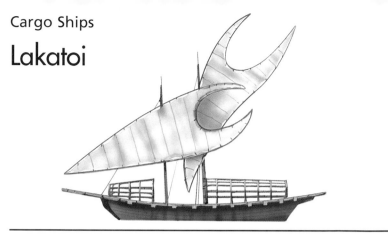

A form of trimaran, this striking vessel from New Guinea consisted of three dugout hulls joined to one another by transverse beams and supporting a deck made of bamboo. Two masts, set close to each other in the midship area, carried the bamboo-framed 'crabclaw' sails found on other ancient South Pacific vessels. The example illustrated here dates from the mid-nineteenth century. Although the *Lakatoi* had no hold, baled cargo such as attap leaves or copra could be carried, lashed to the deck to keep it secure. With cabins built on deck, the *Lakatoi* was certainly a vessel intended for sea voyages. It is the descendant of the large double-hulled craft in which the early Polynesian seafarers traversed vast areas of the Pacific, settling the scattered islands – and inadvertently bringing with them the rats that eventually wiped out much of the native fauna.

Country of origin:	New Guinea
Date of origin:	1850
Length:	c. 12.2m (40ft)
Beam:	c. 4.9m (16ft)
Tonnage:	Not known
Rigging:	Bipod mast; two claw-shaped bamboo-framed sails
Complement:	Not known
Main routes:	South Pacific islands
Cargo:	Tropical produce

Lawhill

The four-masted barque *Lawhill* was built for the jute trade, this strong vegetable fibre being the primary ingredient in the manufacture of ropes and sacking, but was too late to succeed in it and was given over to the carriage of general cargo which included grain and nitrates. In 1900, she was sold to the Anglo-American Oil Company to carry case oil (kerosene) to the Far East and passed into Finnish ownership in 1914. Gustaf Erikson bought her in 1917, and she sailed under his flag until 1941, when she was seized in South Africa. *Lawhill* was later sold to Portuguese interests, but never went to sea again, being scrapped in 1958. In the course of an active career spanning over half a century, *Lawhill* made a total of 50 voyages, not including coastal passages. Most of her early voyages were to India, a principal exporter of jute.

Country of origin:	Britain
Date of origin:	1892
Length:	96.7m (317ft 4in)
Beam:	13.7m (45ft)
Tonnage:	2861 tonnes (2816 tons)
Rigging:	Three masts, square-rigged
Complement:	80
Main routes:	Main ocean routes
Cargo:	General

Cargo Ships

Lorcha

The *Lorcha* was a Chinese vessel in which the traditional style of lugsail junk rig was fitted to a hull built in the European style. The slightly raked stem has a short boom; there was a forecastle, a waist and a raised afterdeck. Lorchas were chiefly built in south China, around Canton and Hong Kong. Originally, they may have been used as pirate-hunters, their finer lines making them swifter than the pirate junks of the South China Sea. That they were probably used in this role is indicated by the boat they carried slung at the stem, ready for boarding operations when a pirate ship had been successfully intercepted. Piracy was rife in the South China Sea during this period and therefore constituted a serious threat to commerce. It was finally suppressed by the Royal Navy in the later years of the nineteenth century.

Country of origin:	China
Date of origin:	1850
Length:	29.9m (98ft)
Beam:	6.7m (22ft)
Tonnage:	Not known
Rigging:	Three masts; lugsail rig with slatted fibre sails
Complement:	4
Main routes:	South China coast
Cargo:	Rice, general

Marie Sophie

The *Marie Sophie* was a brig, a two-masted vessel carrying conventional square sail – usually a course, a single topsail, a single topgallant and a royal – on both masts, with an additional four-sided gaff spanker on the main mast. Sometimes the last sail was laced to a short independent mast stepped immediately about the main, in which case the vessel was properly known as a snow. In a very real sense, a brig was a full-rigged ship reduced to two masts. While this rig was more expensive than that of the brigantine or the schooner, it was more flexible. Two-masted vessels were commonly used in the coastal and short sea trades, and craft such as the brig were favourite subjects for maritime artists, who sought to portray the solid, everyday dependability of Britain's seaborne commerce which was at its height during the later decades of the nineteenth century.

Country of origin:	Britain
Date of origin:	1879
Length:	34.1m (112ft)
Beam:	8.1m (26ft 6in)
Tonnage:	193 tonnes (190 tons)
Rigging:	Two masts, square-rigged
Complement:	10
Main routes:	Coastal, short sea
Cargo:	General

Cargo Ships

Mayflower

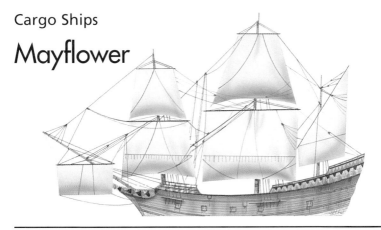

The *Mayflower* plied from London and English south coast ports with such export items as wool and hides, and returned from Bordeaux and Nantes with wine and brandy. She was an entirely typical ship of the galleon type. Her home port was probably Southampton, but the first definite mention of the *Mayflower* occurs in London port papers of 1606, with one Christopher Jones noted as master and co-owner. In 1620, a more momentous voyage was proposed. She was chartered by a group of people who wished to emigrate from England to North America, where they could count on freedom to practise their Puritan religion. The *Mayflower* sailed from Plymouth on 6 September 1620, and the rest is history. The future of her passengers, the Pilgrim Fathers, is well documented; that of the *Mayflower* less so. She returned to England in 1621, but disappeared from the record three years later.

Country of origin:	England
Date of origin:	c. 1606
Length:	c. 27.4m (90ft)
Beam:	c. 7.9m (26ft)
Tonnage:	183 tonnes (180 tons)
Rigging:	Three masts, square-rigged; lateen mizzen
Complement:	About 20 crew, 101 passengers
Main routes:	Normally England–France
Cargo:	Baled wool, wine

Mighty Servant 3

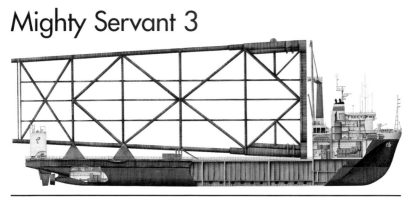

The *Mighty Servant 3* was a semi-submersible heavy-lift ship, specially designed for the transportation of very large objects up to 25,400 tonnes (25,000 tons) in weight. She could take on sufficient water ballast to allow her to be lowered by 10m (33ft), permitting ships with up 7m (23ft) of draught to be loaded. In addition to the ballast tanks, the vessel was equipped with a large hold which had a total cubic capacity of 12,000 cubic metres (423,776 cubic feet), accessible by means of a large hatch and served by a 254-tonne (250-ton) capacity crane. Instead of using water pumps to fill and void the ballast tanks, *Mighty Servant 3* used air compressors, with a capacity such that the whole of the water ballast could be voided in just one hour. Much of *Mighty Servant 3*'s task involved transporting oil rig modules.

Country of origin:	The Netherlands
Date of origin:	1984
Dimensions:	180m x 40m x 12m (590ft 6in x 131ft 3in x 39ft 4in)
Tonnage:	3,978 tonnes (23,600 tons)
Machinery:	Two shafts, diesel-electric engines plus bow thrusters; 16,610hp
Service speed:	14 knots
Cargo:	Heavy components
Constructor:	Oshima, Nagasaki
Built for:	Wijsmuller Transport

Nuestra Señora de Begonia

In 1625, the Spanish government contracted with the Basque shipbuilder Don Martin de Arana for six galleons to carry silver bullion from Spain's colonies in the New World. This was as a result of its awareness of the vulnerability of its treasure ships, especially to the activities of English privateers encouraged by the war between England and Spain, which had been in progress since 1621. One of the six ships was the *Nuestra Señora de Begonia*. Strict guidelines for their construction were laid down, and she and her sister ships, smaller and faster than the usual galleon and normally sailing in convoy formation, all fulfilled their purpose successfully. The reduction in their size enabled the treasure ships to use harbours that were beginning to silt up after more than a century of Spanish exploitation.

Country of origin:	Spain
Date of origin:	1625
Length:	24.6m (80ft 8in)
Beam:	9.5m (31ft 2in)
Tonnage:	457 tonnes (450 tons)
Rigging:	Three masts; square-rigged on fore and main, with lateen mizzen
Complement:	Not known
Main routes:	American harbours – Seville and other Spanish ports
Cargo:	Silver, gold, other ores, field and forest products

Raven

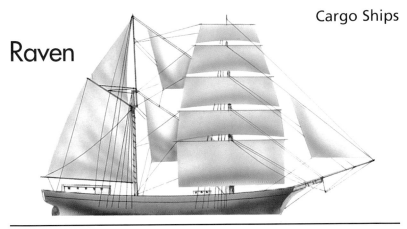

The *Raven* was a brigantine, which, as the name suggests, was a variant of the brig, with an even simpler sail plan – square sails on the foremast to the topgallant, a fore-and-aft gaff course and square topsail on the main. Relative to the spanker carried by ships and barques, the gaff course of the brigantine was larger and more important. When the brigantine's main topsail was replaced by a jib-headed sail, the result was known as a hermaphrodite brig, but this later became the accepted form for the brigantine. *Raven* was simple and straightforward to handle, even when short-handed, and remained popular in the coastal and short sea trades. This particular vessel was built in Canada, but later passed to British ownership and was used on coastal and cross-Channel routes, carrying general cargo. The Royal Navy retained some brigs for use as sail training ships well into the twentieth century.

Country of origin:	Canada
Date of origin:	1875
Length:	27.6m (90ft 6in)
Beam:	7.5m (24ft 6in)
Tonnage:	216 tonnes (213 tons)
Rigging:	See main text
Complement:	8–10
Main routes:	Coastal and short sea routes
Cargo:	General

Result

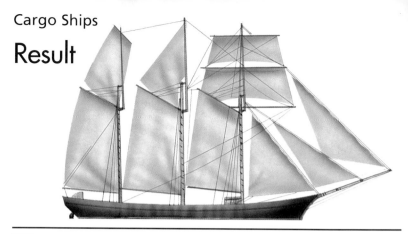

There were comparatively few steel-hulled schooners built in the British Isles; one exception was the *Result*, a three-masted double-topsail schooner constructed in Ulster for a ship owner based in Barrow-in-Furness. The *Result* had a long career in the coastal trade, being fitted with an auxiliary engine and later stripped down to a ketch. She was eventually acquired by the Ulster Folk and Transport Museum, just across Belfast Lough from where she was built. Maritime commerce, however, did not represent the whole story of *Result*'s working life; in 1917 she was taken up by the Royal Navy and armed as a Q-Ship, one of a number of merchant vessels armed with concealed guns to act as decoys in the fight against German U-boats. On one of her voyages in this role, she almost succeeded in sinking the *U-45*, which was later sunk by the RN submarine *D7*.

Country of origin:	Britain
Date of origin:	1893
Length:	37.2m (122ft 2in)
Beam:	6.6m (21ft 9in)
Tonnage:	124 tonnes (122 tons)
Rigging:	Three masts, double-topsail schooner rig
Complement:	12
Main routes:	North Sea, coastal waters
Cargo:	General

Royal William

A wooden-hulled vessel built at Liverpool, England, by William and Thomas Wilson, *Royal William* was one of the first ships to be fitted with watertight bulkheads; they were four in number and made of iron. The ship went into service on the Liverpool–Canada run in 1833 and operated successfully. In a letter of 4 October 1835 to the London *Times*, following various marine disasters, C.W. Williams of Wilson's emphasized the need for higher shipbuilding standards, with special reference to the provision of watertight bulkheads. His point was proven in 1839, when *Royal William* collided with the steamer *Tagus* outside Liverpool; one compartment flooded, but the vessel stayed afloat and was saved. She ended her days as a storage hulk at Dublin, Ireland, where she was broken up in 1888. Another *Royal William*, built at Quebec, also operated on the Canada run at an earlier date.

Country of origin:	Britain
Date of origin:	1831
Length:	53.3m (175ft)
Beam:	8.2m (27ft)
Tonnage:	573 tonnes (564 tons)
Rigging:	Three masts, barquentine rig
Machinery:	Single shaft, steam; 200hp
Complement:	Not known
Cargo:	General goods, passengers

Cargo Ships

Savannah

The *Savannah* was built as an experiment to test the feasibility, both technical and economic, of fitting merchant ships with nuclear power plants. As such, the first two years of her operational life were taken up with demonstration voyages. She then went into (heavily subsidized) service between the United States and Mediterranean ports, first with a small number of paying passengers, latterly with cargo only. Although she was the world's first nuclear-powered freighter, she was not the first nuclear-powered merchant ship. That honour went to the Soviet icebreaker *Lenin*, which made her maiden voyage two months after *Savannah* was launched. *Savannah*, named after the first steamship to cross the Atlantic, was laid up in 1972, having been found uneconomical to operate. A second nuclear-powered freighter, the *Otto Hahn*, was launched in Kiel in June 1964.

Country of origin:	USA
Date of origin:	1959
Dimensions:	181.5m x 23.8m (595ft x 78ft 2in)
Tonnage:	13,817 tonnes (13,599 tons)
Machinery:	Single shaft, nuclear reactor, turbines; 22,000hp
Service speed:	21 knots
Cargo:	General
Constructor:	New York Shipbuilders, Camden, New Jersey
Built for:	US Dept of Commerce/States Marine Lines

Selandia

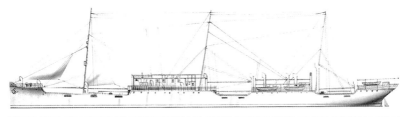

The *Selandia* was the world's first ocean-going motor ship and was built at Copenhagen for the Ostasiatiske Kompanie (East Asia Company), a Danish concern. She carried 7518 tonnes (7400 tons) of cargo and had accommodation for 26 passengers. On her maiden voyage to Bangkok, on 22 February 1912, she covered a total distance of 35,405km (22,000 miles). During the next 12 years, she travelled more than 1,140,000km (600,000 miles), with only 10 days lost in port due to engine trouble. In 1936, she was sold to Norway and renamed *Norseman*. She was wrecked off Japan in January 1942. At the time of *Selandia*'s construction, Dr Rudolf Diesel's engine was a comparatively new concept; this involves compressing air until it becomes hot enough to ignite a lightweight fuel oil. This type of power plant was also known as a compression-ignition engine.

Country of origin:	Denmark
Date of origin:	1911
Dimensions:	117.6m x 16.2m (386ft x 53ft 2in)
Tonnage:	9956 tonnes (9800 tons)
Machinery:	Twin shafts, diesel engines
Service speed:	12 knots
Cargo:	General, plus passengers
Constructor:	Not known
Built for:	Ostasiatiske Kompanie

Slattopare

The Baltic *slattopare* was one of the many regional variations on the basic schooner rig. It was three-masted, generally with all masts of equal height (although a shortened mizzen was also quite common) and carried a square sail from a crossjack (or crojack) yard before the foremast in place of the more normal fore-and-aft staysail. The rig proved enduringly popular in the region where it was developed, and many *slattoparer* made voyages to North America and the Mediterranean. This type of ship was used principally by Denmark, Finland and Sweden. It is not known in which of the three countries it originated, although the name would suggest Finland. During the period when the *slattopare* made its appearance, Finland was joined to the Russian Empire as an autonomous, but not sovereign, Grand Duchy.

Country of origin:	Finland, Denmark, Sweden
Date of origin:	c. 1860
Length:	35m (115ft)
Beam:	7.6m (25ft)
Tonnage:	152 tonnes (150 tons)
Rigging:	See main text
Complement:	Not known
Main routes:	Mainly coastal
Cargo:	General

Speronara

A number of archaic Mediterranean features can be detected in this Maltese craft, although it also sports a jib boom and jib on a long stay in addition to the more traditional lateen sail. With numerous variants of rig, the *speronara* served as a small packet boat and general cargo boat. The hull was double-ended, mostly undecked, and with a low freeboard. The name refers to the vestigial *sperone*, or ram, and not to any specific rig or number of masts. Maltese boat design reflects the island's chequered history and in particular its connection with the Phoenician colony of Carthage. The Carthaginians, who were excellent seafarers, are said to have colonized Malta in ancient times. According to legend, the tomb of the great warrior Hannibal is said to lie hidden on the island. The specifications given below are for a three-masted *speronara*, *La Concetta Immaculata*, of 1882.

Country of origin:	Malta
Date of origin:	1850
Length:	15.5m (50ft 10in)
Beam:	4.4m (14ft 5in)
Tonnage:	17.2 tonnes (17 tons)
Rigging:	Three masts, lateen rig
Complement:	3–4
Main routes:	Malta–Sicily
Cargo:	General, plus passengers

Thomas W. Lawson

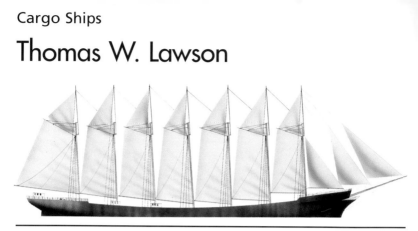

The *Thomas W. Lawson* was the largest sailing schooner ever built, her seven 58m (190ft) masts each carrying a course, a jib-headed topsail and a topmast staysail plus five headsails. She was built of steel by the Fore River Ship & Engine Building Company at Quincy, Massachusetts. Launched in 1902, she was originally employed in the coal trade, carrying 11,177 tonnes (11,000 tons) of coal on each voyage. She was soon converted to carry oil in bulk from the Gulf of Mexico, her draught being too great for the coaling ports. Every halyard, topping lift and sheet aboard the big vessel led to one or other of two large steam winches – one forward, the other on the after deckhouse. As a result, she needed a crew of just 16 men, but was unhandy in anything but strong winds. She was lost in heavy weather off the Scilly Isles on 13 December 1907. Only her captain and one of her crewmen survived.

Country of origin:	USA
Date of origin:	1902
Length:	117.3m (385ft)
Beam:	15.2m (50ft)
Tonnage:	5302 tonnes (5218 tons)
Rigging:	See main text
Complement:	16
Main routes:	US coastal waters, Atlantic
Cargo:	Coal, oil

Topaz

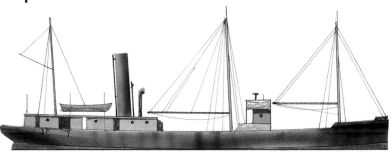

T he *Topaz* was typical of the small coasters that thrived in the British coastal trade from 1900 to 1925, and had a service speed of 8 knots. She was of simple design, with a long quarterdeck extending half the length of the hull, a raised forecastle and a short well deck with a standard bridge at the end. Positioning of the derricks and handling gear varied with the needs of each ship. Aft was a bunker running across the width of the vessel with a capacity of 7.1 tonnes (7 tons) of coal. There was a small mizzen mast right aft for a steadying sail, plus a main mast aft of the bridge and one forward, rising up from the forecastle; all were fitted with derricks. The 'dirty British coasters with their salt-caked smoke-stacks' were once a common sight around the shores of Britain. *Topaz* was scrapped in 1956, having given good service for over 30 years.

Country of origin:	Britain
Date of origin:	1920
Dimensions:	51.2m x 8.2m x 4m (168ft x 27ft x 13ft)
Tonnage:	586 tonnes (577 tons)
Machinery:	Single shaft, triple-expansion
Service speed:	8 knots
Cargo:	General
Constructor:	Lewis
Built for:	W. Robertson, Glasgow

Waterwitch

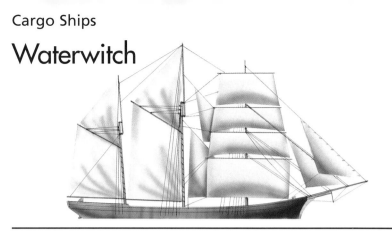

The barquentine was a vessel carrying fore-and-aft sails on all but the foremost of its three or sometimes four masts, the foremost being square-rigged to topgallants. This rig proved to be easily manageable and economical. As it became possible to build longer and longer ships, so additional masts were carried; this rig proved very popular and was to be enduringly so. It was almost as weatherly as the barque rig, in addition to which it was cheaper to construct and needed a smaller crew. Many of the late twentieth-century sailing cruise ships adopted this rig, often with a modified arrangement of courses and staysails. The first ocean cruise of which details survive was a four-month voyage around the Mediterranean, organized by the Peninsular and Orient Steam Navigation Co., starting from Southampton on 26 July 1844.

Country of origin:	Britain
Date of origin:	1872
Length:	62.5m (205ft)
Beam:	10.7m (35ft)
Tonnage:	914 tonnes (900 tons)
Rigging:	See main text
Complement:	15
Main routes:	Principal ocean routes
Cargo:	General

Wyoming

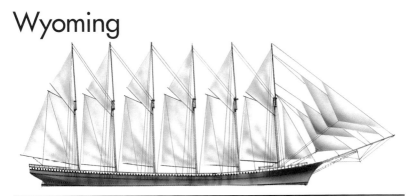

The six-masted schooner *Wyoming*, one of only ten such ships ever constructed, was probably the biggest wooden ship ever built and measured 100.4m (329ft 6in) in length. She was constructed in Bath, Maine, in 1909, by which time the coal trade between New England and the ports serving the Pennsylvania coalfields, for which she was built, had largely passed to steamships. In 1916, the *Wyoming* was sold by her original owners, Percy & Small (also her builders), for the not inconsiderable sum of $350,000. However, she seems to have been a good investment because, by 1 October 1919, she was reported to have paid for herself twice over. In March 1924, while en route from Norfolk to St John, she was overtaken by a storm and foundered with the loss of all 13 hands, a sad end to a splendid and successful vessel.

Country of origin:	USA
Date of origin:	1909
Length:	100.4m (329ft 6in)
Beam:	15.2m (50ft)
Tonnage:	3790 tonnes (3730 tons)
Rigging:	Six masts, schooner-rigged
Complement:	13
Main routes:	Eastern seaboard, USA
Cargo:	Coal

Yeoman Burn

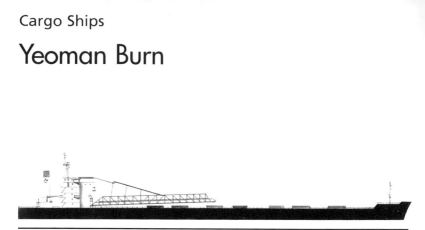

A Norwegian bulk carrier, *Yeoman Burn* was launched in October 1990, her builders entering into a 20-year contract with a British company. The vessel carries iron ore, limestone, salt, and coke or grain in bulk. The hull has nine separate holds and is double-skinned and double-bottomed. *Yeoman Burn* has completely automated loading and unloading equipment and carries a crew of 25. To this day, designers of very large ships such as the *Yeoman Burn* use the so-called Isherwood system of construction, patented by Sir John Isherwood in 1910, which provides the immense longitudinal strength that is required for the carriage of heavy bulk cargoes. The actual stresses involved are known as 'sagging', when the middle of vessel sags due to heavy weight or rough weather, and 'hogging', which means the reverse.

Country of origin:	Norway
Date of origin:	1990
Dimensions:	245m x 32.2m x 14m (830ft 10in x 105ft 8in x 46ft)
Tonnage:	78,740 tonnes (77,500 tons)
Machinery:	Single shaft, diesel engines
Service speed:	14.6 knots
Cargo:	Bulk
Constructor:	Not known
Built for:	Not known

A. J. Meerwald

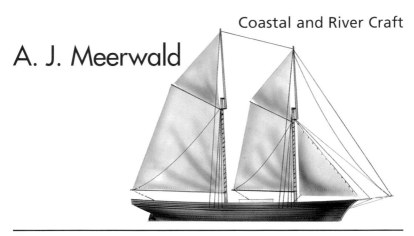

The *A. J. Meerwald*, a schooner-rigged oyster dredger, was to have a second lease of life as a working feature of a maritime exhibition and as an occasional sail training vessel. She was originally constructed in Dorchester, New Jersey, near the mouth of the short Maurice River, which runs into Delaware Bay. The vessel ran the fresh-dredged shellfish to markets in nearby Wilmington, Philadelphia and Camden, up the Delaware River. *A. J. Meerwald* was typical of the Delaware Bay oyster dredger schooners; she was substantially rebuilt after half a century and put back into commission in her original form. At the height of *A. J. Meerwald*'s career, Delaware Bay was one of the most prolific oyster fisheries in North America, rivalled only by Chesapeake Bay. *A. J. Meerwald* was named after the company that bought her, which was based in South Dennis, New Jersey.

Country of origin:	USA
Date of origin:	1928
Length:	23.3m (76ft 4in)
Beam:	6.8m (22ft 2in)
Tonnage:	57.9 tonnes (57 tons)
Rigging:	Two masts, schooner-rigged
Machinery:	Single shaft, auxiliary diesel; 100hp
Main routes:	Delaware River
Cargo:	Oysters

Adelaide

The *Adelaide* was believed to be the oldest wooden-hulled steamer still operating in 2000, 134 years after she was built in Echuca, Victoria, Australia. She was built for towing barges laden with wool up and down the Murray River; however, for most of her working life (from 1872 to 1957), she hauled trains of barges laden with red gum logs to the Echuca sawmills. She was laid up ashore between 1963 and 1984, but was then entirely refurbished and refloated, to operate in conjunction with a restored barge, *D26*. The *Adelaide* still runs on her original engine, built by Fulton & Shaw in Melbourne; like most power units on Murray River vessels, it was wood-fired, and can generate up to 36hp. The *Adelaide* herself was built by G. Link of Echuca, Victoria. She is now owned by the City of Echuca.

Country of origin:	Australia
Date of origin:	1866
Length:	23.3m (76ft 5in)
Beam:	5.2m (17ft)
Tonnage:	58.9 tonnes (58 tons)
Machinery:	Side wheels, two-cylinder reciprocating; 36hp
Complement:	4
Main routes:	Murray River
Cargo:	Timber

Anchor Hoy

O riginally mostly coastal traders, hoys found a specialized use as service
vessels to large naval ships. The anchor hoy was used in naval anchorages to
transport the massive anchors required by ships of the line and was equipped with
two capstans in order to distribute the weight. It could also be used to warp big
ships from their moorings when they could not use their sails and to transport
provisions from a harbour to ships lying close inshore. The mainsail was mounted
in a trysail mast, as the mainmast was fitted with the tackle used for hoisting the
anchors. It may be claimed with justification that the hoy was the original harbour
service vessel, and it remained an important asset until the advent of the steam
tug, which revolutionized the movement of shipping in the confined environment
of a port.

Country of origin:	USA and others
Date of origin:	1820
Length:	18.6m (61ft)
Beam:	6.1m (20ft)
Tonnage:	Not known
Rigging:	Single mast with topmast and trysail mast; fore-and-aft rig
Complement:	4
Main routes:	Naval anchorages
Cargo:	Anchors

Baikal

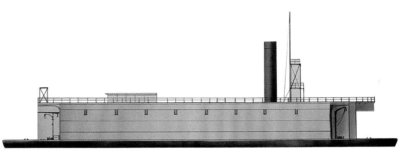

The trains of the Trans-Siberian Railway, which was completed in 1901, originally crossed Lake Baikal – some 645km (400 miles) long and 100km (60 miles) wide – aboard a ferry named after the lake. The *Baikal* was constructed by Armstrong shipbuilders at Elswick, on the River Tyne, England, and was broken down into manageable sections for the long overland journey across Russia to her destination, where she was reassembled. She was one of the largest vessels ever to be prefabricated, transported in sections and assembeld on site. *Baikal* had a strengthened hull and had a secondary role as an icebreaker in the winter. She remained in service until the railway was extended around the lake's southern tip. The Trans-Siberian Railway is the longest railway in the world, covering 9334km (5799 miles) from Moscow to Nakhoda in the Far East. There are 97 stops in all.

Country of origin:	Russia
Date of origin:	1900
Length:	76.2m (250ft)
Beam:	19.2m (63ft)
Tonnage:	2845 tonnes (2800 tons)
Machinery:	Two shafts, vertical triple-expansion
Complement:	Not known
Route:	Lake Baikal
Cargo:	Rolling stock

Bertha

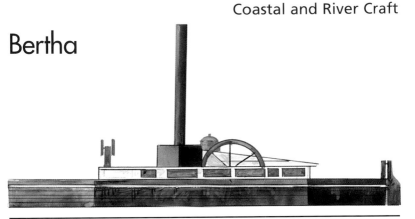

Designed by Isambard Kingdom Brunel and built by Lunel & Co in Bristol, *Bertha* is the oldest steam vessel still afloat. Her long working life was spent scraping mud from bridgewater docks in Somerset with a dozer blade fixed to the end of a long pole mounted aft. She was retired in 1968 when the docks closed and is now on display at Bristol as one of the 'core collection' of British heritage ships. *Bertha*'s official designation was that of a 'drag boat', as she hauled herself along on chains fixed to the quaysides. The talent for marine engineering was something Brunel inherited from his father, an inventor of machines which made, among many other things, blocks for the navy's rigging and boots for the army. Brunel senior was the first to persuade the British Admiralty to investigate the concept of the steam tug.

Country of origin:	Britain
Date of origin:	1844
Length:	16.5m (54ft)
Beam:	4.2m (13ft 9in)
Tonnage:	65 tonnes (64 tons)
Machinery:	Single-acting
Complement:	Not known
Main routes:	River Parrett, England
Cargo:	Not applicable

Boier

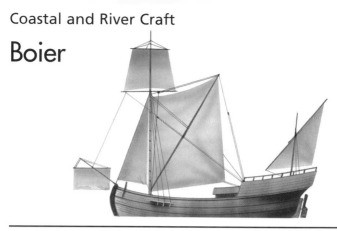

In the sixteenth and seventeenth centuries, the Dutch excelled in building the bulk carriers of their day. The *boier* (or *boejer*) was one such vessel, widely in use by 1575, and an effective short-sea merchant ship. The foresail, not attached to the bowsprit, is a very early example on a seagoing ship. The original rig, with topsail and lateen on the mizzen, gave way over the next century or so to a single-masted spritsail rig and a simpler hull with no quarterdeck. The big spritsail, in its turn, was found to be unwieldy, and in time it gave way to the more manageable gaff rig found on later versions of the *boier*. At about the time of the *boier*'s appearance, trade in the Netherlands was severely disrupted by a revolt of the Dutch population against occupying Spanish forces; much of the country was deliberately flooded.

Country of origin:	The Netherlands
Date of origin:	1565
Length:	21.3m (70ft)
Beam:	6.1m (20ft)
Tonnage:	101.6 tonnes (100 tons)
Rigging:	Two masts; mainmast with spritsail, square topsail and jib; lateen mizzen; spritsail
Complement:	4–6
Main routes:	Dutch and North German coasts
Cargo:	Baled and barrelled goods

Bucintoro

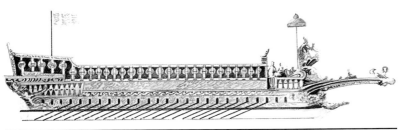

The galley was the traditional vessel used for centuries in the Mediterranean. It served both as a warship and a merchant vessel, although its cargo capacity compares unfavourably with that of the short, rounded hull form of the carrack from the same period. Galleys were widely used to transport soldiers on short journeys, and Venetian galleys provided the bulk of the Christian army's transport during the Crusades. The *Bucintoro* was the state galley of the Doge (Duke) of Venice and was brought out for ceremonial occasions. She had two decks, was ornately carved and gilded, and was propelled by 42 oars. There were several state galleys named *Bucintoro* during the lifetime of the Venetian Republic, which in its heyday extended its influence over much of the central Mediterranean; the last one was broken up in 1824.

Country of origin:	Venetian Republic
Date of origin:	Various
Length:	30m (100ft)
Beam:	6m (20ft)
Tonnage:	Not known
Rigging:	None (oar-propelled)
Complement:	Not known
Main routes:	Mediterranean coasts and rivers
Cargo:	VIP passengers

Cephée

The canal barge *Cephée* was a late example of those used to transport goods from the industrial centres of Belgium and northern France to the port of Antwerp. The basic style of the barges in this region changed little over more than a century and a half, the canal system remaining in everyday use until after World War II. They were exclusively horse-drawn, usually by two teams. In the summer of 1940, many hundreds of motorized barges were requisitioned by the Germans from all over occupied Europe and assembled at the English Channel ports, to be used as troop transports in Hitler's planned invasion of England. The invasion never took place, the Germans having failed to establish air superiority over southern England, and a great many barges were bombed and destroyed in their harbours by the Royal Air Force.

Country of origin:	Belgium
Date of origin:	1937
Length:	38.5m (126ft 5in)
Beam:	5.1m (16ft 7in)
Tonnage:	Not known
Complement:	2–3
Cargo:	General
Constructor:	Pruvost Fräres, Merville
Built for:	Marcel Ruyffelaere

Chaperon

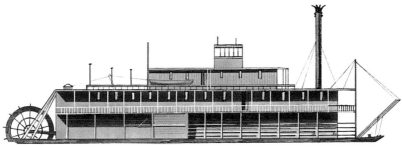

The *Chaperon* was one of more than 5000 paddle steamers built for service on the Mississippi and its tributaries during the nineteenth century. She was built entirely of wood and, as was usual with this kind of craft, had a long, low hull with minimum draught. Like all Mississippi steamers, she was strengthened fore and aft with sturdy supporting trusses stretched over spars above the upper deck. Paddle steamers of this type were ideal transports on the four great western rivers of the United States – the Mississippi, the Ohio, the Tennessee and the Cumberland. They were used extensively by both sides to transport troops and supplies during the American Civil War, and, in 1861, an American Union general, Winfield C. Scott, planned to use them to keep troops supplied as they advanced along these four rivers.

Country of origin:	USA
Date of origin:	1884
Dimensions:	37m x 6m x 2m (121ft x 21ft x 7ft)
Tonnage:	812 tonnes (800 tons)
Machinery:	Stern paddle wheel, compound engine
Service speed:	8 knots
Cargo:	Passengers, mail, light freight
Constructor:	Not known
Built for:	Not known

Charlotte Dundas

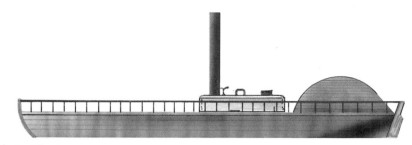

The *Charlotte Dundas* was the first practical steamboat and was used in experiments to test the viability of steamboats in place of horse-drawn canal barges. She was built of wood and had a single engine of 10hp with a single cylinder. A boiler next to the engine provided steam. The paddle wheel was at the stern, and she had two rudders. The *Charlotte Dundas*'s main routes were along the Forth and Clyde canals in Scotland. In March 1802, she took six hours to tow two loaded 70-tonne (688-ton) barges along 31km (19.5 miles) of the Forth and Clyde canal against a strong wind. Although a success, drainage problems caused by the wash to the canal banks as she passed forced her to be abandoned, and she was left to rot in a creek before being broken up in 1861. Her designer, William Symington, was a talented engineer well ahead of his time, but died a pauper in London in 1831.

Country of origin:	Britain
Date of origin:	1801
Dimensions:	17m x 5.5m x 2.4m (56ft x 18ft x 8ft)
Tonnage:	Not known
Machinery:	Paddle wheel, horizontal reciprocating engine
Service speed:	4 knots
Cargo:	General
Constructor:	William Symington
Built for:	Experimental purposes

Clermont

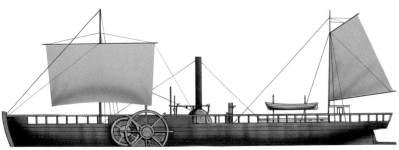

Originally known as steamboat, then North River Steamboat, *Clermont* can claim to be the first steamship in regular service. She was built at Corlear's Hook, New York, in 1807 and was designed by the prolific Robert Fulton. Fulton had earlier designed a man-powered submersible craft and offered it to the British Admiralty, who did not like the idea and turned it down. *Clermont*'s engine was made in England by Boulton & Watt, and the vessel also had two masts – she was square-sailed on the main and had a gaff mizzen. Nicknamed 'Fulton's Folly', she actually operated very successfully on the Hudson River between New York and Albany until 1814, when she was retired from service. Capable of outperforming both land coaches and river sloops, *Clermont* could carry up to 140 passengers. She was joined by a second steamer in 1809.

Country of origin:	USA
Date of origin:	1807
Dimensions:	40.5m x 4m x 2.1m (133ft x 13ft x 7ft)
Tonnage:	101.6 tonnes (100 tons)
Machinery:	Side paddle wheels, reciprocating engine
Service speed:	Not known
Complement:	Not known
Main route:	Hudson River
Cargo:	Passengers

Comet

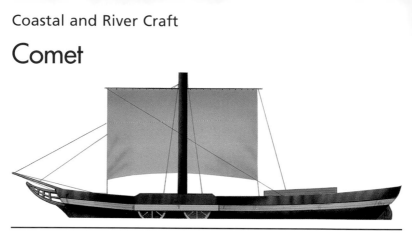

The first European steamship in commercial service, *Comet* was built on the River Clyde by John Wood and Company. Her designer, Henry Bell, had her built as a speculative venture. Although her arrival stimulated the building of further steamships, she was not a commercial success, partly because she was overtaken by the greatly improved designs that quickly followed after her. When first completed, *Comet* had two small paddle wheels on each side, but these were later replaced by larger wheels which raised her speed from 5 knots to 6.7 knots. She ran passengers on the west coast of Scotland until 13 December 1820, when she ran aground in Argyll and became a total loss. *Comet*'s engine, a vertical single-cylinder power plant, is today preserved as an exhibit at the Science Museum in London.

Country of origin:	Britain
Date of origin:	1812
Length:	13.3m (43ft 5in)
Beam:	3.4m (11ft 3in)
Tonnage:	23.36 tonnes (23 tons)
Machinery:	Side wheels, reciprocating; 4hp
Complement:	6, plus piper
Main routes:	West coast of Scotland
Cargo:	50 passengers

Cretecable

Due to the shortage of materials at the end of World War I, the British government decided to use ferro-concrete in the construction of tugs and small transports with a displacement of up to 1016 tonnes (1000 tons). Not only was it a more durable material than wood, but it was also far easier to work. Given the shortage of skilled labour as well, an additional bonus was that the use of ferro-concrete meant that hulls could be built at new, open sites away from traditional shipyards. The British Admiralty therefore initiated a comprehensive construction programme of new barges and tugs, one of which was *Cretecable*. Launched in 1919, she was completed four months later. A single-screw steam tug designed for harbour and coastal operations, she had a brief career, being wrecked in October 1920 after less than 18 months in service.

Country of origin:	Britain
Date of origin:	1919
Dimensions:	38m x 8.5m x 4m (125ft x 27ft 6in x 13ft 4in)
Tonnage:	266 tonnes (262 tons)
Machinery:	Single shaft, vertical triple-expansion
Service speed:	10 knots
Cargo:	None
Constructor:	Not known
Built for:	British Admiralty

Elizabeth

Charles Baird, a Scot living in St Petersburg, converted a wooden barge into Russia's first steamboat, the *Elizabeth*. She went into regular service on the Neva River between St Petersburg and its port of Kronstadt on the Gulf of Finland. Baird built a side-lever engine that could drive the side wheels at up to six knots; the vessel's 'funnel' was built of brick. The *Elizabeth* was the first paddle vessel to have self-feathering paddle blades, which ensured a clean vertical entry into the water. Other steam-driven craft soon followed once the Elizabeth had proven the concept viable, as the wide rivers of Russia, as in the United States, were ideally suited to early steamboat operations. At this time there were very strong ties between Great Britain and Imperial Russia, and many Russian ships were built using the expertise of British engineers.

Country of origin:	Russia
Date of origin:	1815
Length:	21.9m (72ft)
Beam:	4.8m (15ft 9in)
Tonnage:	38.6 tonnes (38 tons)
Machinery:	Side wheels, side lever; 20hp
Complement:	3
Main routes:	Neva estuary
Cargo:	Passengers, light freight

Ferdinando Primo

The *Ferdinando Primo* was the first passenger steamer to operate in the Mediterranean. She was built in Naples for the newly formed Societa Napoletana Pietro Andriel. The founder of the new company, Captain Pierre Andriel, was a steam pioneer who had commanded the first steamship to cross the English Channel in 1816. *Ferdinando Primo* was a wooden three-masted vessel, with two paddle wheels. Her engine was a side-lever unit built by James Cook of Tradeston, Scotland, and developed 32hp. This drove two paddle wheels of 4m (13ft) diameter, each of which had eight paddles. The vessel had good passenger accommodation for a ship of her size, with 16 private cabins and a spacious saloon seating 50 people. Her maiden voyage was in October 1818, when she sailed from Naples to Genoa. Later, she became the first passenger steamer to enter the port of Marseille.

Country of origin:	Italy
Date of origin:	1818
Dimensions:	38m x 6m x 1.9m (127ft 4in x 20ft 2in x 6ft 5in)
Tonnage:	250 tonnes (247 tons)
Machinery:	Paddle wheels, side-lever twin-cylinder engine
Service speed:	6 knots
Complement:	Not known
Main routes:	Northern Mediterranean coast
Cargo:	Passengers, mail

Ferry Scow

E ven as late as the 1950s, wooden scows were still being constructed in much of central Europe. Scows are among the simplest vessels of all. They have little more form to their hull than a lighter, but are generally flat-bottomed and usually have external propulsion, such as a towing tractor or a horse (the latter much more likely in the poorer rural areas), and no machinery of their own (although some were rowed). Many were in use as vehicle ferries across major and minor inland waterways. Small riverine craft such as the ferry scows were completely unsophisticated and were built locally from available materials. Most had a very short life span. Scows were once a familiar sight on the waterways of western Russia and Poland, and on the upper reaches of the Rhine. Details below apply to the craft illustrated.

Country of origin:	Germany
Date of origin:	1954
Dimensions:	15.65m x 4.35m (51ft 4in x 14ft 3in)
Tonnage:	Not applicable
Machinery:	Not applicable
Service speed:	Not applicable
Complement:	2
Main route:	River Danube
Owner:	Deutsches Schiff-fahrtsmuseum

Fishing Vessel

In the eighteenth century, the fishing fleets of Europe and North America converged, every season, on the Grand Banks, the shoal waters to the south of Newfoundland, which teemed with cod. The waters of the Grand Banks were shallow enough to permit vessels to anchor while fishing. Weather permitting, the vessel was kept beam on to the wind while the fishermen fished, using single lines, from a platform set up along the weather side of the ship, protected from the wind. Other members of the crew were stationed at each end of the ship with nets, to catch any fish that fell from the lines. Still others, less fortunate, were deployed in longboats, with orders not to return without a full catch. The large Normandy fishing vessel of about 1780 shown here was typical of the type seen in great numbers off the Grand Banks.

Country of origin:	France
Date of origin:	1780
Length:	31m (27ft)
Beam:	8.2m (27ft)
Tonnage:	406 tonnes (400 tons)
Rigging:	Three masts, square rig
Complement:	Not known
Main routes:	Newfoundland fishing grounds
Cargo:	Fish, mainly cod

Fulton

In the early years of the nineteenth century, the American entrepreneur and engineer Robert Fulton constructed two early sidewheel steamships in Paris, financial support being provided by the US Ambassador. The first one sank, but the machinery was retrieved and installed in a stronger hull. Tried out on 9 August 1803, it caused a considerable sensation, towing two barges against the current. Fulton's hull was long and narrow, with the engine installed on deck. Fulton had started experimenting with a steam engine suitable for propelling a small boat in 1794. Four years later, he developed a screw propeller, although all his earlier boats were driven by paddles. Despite the success of his projects, Fulton found little support in France or England. He returned to the United States in 1806, where he continued to build innovative ships.

Country of origin:	France
Date of origin:	1803
Length:	27.4m (90ft)
Beam:	4.9m (16ft)
Tonnage:	25.5 tonnes (25 tons)
Machinery:	Side wheels, single-cylinder beam engine
Complement:	4
Main routes:	River Seine
Cargo:	Experimental only

Gaiassa

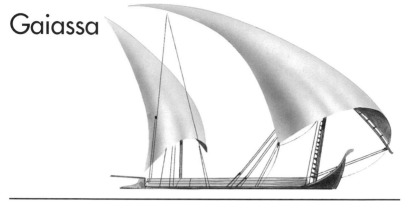

The *Gaiassa* was a sailing barge used for Nile cargo transport, probably in a form little changed for centuries apart from the provision of a tiller to replace a steering oar. According to size, the vessel was equipped with from one to three masts – most often two – placed well forward and aft in order to provide maximum loading space. The cargo carried by this nineteenth century vessel had also changed little from that carried by Nile river boats of earlier centuries. The high-raised prow, with an anchor slung from a block at the tip, has no apparent purpose and may be an archaic feature. Navigating the cataracts of the upper Nile, in the days before dams were built, could be a hazardous undertaking, with the flow of the river boiling and tumbling over and around the rocks. Techniques were subsequently developed to haul boats from one stretch of clear water to the next.

Country of origin:	Egypt
Date of origin:	1850
Length:	26.5m (87ft)
Beam:	5.5m (18ft)
Tonnage:	Not known
Rigging:	Two masts, lateen rig
Complement:	2
Main routes:	Nile river and delta
Cargo:	Grain, papyrus, barrelled and baled goods

Coastal and River Craft

Ghanja

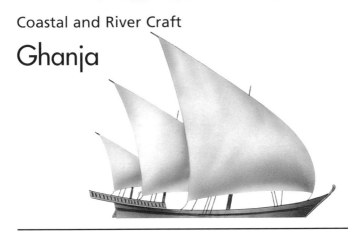

Although some of its detail is conjectural, the *ghanja* appears to have been a three-masted vessel, and would certainly have been lateen rigged, as illustrated here. Its lines were longer than those of the *sambuk* and it had the sort of extended stern platform, probably grating-decked, also seen on the Mediterranean *chebeck*. It may have been used more as a warship than as a merchant vessel; certainly it looks built for speed, although there is no evidence that it carried any form of armament. Its size and speed would also have made the *ghanja* a useful ship for piracy, coastal raids and smuggling along the lengthy Red Sea and Gulf coasts. Like the *baghla*, boom and *sambuk*, the other types of boat developed in the region, the *ghanja* would generally have been referred to by non-Arabs simply as a *dhow*.

Country of origin:	Arab States
Date of origin:	1850
Length:	c. 33.5m (110ft)
Beam:	c. 6.7m (22ft)
Tonnage:	Not known
Rigging:	Three masts, lateen rig
Complement:	Not known
Main routes:	Arabian coasts
Cargo:	Passengers, light goods

Ghe Luoi Rung

Shaped like a slice of melon, this Korean coastal craft had a very distinctive rig, its three masts comprising a large mainmast and two small foremasts. All three masts were like trysail masts and were fitted with triangular sails in an oriental version of the gunter rig. With a 'seeing eye' painted on the bow and the yin-yang symbol on its side, the *Ghe Luoi Rung* was protected against water hazards and demons. Probably used chiefly as a fishing boat, the *Ghe Luoi Rung* was furnished with a small deck shelter made out of bamboo fibre for use by its small crew. Unlike neighbouring China, whose seagoing junks had been active for centuries, Korea never had any serious seafaring tradition, relying on Japanese sailing vessels to transport her goods abroad (mostly to Japan itself) in the nineteenth century.

Country of origin:	Korea
Date of origin:	1850
Length:	c. 6.1m (20ft)
Beam:	c. 1.8m (6ft)
Tonnage:	Not known
Rigging:	Three trysail masts; triangular fore-and-aft sails
Complement:	Not known
Main routes:	Korean coast
Cargo:	Fish

Greek Coaster

Greek coastal sailing vessels had a variety of hulls and rigs, and had type names with a confusing tendency to overlap. This is a form of the *bratsera*, a craft that was not only good-looking, but also of an intensely practical appearance. The rig was entirely fore-and-aft, although the lugsails were very old-fashioned and would usually be replaced by gaffsails in a nineteenth-century vessel, with a large spanker set on the mainmast. Topmasts and up to three levels of topsails could be fitted to the foremast. The *bratsera* was a multipurpose ship, but was used chiefly to carry inter-island cargoes in the Ionian Sea. Trade between the many scattered Greek islands flourished in the nineteenth century, and the owners of the vessels that carried it often amassed considerable wealth. Greece today still has a strong tradition in merchant ship building.

Country of origin:	Greece
Date of origin:	Nineteenth century
Length:	18.3m (60ft)
Beam:	4.3m (14ft)
Tonnage:	c. 40.6 tonnes (40 tons)
Rigging:	Two masts; lugsails with fore staysail set to lugsail
Complement:	3
Main routes:	Greek western coasts and islands
Cargo:	General

Hektjalk

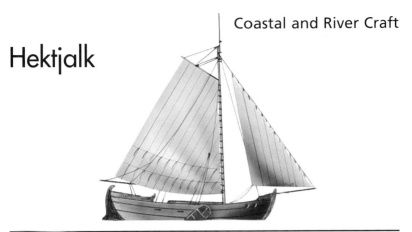

Built with a curved stempost and single-masted with a fore-and-aft rig, the *hektjalk* was the most common form of the Dutch *tjalk*, or keel barge, although there were many regional variations in size and detail; the type had evolved over a period of some 200 years. The mainsail was much wider at the foot than at the top, bent from a short gaff to a long boom that reached to the vessel's stern. Like most others of its kind, it was fitted with a leeboard on the starboard side. In the seventeenth century, these vessels were generally spritsail-rigged. The *hektjalk* bore a strong resemblance to craft that earned their keep across the North Sea, in the Humber estuary and the harbours of East Anglia; perhaps the resemblance was not so surprising, in view of the fact that the vessels were developed to meet a mutual requirement.

Country of origin:	The Netherlands
Date of origin:	Eighteenth century
Length:	19.5m (64ft)
Beam:	4.9m (16ft)
Tonnage:	61–81 tonnes (60–80 tons)
Rigging:	Single mast; fore-and-aft rig with gaff, fore staysail and jib
Complement:	2
Main routes:	Dutch inland waterways
Cargo:	Agricultural goods, beer, timber

Industry

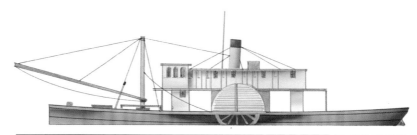

The shallow-draught sidewheel paddle steamer *Industry* was built for the State of South Australia to keep the channels of the Murray River free of obstructions and clear for navigation. She was a versatile craft, and was variously employed as a snag boat to remove floating logs, as a bucket dredger and as a floating workshop for lock repair. She remained on active service until 1969 and was eventually restored to original condition and put on display at Renmark in South Australia. With her shallow draught, low freeboard and equipped with a sizeable derrick, the *Industry* was typical of the fleet of small ships employed to maintain navigation channels in Australia's rivers. With vessels such as *Industry* and the steamer *Adelaide* of 1866 operating on it, the Murray River itself was virtually an open-air museum.

Country of origin:	Australia
Date of origin:	1911
Length:	34.1m (112ft)
Beam:	5.6m (18ft 6in)
Tonnage:	92.5 tonnes (91 tons)
Machinery:	Side wheels, steam; 30hp
Complement:	4
Main route:	Murray River
Cargo:	None

Jagt

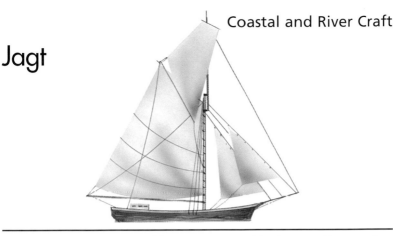

F inland has a long coastline with innumerable tiny islands grouped in two main archipelagos (the largest of which, the Aland Archipelago, consists of some 300 small islands at the entrance to the Gulf of Bothnia, a northern arm of the Baltic Sea between Sweden and Finland). The Finnish *jagt*, used both for cargo and passenger services, was an elegant-looking ship with a clipper bow. The single mast carried considerable spread of sail, the driver being a very large fore-and-aft sail rigged to gaff and boom; a form of spritsail topsail, found also in some other Nordic *jagt* types, was rigged from a short gaff. The name *jagt* is a form of the Dutch *jacht*, which originally implied a hunting vessel, and the lines of the craft suggest that it had a fair turn of speed. In 1939, there were still 110 sailing vessels in Finland's merchant fleet.

Country of origin:	Finland
Date of origin:	Nineteenth century
Length:	c. 16.8m (55ft)
Beam:	c. 4.3m (14ft)
Tonnage:	c. 45.7 tonnes (45 tons)
Rigging:	Single mast, spanker and gaff topsail; two jibs and fore staysail
Complement:	4
Main routes:	Finnish coast and islands
Cargo:	Passengers, light freight

James Watt

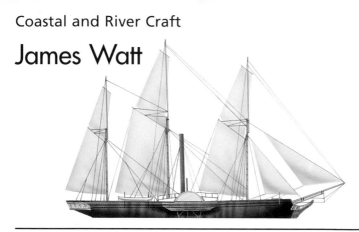

When the first working paddlewheel steamship appeared, it was the culmination of centuries of experimentation. The ancient Egyptians had already realized the potential of the paddle wheel as a form of propulsion, and, as early as 1685, the Frenchman Denis Papin had designed a single steam cylinder which drove a piston. By the early 1800s, several successful small steamships were in operation, and *James Watt* was the largest of them all at the time of her completion. She entered service as a passenger and cargo vessel, and spent her career working Britain's east coast between Leith (for Edinburgh) and London. In the days before railways, a sea passage was the fastest way between the two cities. *James Watt* was the first steamship to be entered in Lloyd's Register of Shipping, an indication that steam power was here to stay.

Country of origin:	Britain
Date of origin:	1821
Dimensions:	43m x 14.3m (141ft 8in x 47ft)
Tonnage:	455 tonnes (448 tons)
Machinery:	Paddle wheels, twin-cylinder engine
Rigging:	Three masts, square-rigged on fore and main, gaffsail on mizzen
Complement:	Not known
Main route:	Edinburgh–London
Cargo:	Passengers, light goods

Japanese Junk

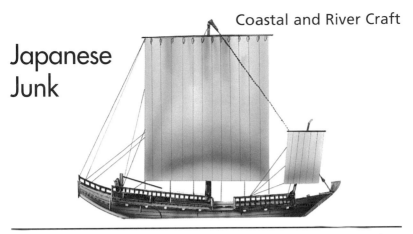

Q uite a different vessel from the Chinese junk, this Japanese junk has a number of apparently archaic features, including the way in which the deck is built out in wings towards the stern, suggesting one-time steering oar positions. Driven by a single square mainsail, with a small square foresail on what is more of a bowsprit than a foremast, it was a solid craft, but with a reputation as a poor sailer. The Japanese junk of 1850 would not differ greatly from the vessels in service some 600 years earlier, when the Mongol Emperor Kublai Khan launched a massive expedition with the intention of conquering the Japanese islands. The Japanese had no vessels capable of matching Kublai's in a sea battle, and owed their deliverance this time to a typhoon which dispersed his ships. They called the storm the Divine Wind – *kamikaze*.

Country of origin:	Japan
Date of origin:	Twelfth century
Length:	9.8m (32ft)
Beam:	2.4m (8ft)
Tonnage:	Not known
Rigging:	Single mast with square sail; small bowsprit type mast with square sail
Complement:	3
Main routes:	Japanese coast
Cargo:	General freight

Coastal and River Craft

Jekt

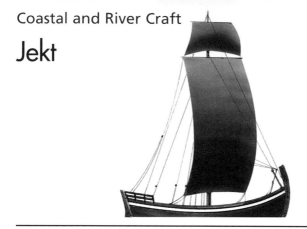

The Dutch word *jacht* was picked up by the Scandinavian countries and applied to a variety of smaller vessels, most of which did not come directly from the Dutch tradition; the Finnish *jagt* was one classic example and so was the Norwegian *jekt*, seen here. This craft has a strong resemblance in the stem to the old Viking boat; it is clinker-built and has a single pole mast, but the hull is wider in relation to the relatively short length, and the square stern shows the influence of North Sea trading vessels. Light and flexible, the *jekt* was built to cope with the squalls and variable winds of the long Norwegian fjords, where the weather conditions can literally change within minutes. Boats such as the *jekt* provided relatively quick means of moving perishable foodstuffs and light cargo from one place to another.

Country of origin:	Norway
Date of origin:	Nineteenth century
Length:	10.5m (34ft 6in)
Beam:	3.4m (11ft)
Tonnage:	Not known
Rigging:	Single pole mast; square sail, sometimes square topsail
Complement:	2
Main routes:	Norwegian fjords and inner coast
Cargo:	Farm produce

Ketch

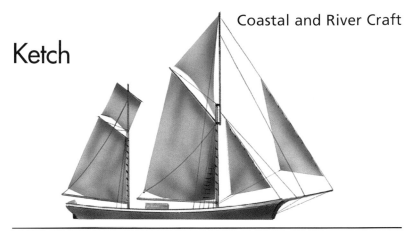

A mongst the smallest of eighteenth-century square-rigged vessels was the ketch, which was widely used in the short sea trade. The name refers to the rig, which was changed around the mid-nineteenth century. It usually became wholly fore-and-aft in nature, with gaff topsails replacing a square topsail and topgallant on the mainmast and a spanker replacing the lateen mizzen. This rig was simpler and cheaper for a vessel often manned by only a 'master and boy'. The foremast of the English ketch was set well back from the bow, enabling it to mount two staysails, a jib and a flying jib. The ketch was the standard British coaster of its day, and many seafarers destined to go on to greater things learned their trade in these humble, sturdy craft, which carried a wide variety of cargoes along an equally diverse set of coastal routes.

Country of origin:	Britain
Date of origin:	Eighteenth century
Length:	17.8m (58ft 6in)
Beam:	6.5m (21ft 4in)
Tonnage:	107.7 tonnes (106 tons)
Rigging:	Two masts; mainmast with gaffsail and boom, triangular topsail, two jibs, two staysails; mizzen with spanker and spritsail topsail
Complement:	3 or 4
Main routes:	British coastal routes
Cargo:	Coal, china clay, grain, bricks etc.

Lady Hopetoun

The *Lady Hopetoun* was constructed by Watty Ford for Sydney's Maritime Services Board, ostensibly as an inspection vessel, for use in Sydney Harbour. She was very well appointed, as befitted the personal transportation of the Board's senior officials. She enjoyed a long and active career, during the course of which she inevitably deteriorated, and was acquired for restoration and preservation as an operating museum exhibit in 1967. The restoration was completed in 1991, and the vessel is now owned by the Sydney Maritime Museum where she is on display. The *Lady Hopetoun* was an excellent example of a turn-of-the-century steam pinnace, many of which were in service throughout the British Empire. The majority of these vessels were employed in government service or some kind of official duty.

Country of origin:	Australia
Date of origin:	1902
Dimensions:	23.45m x 4.2m x 2.05m (70ft x 13ft 9in x 6ft 9in)
Tonnage:	38.6 tonnes (38 tons)
Machinery:	Single shaft, triple-expansion
Service speed:	Not known
Complement:	6
Main route:	Sydney harbour
Cargo:	VIP passengers

Mahovna

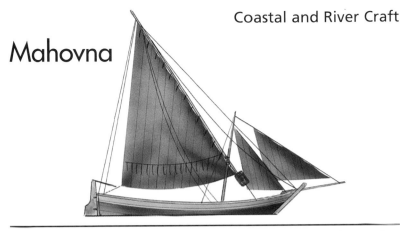

A smaller version of the *cektirme*, the Turkish *mahovna* would have been used to take passengers off vessels moored in a seaway, as well as for trans-shipping the great variety of goods arriving at a large port. The craft had a very stumpy mast and a long sprit boom supporting a triangular sail. The purpose of this may have been to enable the vessel to pass under the low Galata Bridge at Constantinople (Istanbul) with the sprit lowered. The *mahovna* is a different vessel from the older, seagoing *mahona*, which was a lateen-rigged *galleas*. During the nineteenth century, Constantinople stood at the crossroads between Europe and Asia, and the Bosporus seaway handled a huge amount of sea traffic, most of it served by fleets of *mahovnas*. The need for such craft disappeared with the modernization of navigation channels and harbour facilities.

Country of origin:	Turkey
Date of origin:	Nineteenth century
Length:	8.5m (28ft)
Beam:	2.7m (9ft)
Tonnage:	Not known
Rigging:	Stump mast; spritsail gaff, short jib and staysail
Complement:	2
Main route:	Bosporus
Cargo:	Hay, foodstuffs, wood, passengers

Moliciero

A light barge with an extraordinary upswept prow somewhat resembling that of a Venetian *gondola*, this Portuguese craft preserved an antique appearance into the nineteenth century. The *moliciero* was fitted with a small spritsail and was probably also equipped with oars, and her shallow draught enabled her to go a considerable way up rivers such as the Tagus and Douro, transporting casks and other material for the port wine producers. The gondola-like prow, in fact, may be a throwback to the time of the Portuguese King Diniz (1279–1325), who called in Genoese and Venetian experts to advise him in the construction of a navy. Italian influence on Portuguese ship and boat building was therefore very strong, and some design traditions, like the one mentioned here, may have endured for centuries.

Country of origin:	Portugal
Date of origin:	Eighteenth century
Length:	c. 7.6m (25ft)
Beam:	c. 1.8m (6ft)
Tonnage:	Not known
Rigging:	Single mast; spritsail rig
Complement:	2
Main routes:	Portuguese rivers
Cargo:	Barrels, farm produce

Natchez

The *Natchez* of 1869 was the sixth of seven river boats of the same name built for Thomas P. Leathers. Said to be an ungainly-looking craft, she soon acquired a well-deserved reputation for speed; in 1870, she steamed the 1672km (1039 miles) from New Orleans to St Louis at an average of 11.17 knots, breaking a record which had stood for a quarter of a century. She was perhaps best known for the celebrated (but inconclusive) race against the *Rob't E. Lee* that same year. She remained in service until 1879. Sidewheel river boats such as the *Natchez* and *Rob't E. Lee* were faster and much more manoeuvrable than sternwheel river boats. They became symbols of the refined gentility of the southern American states, something that the Civil War had not entirely destroyed. *Natchez* was built at the Cincinnati Marine Ways, Cincinnati, Ohio.

Country of origin:	USA
Date of origin:	1869
Length:	91.7m (301ft)
Beam:	13m (42ft 6in)
Tonnage:	1572 tonnes (1547 tons)
Machinery:	Side wheel, engine type not known
Complement:	Not known; variable
Main route:	Mississippi River
Cargo:	Passengers, mail, light freight

Navicello

Racy-looking with its clipper-type bow, this coastal trading vessel shows an interesting combination of Mediterranean and 'international' features. The short foremast is angled forwards, as in older Mediterranean craft, and supports a jib. A gaffsail is the main driver, with a triangular topsail; however, between the foremast and mainmast there is another gaffsail, without a spar, rigged to a line between the masts, and a staysail above it. The flush hull has a modern look. The *navicello* was used on Italy's Ligurian coast, from Livorno to west of Genoa, and on the island of Elba. Elba, it will be recalled, was where Napoleon Bonaparte was sent into exile after his defeat at the hands of the Allied Coalition in April 1814, only to re-enter France a year later to wage his famous 'Hundred Days' campaign, culminating in the Battle of Waterloo.

Country of origin:	Italy
Date of origin:	Nineteenth century
Length:	19.3m (63ft 4in)
Beam:	5.5m (18ft)
Tonnage:	Not known
Rigging:	Two masts; fore-and-aft gaff rig with staysails and jib
Complement:	6–8
Main routes:	Ligurian Sea
Cargo:	General goods

Portland

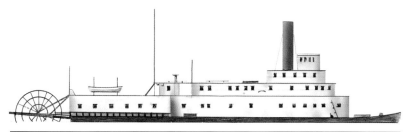

Although they were much less efficient than vessels with screw propellers, sternwheel paddleboats had important advantages as riverboats; they were of relatively shallow draught and offered good resistance to snagging. Small numbers were built in the United States even after World War II, and some remained in operation as service craft into the 1980s. The last remaining example on the Columbia River in the Pacific Northwest was the *Portland*, which was preserved in working order in the city from which she took her name. She is owned by the Port Authority of Portland, for which she was originally built by the Northwest Marine Iron works, Oregon. Although the age of the paddle steamers is remembered for the boats that plied the great rivers of the South, there were many smaller working boats of this type which have passed almost unnoticed into history.

Country of origin:	USA
Date of origin:	1947
Length:	56.7m (186ft)
Beam:	12.8m (42ft)
Tonnage:	943 tonnes (928 tons)
Machinery:	Sternwheel, engine type not known; 1800hp
Complement:	Not known
Main routes:	Columbia River
Cargo:	General

Rascona

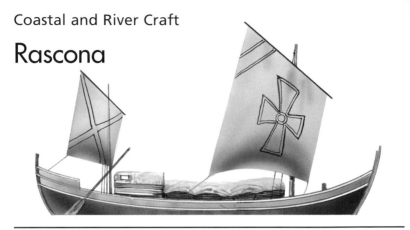

With a distinct resemblance to its passenger-carrying relative, the *gondola*, this two-masted sailing craft operated in and perhaps beyond the Venetian lagoon, carrying bulk supplies to and from the numerous islands and coastal ports. It was fitted with a steering oar, not a rudder, and was lugsail-rigged. A lugsail was a quadrilateral sail which was hoisted up and down from a yard. Often the *rascona* must have been poled along in shallow water on windless days by its two man crew. The small deck cabin located towards the aft of the ship suggests that the *rascona* might have gone on voyages beyond the lagoon, for which the two man crew would require some shelter; however, it can only have been a slow sailer. Small craft such as this were used to transport food, wine and other perishable goods between the many islands in the Venetian lagoon.

Country of origin:	Italy
Date of origin:	Nineteenth century
Length:	13.7m (45ft)
Beam:	4.9m (16ft)
Tonnage:	Not known
Rigging:	Two masts; lugsail rig
Complement:	2
Main routes:	Venice and northern Adriatic Sea
Cargo:	Rice, grain, sand, wood, wine

Roslagsjakt

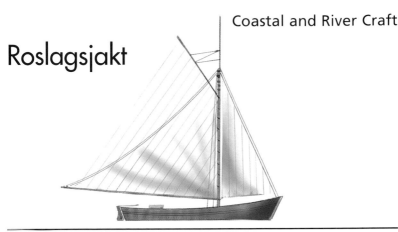

Of the various Scandinavian single-masted coastal craft whose names derive from the Dutch *jacht*, this sloop has one of the most simple rigs, with no bowsprit. Its form emerged from that of the *storbat*, and it was a common carrier of passengers and cargo in the Stockholm archipelago during the nineteenth century. Able to operate with a minimal crew, it was economical to fit out and maintain. A notable feature of the *roslagsjakt* was the lengthy boom extending well abaft the stern and secured by a long stay to the mast. Apart from passengers, the main commodities carried by these small and handy craft would be oats, wheat, rye, barley and potatoes, as well as grasses for animal fodder and products such as light timber, pitch and tar. Sweden's neighbour, Finland, developed its own *jagt* for the same purpose.

Country of origin:	Sweden
Date of origin:	Nineteenth century
Length:	c. 9.1m (30ft)
Beam:	c. 2.4m (8ft)
Tonnage:	Not known
Rigging:	Single mast; gaff-and-boom-rigged driver; foresail
Complement:	1 or 2
Main routes:	Islands around Stockholm
Cargo:	Passenger, light goods

Coastal and River Craft

Sambuk

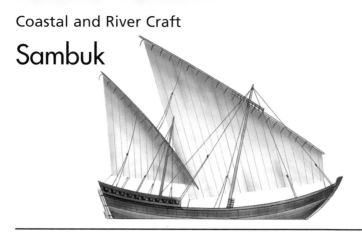

One of the numerous craft known collectively as *dhows*, the *sambuk* was a two-masted Arab trader of similar rig to the *baghla*, but longer and lower; in fact, it was more of a cargo carrier. The main distinguishing feature was the curved stemhead. Like the *baghla*, the *sambuk*'s lateen sails were four-sided; this was known as a settee rig. As with other larger Arab craft, the *sambuk* usually had fine carving applied to the quarter strakes. Arab trading vessels ventured surprisingly long distances down the east coast of Africa, maintaining contact with the indigenous African tribes. Trade between the semitic peoples of Arabia and the peoples of East Africa was established many centuries ago, when merchants in craft not very different from the *sambuk* traded such goods as knives, tools and utensils for ivory.

Country of origin:	Arab States
Date of origin:	Nineteenth century
Length:	c. 16.8m (55ft)
Beam:	3.7m (12ft)
Tonnage:	c. 101.6 tonnes (100 tons)
Rigging:	Two masts, lateen rig
Complement:	2–3
Main routes:	Arabian and East African ports
Cargo:	Foodstuffs, fish, general

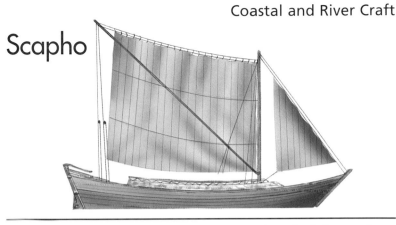

Scapho

The word *scapho* is Greek for 'boat', and this type of vessel sailed among the Aegean islands and the promontories of the mainland and is one of the larger Greek merchant vessels. Its unusual rig seems to be an adaptation of the spritsail, with the sprit rigged derrick-fashion and stayed to each gunwale close to the stern. The sail was mounted curtain-style, enabling it to be 'drawn' rapidly. Loose-footed, it could be hauled across the sheet to cope with changing winds or direction. This curtain-style rig was also seen in a few Turkish ship types of similar size and function. There is no bowsprit, but the forestay is fixed to the extended stempost. Many Greek sailing vessels of the nineteenth century were modelled on older types of boat; Greek seamen had a strong ability to adapt old techniques to meet new requirements.

Country of origin:	Greece
Date of origin:	Late nineteenth century
Length:	17.1m (56ft)
Beam:	4.3m (14ft)
Tonnage:	Not known
Rigging:	Single mast; derrick-type gaff and curtain rig mainsail; fore staysail
Complement:	2
Main routes:	Inner Aegean islands
Cargo:	General, mainly foodstuffs

Smack

The smallest of all the Northern European commercial craft of the late nineteenth century, measuring just 15.25m (50ft) in length, the smack was the maid-of-all-work of the coastal trade, equally at home hauling general cargo or being employed as a fishing vessel. Single-masted, gaff-rigged and often with a jackstaff topsail, smacks were very easy to sail, and were often manned by no more than a man and a boy. Nevertheless, they were capable of a surprising turn of speed under the right conditions. Smacks were still in use in the west of England at the beginning of World War II, and some took part in the evacuation of Dunkirk in May 1940. Long before then, however, many were converted to power of some sort. Like so many nautical terms, the name 'smack' is of Dutch origin, a corruption of *smak*, which in itself is derived from an earlier word, *smacke*.

Country of origin:	Northern Europe
Date of origin:	c. 1860
Length:	15.25m (50ft)
Beam:	6.35m (17ft 6in)
Tonnage:	25.4 tonnes (25 tons)
Rigging:	Single-masted, gaff-rigged
Complement:	2 or 3
Main routes:	Coastal
Cargo:	General

Storbat

For at least 300 years up to the nineteenth century, the *storbat* ('big boat') was used by Swedish farmers to transport their produce to the markets of Stockholm, the Swedish capital. Usually two-masted, the *storbat* was double-ended, clinker-built – as was the fashion with Scandinavian boats since the days of the Vikings – and featured a small cabin built into the stern, earning the vessel its other name of *kajutbot* (cabin boat). The cabin had a rounded plank-tile roof. The square sails originally used by these vessels were replaced by fore-and-aft rig at some point in the nineteenth century. Vessels similar to the *storbat* were used by coastal farms in other parts of Scandinavia, the sea often being by far the most rapid means of shipping goods, especially foodstuffs and perishable goods, from one point to another.

Country of origin:	Sweden
Date of origin:	Sixteenth century
Length:	9.1m (30ft)
Beam:	4.3m (14ft)
Tonnage:	Not known
Rigging:	Two masts; one square-rig sail on each; headsail
Complement:	1–2
Main routes:	Swedish coast and islands
Cargo:	Farm produce

Sump

The sixteenth and seventeenth centuries marked an era of growth for the countries around the Baltic Sea. The Hanseatic League still controlled all commerce in these northern waters, and the cities of northern Germany flourished through the Baltic trade in timber, copper, pitch and iron, and luxuries such as amber and furst. Above all, however, they flourished on the export of barrelled herring, the staple diet of Catholic Europe on Fridays and during Lent. The increased trade led to a corresponding increase in specialized vessels, their size and capacity varying according to requirements. The sump was a relatively small single-masted vessel suitable for the coastal trade, able to carry mixed cargo, but with no deck covering. A small covered space was provided for the crew of two or three, its flat roof acting as a deck for the helmsman.

Country of origin:	Sweden
Date of origin:	Seventeenth century
Length:	12.3m (40ft 6in)
Beam:	4m (14ft)
Tonnage:	30.5 tonnes (30 tons)
Rigging:	Ketch
Complement:	2–3
Main routes:	Coastal waters, Baltic Sea
Cargo:	General

Trekandiri

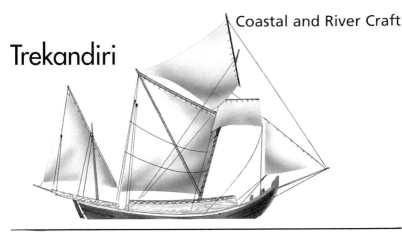

As coastal vessels go, this Greek example cut more of a dash than most, with her double-ended hull upswept to stem and stern, and a high stern platform built far out, with a bumkin pole beyond it to secure the corner of the lateen mizzen. The *trekandiri* was similar to another Greek coastal vessel, the *bratsera*, but her masts were not parallel, and she was normally smaller (measuring just 9.8m [32ft] in length) than the even more flamboyant *sacoleva*, a ship capable of taking to the open sea and voyaging as far as Crete and Rhodes. By the nineteenth century, the *trekandiri* tended to have only a single mast. Low slung in the waist to facilitate the handling of cargo, vessels of the *trekandiri* type usually carried weatherboards to help provide shelter in that area of the vessel. Like the *sambuk* of the Arabian states, the trekandiri had a markedly curved stemhead.

Country of origin:	Greece
Date of origin:	Nineteenth century
Length:	c. 9.8m (32ft)
Beam:	c. 2.7m (9ft)
Tonnage:	Not known
Rigging:	Two masts; main with sprit mainsail and topsail; square topsail, jib; lateen mizzen
Complement:	Not known
Main routes:	Greek coast and islands
Cargo:	General

Turkish Coaster

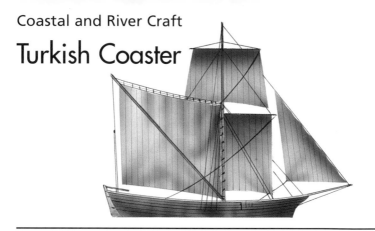

Like the similar-sized Greek *sacoleva*, this ship mounted a varied rig on a single mast; square-rigged with course and topsail, there is also a staysail and jib. The derrick-rigged sprit supported not a spritsail, but a curtain-like sail similar to that of the Greek *scapho*, suspended on rings and furled by being drawn back towards the mast. Ships rigged in this fashion plied the Black Sea coast into the twentieth century; Turkish coastal transport was very much focused on supplying the needs of Constantinople (Istanbul) with food, fuel and fodder for animals. The capture of Constantinople by the Ottoman Turks in the fifteenth century did not at first have a disastrous effect on Mediterranean trade; this happened later, when the Ottomans conquered North Africa and cut off trade with Egypt. By the time of this coaster, the Ottoman Empire had greatly declined, eventually collapsing after World War I.

Country of origin:	Turkey
Date of origin:	Nineteenth century
Length:	15.2m (50ft)
Beam:	4m (13ft)
Tonnage:	c. 45.7 tonnes (45 tons)
Rigging:	Single mast with square sails and jib; fore and-aft curtain mainsail from sprit
Complement:	4
Main routes:	Black Sea coast, Bosporus
Cargo:	General, mainly foodstuffs

Vinco

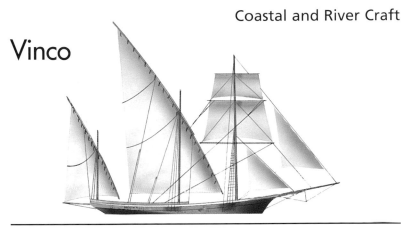

After many years in decline, Genoa grew in importance as a port once again in the nineteenth century, and many ships traded from this location. One was the *vinco*, which appears to have been a local type produced in the province of Piedmont. She was three-masted, with a long, raised quarterdeck. Her rig was distinctive even by Mediterranean standards, with its combination of square-rigged foremast, lateen-rigged mainmast and lateen mizzen perched on the sternpost. The mixed rig again demonstrates the versatility of the Mediterranean seamen, ready to confront the highly variable wind conditions of the Ligurian Sea. Vessels of the *vinco* type could have made a rapid voyage to Corsica or Elba, or indeed even farther afield. These boats carried farm produce, industrial products and other general cargo.

Country of origin:	Piedmont (Italy)
Date of origin:	1850
Length:	c. 29m (95ft)
Beam:	c. 7.6m (25ft)
Tonnage:	c. 183 tonnes (180 tons)
Rigging:	Three masts; square-rigged with topmast on foremast; two jibs and foresail; lateen rig on mainmast and mizzen
Complement:	Not known
Main routes:	Genoa to Tuscan coast, Elba and Corsica
Cargo:	General

Wine Barge

A vessel of conservative style, with upswept prow and stern and a remarkably long steering oar fixed to the sternpost (one contemporary illustration shows three men wielding it), this barge carried hogsheads of the rich red wine known to the world simply as 'port' up and down the Douro River at Oporto and out to cargo ships. A scaffolding along the deck acted as a barrel rack, and this was raised aft to make a gantry for the helmsman. A line was made to the middle of the square sail's foot to draw it up. Substantial rowlocks towards the bow suggest that the vessel was often manoeuvred in the waterway using sweeps. Wine barges remained an important facet of Portugal's commercial life until they were replaced by faster forms of transport. As an aside, Portuguese bargees had the reputation of being fine singers.

Country of origin:	Portugal
Date of origin:	1847
Length:	c. 12.8m (42ft)
Beam:	c. 5m (16ft 6in)
Tonnage:	Not known
Rigging:	Single mast, square sail
Complement:	3
Main routes:	River Douro
Cargo:	Wine barrels

Ever Globe

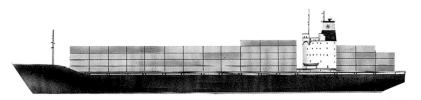

Launched in 1984, *Ever Globe* was one of the large, expanding fleet of container ships owned in the mid-1980s by the Evergreen Marine Corporation, a company based in Taiwan and registered in Panama. *Ever Globe* had three holds for containers, plus a massive deck area where more could be stacked up to five deep. Container ships of this kind, which revolutionized cargo handling and transportation, were first introduced in the 1960s, although the concept of container transport is much older than that. In fact, it was first introduced by the British haulage firm Pickford's, by agreement with the Liverpool and Manchester Railway Company, in November 1830. Containers designed for motor transport made their appearance with Hays Wharf Cartage, West Smithfield, London, in 1926.

Country of origin:	Taiwan
Date of origin:	1984
Dimensions:	231m x 32m (757ft 10in x 105ft)
Tonnage:	43,978 tonnes (43,285 tons)
Machinery:	Single shaft, diesel engine
Service speed:	20 knots
Cargo:	General
Capacity:	Not known
Constructor:	Not known

Geest St Lucia

Ordered in 1993 by the Southampton-based Geest Line, the *Geest St Lucia* and her sister ship, the *Geest Dominica*, were brought into service in response to a need for new vessels with superior capacity for transporting bananas and exotic fruits from the Caribbean to northern Europe. *Geest St Lucia* has four holds, each divided into 18 separate compartments, and her refrigeration system can maintain the goods she carries at temperatures between minus 29 degrees Celsius and plus 13 degrees Celsius, the latter being the optimum temperature for the carriage of bananas. The vessel carries a full navigation suite which includes X-band radar, a global positioning system (GPS), Loran and Decca navigator. The vessel's fully automated systems can be monitored from the bridge by a single person, if necessary.

Country of origin:	Britain
Date of origin:	1993
Dimensions:	158m x 24.4m (518ft x 80ft)
Tonnage:	14,000 tonnes (14,224 tons)
Machinery:	Single screw, diesel engine; 16,520hp
Service speed:	21.4 knots
Cargo:	Refrigerated fruits, vegetables, rum, spices
Capacity:	18,000 cubic metres (23,543 cubic yards)
Constructor:	Danyard, Frederikshavn, Denmark

Hannover Express

The *Hannover Express* was the first in a class of five container ships that were improvements on an already successful design. She had an increased container-carrying capacity made possible, in part, by using high-tensile steel in her construction, The resulting saving in weight allows 11 tiers of containers to be stowed in the hull instead of 10. In addition, the rearrangement of the longitudinal beams made it possible for the vessel to carry heavy-lift cargoes, which is not usually practicable with this type of ship. The *Hannover Express* is automated to such a degree that, despite her size, she requires a crew of only 21. She is among a minority of container ships designed to operate at 24 knots instead of 20 knots. Ships of this type were almost always built to the 'Panamax' limit of 32.3m (106ft) breadth.

Country of origin:	Germany
Date of origin:	1990
Dimensions:	294.3m x 32.25m x 13.5m (965ft 8in x 105ft 10in x 44ft 4in)
Tonnage:	54,646 tonnes (53,783 tons)
Machinery:	Single shaft, diesel; 48,240hp
Service speed:	24 knots
Cargo:	General
Capacity:	4100 TEU
Constructor:	Samsung Shipbuilding

Hyundai Admiral

Fitted with the world's most powerful diesel engine, developing more than 67,000bhp, *Hyundai Admiral* was the first of five new large container ships built at the massive Hyundai shipyard at Ulsan, South Korea, and designed for service on the Far East – West Coast shipping routes of the Hyundai Corporation. The ship is largely automated, with surveillance monitors in each control centre; this arrangement means that a single watch-keeping system can be employed to monitor all systems. There are seven holds, which can carry more than 4400 containers, and an area is set aside in the forward holds for the carriage of dangerous cargo. *Hyundai Admiral* has a double hull, the rigidity of which is maintained by box passages. The ship's single propeller weighs 82.5 tonnes (81 tons).

Country of origin:	South Korea
Date of origin:	1992
Dimensions:	275m x 37m x 13.6m (902ft 3in x 121ft 9in x 44ft 7in)
Tonnage:	62,131 tonnes (61,153 tons)
Machinery:	Single shaft, diesel engine; 67,000hp
Service speed:	20 knots
Cargo:	General
Capacity:	4400 TEU
Constructor:	Hyundai Shipyard

Jervis Bay

P&O Nedlloyd's *Jervis Bay* is a fast container ship with a capacity of more than 4000 6m (20ft) equivalent units, some 240 of which can be refrigerated. She and her sister ships were intended to be used mainly on the Europe–Far East run, being capable of making the round trip from Southampton to Yokohama and back in 63 days, with a turnaround time of 24 hours. *Jervis Bay*, like most other container vessels, is a so-called 'Panamx' ship, which means that her beam measurement is marginally within the maximum capable of passing through the locks of the Panama Canal. *Jervis Bay* bears a proud name. At the outbreak of World War II, the fast passenger liner *Jervis Bay* was requisitioned by the Admiralty and converted to an armed merchant cruiser. In 1940, while gallantly defending an Atlantic convoy, she was sunk by the German heavy cruiser *Admiral Scheer*.

Country of origin:	Britain
Date of origin:	1992
Dimensions:	292.15m x 32.2m x 11.2m (958ft 6in x 105ft 6in x 36ft 9in)
Tonnage:	51,818 tonnes (51,000 tons)
Machinery:	Single shaft, diesel; 46,800hp
Service speed:	23.5 knots
Cargo:	General
Capacity:	4038 TEU
Constructor:	Ishikawajima-Harima Heavy Industries, Kure

Kota Wijaya

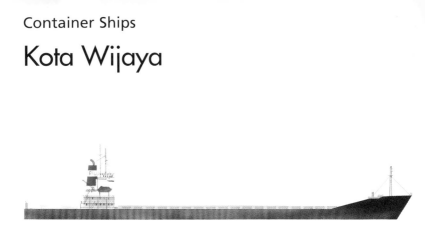

Built for Pacific International Lines, the Singapore-registered *Kota Wijaya* is a container ship with a capacity of just 1160 6m (20ft) equivalent units, barely a quarter of that of the real giants of the trade. As a result, she is considered more economical to operate; in particular, she can be loaded and unloaded very quickly. She is double-hulled, carrying her fuel in wing tanks; a heeling tank, to be filled with water as ballast, is fitted to starboard to assist in loading and unloading operations. The *Kota Wijaya* is typical of small container ships; she can accommodate both 6m (20ft) and 12m (40ft) containers, up to 120 of which can be refrigerated. The hull is double-skinned over the midships section. *Kota Wijaya*'s engines consume some 40.8 tonnes (40.2 tons) of fuel a day under normal cruise conditions.

Country of origin:	Singapore
Date of origin:	1991
Dimensions:	184.5m x 27.6m x 9m (605ft 4in x 90ft 6in x 29ft 6in)
Tonnage:	16,998 tonnes (16,730 tons)
Machinery:	Single shaft, diesel; 14,400hp
Service speed:	19 knots
Cargo:	general
Capacity:	1160 TEU
Constructor:	Kanasishi

Nedlloyd Europa

P&O Nedlloyd's fast container ship *Nedlloyd Europa* was the second of a class of five ships originally built for service between Europe and the Far East. She is of an unusual design which does away with standard hatch covers to the cargo holds; instead, she features container guides which extend from the holds up above the deck to secure deck-carried containers. This system ensures greater security for the cargo in transit, minimizing the risk of loss or damage in heavy weather. Tests proved the safety of the design, confirming that hatch covers do not add strength to the structure of the hull. Removal of any water that finds its way into a hatchless vessel has to be a priority, however, and duplicate pumping and drainage systems are incorporated. *Nedlloyd Europa* has seven cargo holds, two of them positioned aft in the bridge structure.

Country of origin:	The Netherlands
Date of origin:	1991
Dimensions:	266m x 32.2m x 13m (872ft 9in x 105ft 9in x 42ft 8in)
Tonnage:	48,768 tonnes (48,000 tons)
Machinery:	Single shaft, diesel; 41,600hp
Service speed:	23.5 knots
Cargo:	General
Capacity:	3568 TEU
Constructor:	Mitsubishi Heavy Industries, Kobe, Japan

Acadia

The *Acadia* was built by Swan, Hunter & Wigham Richardson in Newcastle upon Tyne for the Canadian government and was one of the first vessels commissioned into the recently formed Royal Canadian Navy. She was employed for many years as a hydrographic research ship; at the end of her useful life, the *Acadia* was preserved, unchanged both internally and externally, at the Maritime Museum of the Atlantic in the port of Halifax, Nova Scotia. The *Acadia* was one of the first purpose-built hydrographic survey ships. She added a great deal to our knowledge of the often treacherous waters off Canada's east coast – in particular, the Newfoundland Grand Banks, the area that saw the sinking of the *Titanic* only a year before *Acadia* was launched, infamous for its sudden dense fogs and icebergs, the cause of *Titanic*'s demise.

Country of origin:	Canada
Date of origin:	1913
Length:	51.8m (170ft)
Beam:	10.2m (33ft 6in)
Displacement:	859 tonnes (846 tons)
Machinery:	Single shaft, vertical triple-expansion; about 1750hp
Service speed:	Not known
Constructor:	Swan, Hunter & Wigham Richardson, Wallsend
Built for:	Canadian government

Aluminaut

The deep submergence vehicle *Aluminaut* became famous when she helped to recover an H-bomb which had fallen from an American B-52 bomber involved in a mid-air collision with a KC-135 tanker aircraft over Spain in 1966. Built in 1965, *Aluminaut* was capable of exploring to depths of up to 4475m (14,682ft), although most routine underwater explorations missions never reach such depths. Even the most advanced military submarines go down no further than 900m (2952ft); any deeper and the costs of hull strengthening and engine uprating are prohibitive. *Aluminaut* is equipped with a side-scan sonar which builds up a map of the terrain. Manned submersibles dominate in commercial and scientific work in coastal waters; pressures are within comfortable engineering limits, and crews have made impressive advances in undersea archaeology and oil exploration.

Country of origin:	USA
Date of origin:	1965
Length:	Not known
Beam:	Not known
Displacement:	81 tonnes (80 tons) submerged
Machinery:	Diesel/electric
Service speed:	3 knots submerged
Complement:	3
Constructor:	Not known

Argonaut

The *Argonaut* was built by Simon Lake at his own expense as a salvage vessel for inshore waters. A 30hp gasoline engine drove the single screw, and the engine could be connected to the twin front wheels for movement along the sea bed; a third wheel aft steered the craft. There was an air chamber forward to allow divers to enter and leave. The vessel was rebuilt in 1899 and once made a trip of 3200km (1725 nautical miles) on the surface. Successful trials led to a number of export orders, but by that time Lake had lost the submarine design initiative to John Holland in the eyes of the US Navy, the senior officers of which were not impressed by the idea of a wooden-hulled craft trundling along the sea bed. The idea was to be resurrected nearly a century later, however, when designs for 'ocean crawling' submarines were again proposed.

Country of origin:	USA
Date of origin:	1897
Length:	11m (36ft)
Beam:	2.7m (9ft)
Displacement:	60 tonnes (59 tons) submerged
Machinery:	Gasoline engine
Service speed:	5 knots surfaced/submerged
Complement:	5
Constructor:	Simon Lake

Artiglio II

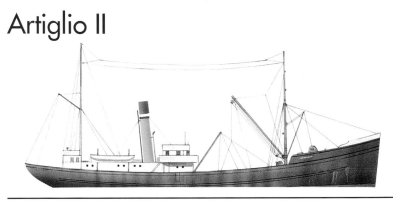

The *Artiglio II* was built to the order of the Italian salvage firm Sorima in 1931 to act as the support ship in an operation aimed at recovering gold from the P&O liner *Egypt*, which had sunk in 70 fathoms (130m) of water off Ushant in 1922. The first *Artiglio* was destroyed by accident while divers were clearing the wreck of an ammunition ship at St Nazaire. Sorima eventually recovered bullion worth $1,183,000 from the wreck of the *Egypt*, a total that represented most of the gold the vessel had been carrying. Underwater salvage rarely yields such vast financial gains, but has contributed much to marine archaeology and maritime history. The recovery marked the start of a new era in underwater salvage, as the wreck of the *Egypt* lay at a depth that could not be reached by conventional diving gear. A new type of diving suit had to be specially designed for the operation.

Country of origin:	Italy
Date of origin:	1931
Length:	42.6m (139ft 9in)
Beam:	7.6m (25ft)
Displacement:	305 tonnes (300 tons)
Machinery:	Single shaft, vertical triple expansion, 400hp
Service speed:	14 knots
Complement:	20
Built for:	Sorima

Batcombe

Launched in 1970, the *Batcombe* is a dual-purpose vessel: she is a tugboat that is also equipped for fire-fighting, carrying high-pressure hoses with which she is able quickly to cover a burning vessel with a blanket of foam and water. The foam and water hoses are mounted on the bridge, which has good all-round visibility because of its curved structure. Many tugs of this period had a dual role, including those vessels produced for the Royal Navy. The larger naval tugs were also fitted for ocean salvage, and some had a machinery arrangement of two diesels geared to a single shaft, with a controllable-pitch propeller. The Royal Navy also employed a sizeable number of diesel-electric paddle tugs on harbour service and in Her Majesty's dockyards. While not blessed with the most elegant lines, versatile boats such as these perform very valuable work.

Country of origin:	Britain
Date of origin:	1970
Length:	18.3m (60ft)
Beam:	5.5m (18ft)
Displacement:	Not known
Machinery:	Single shaft, diesel
Service speed:	12 knots
Constructor:	Not known
Built for:	British Ports Authority

Beagle

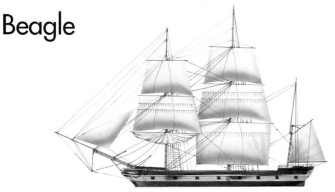

L aunched at Woolwich Dockyard as a 10-gun brig of the Cherokee class, *Beagle* was converted almost immediately to a barque rig, which she then retained. Although her name is always associated with that of Charles Darwin, the ship had already made a major voyage to South America in 1826–30. This journey resulted in her name being given to the Beagle Channel south of Tierra del Fuego, before Darwin's more famous expedition of 1831–36. Darwin's observations laid the foundation for his revolutionary treatise *The Origin of the Species*, published in 1859. In 1837, the *Beagle* sailed again for Australia, surveying the west and south-eastern coasts before moving to the north coast in 1839. Returning to Britain in 1843, she was paid off as a naval vessel in 1845. She was then used as an anti-smuggling ship by the Revenue Service, moored on the Essex coast, before being broken up in 1870.

Country of origin:	Britain
Date of origin:	1820
Length:	27.4m (90ft)
Beam:	7.5m (24ft 6in)
Tonnage:	238 tonnes (235 tons)
Rigging:	Three masts, barque rig; square sails on fore and main; spanker on mizzen
Armament:	10 guns, reduced to six as survey vessel
Complement:	70
Main routes:	Various, including global circumnavigation

Bounty

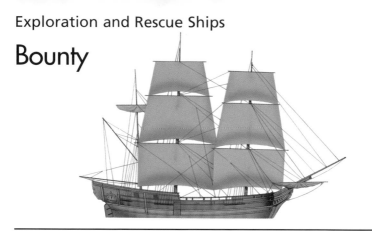

The *Bounty* began as the merchant vessel *Bethia*, a ship-rigged craft of 224 tonnes (220 tons), built in the port of Hull in 1784; she was purchased by the Admiralty three years later. English merchants had made vast investments in slave-tended plantations in the West Indies, and voyages to the South Pacific had shown that the breadfruit found growing in the Society Islands could provide the ideal food to keep slaves well nourished cheaply. Under her commander, Lieutenant William Bligh, *Bounty*'s task was to transport breadfruit plants from the South Pacific to the Caribbean. Ventilated with gratings and scuttles, she duly loaded at Tahiti, where her crew revelled in the easy-going life. On the way back, on 28 April 1789, the crew mutinied under Fletcher Christian, setting Bligh and some loyal men adrift. The mutineers sailed *Bounty* to Pitcairn Island and burned her.

Country of origin:	Britain
Date of origin:	1784
Length:	27.7m (91ft)
Beam:	7.4m (24ft 4in)
Tonnage:	223 tonnes (220 tons)
Rigging:	Three masts; square rig
Armament:	Four guns
Complement:	45
Main routes:	South Pacific–Caribbean

Calshot Spit

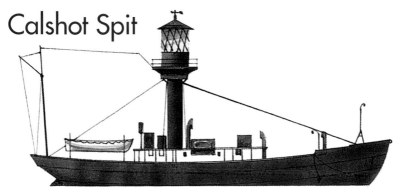

The *Calshot Spit* was a lightship stationed in the English Channel and owned by the Corporation of Trinity House. She was permanently anchored to mark the passage between the River Bramble and the shore near Southampton's busy waterways. The constricted waters here race between the Isle of Wight and the mainland at speeds of up to five and a half knots, creating a dangerous navigational area for shipping. *Calshot Spit* had a single powerful light mounted on top of a tall tower, which flashed every 15 seconds. It could be seen over a radius of up to 19km (10 miles). The seas around the coastline of the British Isles are among the most difficult in the world to navigate. Dense shipping traffic, frequent fogs and the shallowness of inshore waters create unpredictable and often hazardous conditions for mariners.

Country of origin:	Britain
Date of origin:	1920
Length:	21.3m (70ft)
Beam:	5.2m (17ft)
Tonnage:	213 tonnes (210 tons)
Machinery:	Not applicable
Service speed:	Not applicable
Complement:	7
Constructor:	Corporation of Trinity House

D'Halve Maen

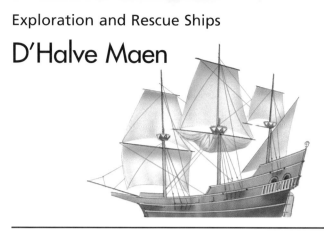

Built at Amsterdam in 1608 for the Dutch East India Company, *D'Halve Maen* (*Half Moon*) had four guns mounted as two ports to each side. The guns were mainly for show, as she was essentially a merchant vessel. In 1609, the English Explorer Henry Hudson crossed the North Atlantic in *D'Halve Maen* and sailed 237km (147 miles) up the US river that now bears his name. The voyage was by no means prompted by mere curiosity. Hudson made land claims on behalf of both the Dutch, who were sponsors of his expedition, and the English. On his return to England, he docked at Dartmouth, where he left his ship; she was returned to the Dutch in the following year and sailed to the East Indies. According to one report, *D'Halve Maen* was wrecked off Mauritius in 1611; other reports suggest she was wrecked off Sumatra in 1616, or burned by the English in 1618.

Country of origin:	The Netherlands
Date of origin:	1608
Length:	19.8m (65ft)
Beam:	5.3m (17ft 3in)
Tonnage:	81 tonnes (80 tons)
Rigging:	Three masts, square-rigged on fore and main with topsails; lateen mizzen; bowsprit
Complement:	17–20
Main routes:	Hudson River; Indian Ocean
Cargo:	Sandalwood, spices, ores

Deep Quest

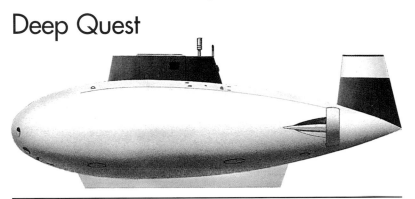

The *Deep Quest* was the first submersible built with a fairing around a double sphere, one for the crew, the other for the propulsion unit. She worked as a commercial deep search and recovery submarine, and could descend to 2438m (8000ft). Even the most advanced naval submarines go down no further than 300m (1000ft). The pressure is crushing – 60 atmospheres at 600m (2000ft) , reaching 500 on the mid-ocean bed. Pressure can exceed 1000 atmospheres in the deepest ocean trenches, a force of almost seven tons per square inch. Vessels such as *Deep Quest* spend much of their time surveying the sea bed for cable-laying and pipeline operations. Another famous vessel of similar age and type was the Alvin, used to help retrieve an H-bomb from the Mediterranean in 1966; the weapon had fallen from a B-52 bomber.

Country of origin:	USA
Date of origin:	1967
Length:	12m (39ft 4in)
Beam:	4.6m (15ft)
Displacement:	5 tonnes (5 tons) surfaced
Machinery:	Twin reversible-thrust motors
Service speed:	4.5 knots surfaced
Complement:	1–3
Constructor:	Lockheed Missile and Space Company

Deepstar 4000

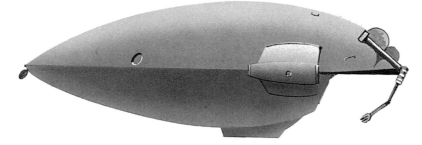

The *Deepstar 4000* was built between 1962 and 1964 by the Westinghouse Electric Corporation and the Jacques Cousteau group OFRS. The hull consisted of a steel sphere with 11 observation portholes, and the craft carried a wide range of scientific equipment. She was capable of operating at a depth of up to 1000m (3280ft). Existing technology has always placed limits on the depths at which manned submersibles can operate, and, during the 1980s and 1990s, great progress was made in the development of automatic or robotic deep-sea diving vehicles. At the beginning of the twenty-first century, however, manned submersibles are increasing in their scope. Hawkes Ocean Technologies in the United States has developed *Deep Flight*, a torpedo-shaped probe designed to take one man to the bottom of the Pacific Ocean.

Country of origin:	France
Date of origin:	1965
Length:	5.4m (17ft 9in)
Beam:	3.5m (11ft 6in)
Displacement:	Not known
Machinery:	Two fixed, reversible 5hp AC motors
Service speed:	3 knots surfaced
Complement:	1
Constructor:	Westinghouse Electric Corporation/OFRS

Discovery

The *Discovery* was built in 1901 in Dundee, Scotland, then a major whaling port as well as a centre for the jute industry. Her design was based on an earlier whaling ship of the same name, which had carried an 1875 expedition to the Arctic. She had a reinforced hull, and both screw and rudder could be lifted clear of the water to prevent ice damage. Her maiden voyage in 1901, under the command of Robert Falcon Scott, took her to the Ross Sea in Antarctica, where she remained until 1904, having been frozen into the ice. On her return to Britain, the *Discovery* was sold to the Hudson's Bay Company. She was laid up from 1912 to 1915, and again from 1931 to 1936, having previously been used as a research ship by the Crown Agents. After use as Sea Scouts training ship, moored on the Thames, she was restored and placed on display by her owners, the Dundee Heritage Trust.

Country of origin:	Britain
Date of origin:	1901
Length:	52.1m (171ft)
Beam:	10.3m (33ft 9in)
Tonnage:	1595 tonnes (1570 tons)
Machinery:	Single shaft, auxiliary triple-expansion; 450hp
Rigging:	Three masts, barque-rigged
Complement:	Not known
Main routes:	Antarctica

Exploration and Rescue Ships

Eendracht

Within a few years of their declaration of independence in the early 1580s, the Dutch had become the prominent trading power in the East. The rapid ascendancy of the Dutch as a trading nation was due largely to their single-minded pursuit of commerce alone, unlike their rivals who spent much time and effort in seeking to 'convert' the peoples with whom they traded. The Dutch East India Company soon controlled the Cape of Good Hope route, and, in 1615, an expedition was launched to find a new route to the Far East. Two ships, the *Eeendracht* and the *Hoorn*, set out, but the *Hoorn* caught fire and *Eendracht* sailed on alone. In January 1616, she sailed round the tip of South America, which the explorers named Cape Hoorn after their lost ship and home town. Upon arrival at Bantam in the Dutch East Indies, the captain's story of *Eendracht*'s new route was at first ridiculed.

Country of origin:	The Netherlands
Date:	1614
Length:	Not known
Beam:	Not known
Tonnage:	366 tonnes (360 tons)
Rigging:	Three masts, square-rigged on fore and main; lateen mizzen; spritsail
Armament:	19 guns, 12 swivel cannon
Complement:	87
Main routes:	South Seas

Endeavour

This is the first 'discovery ship' of which detailed descriptions are available. Launched at Whitby in 1764 as the cat-built collier barque *Earl of Pembroke*, she was purchased by the British Admiralty and fitted out for a scientific journey to the South Seas, to observe the transit of Venus from Tahiti and also to ascertain whether a southern continent really existed. In command was Lieutenant James Cook. The expedition left Plymouth on 25 August 1768 and returned on 12 July 1771, having made many discoveries. After a refit, *Endeavour* made three voyages to the Falkland Islands before being sold by the Admiralty and reverting to the collier trade. In 1790, she passed into French ownership as *La Liberté* and was used as a whaler. She ran aground off Newport, Rhode Island, in 1793 and was later broken up.

Country of origin:	Britain
Date of origin:	1764
Length:	29.8m(97ft 8in)
Beam:	8.9m (29ft 4in)
Tonnage:	372 tonnes (366 tons)
Rigging:	Three masts, square rig
Armament:	Six swivel guns
Complement:	85
Main routes:	South Seas

Endurance

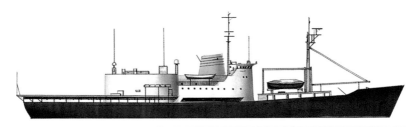

Originally named *Anita Dan*, *Endurance* was built by Krîgerwerft, Rendsburg, for the Lauritzen Line. In 1967, she was purchased by the British government for use as an ice patrol vessel in the South Atlantic and was converted at the Harland & Wolff yard in Belfast, Northern Ireland. As well as having extra equipment fitted, her hull was strengthened for operations in icy waters. She entered service as a support ship to the British Antarctic Survey in 1968, and her red-painted hull became a welcome sight to many a scientist and explorer. One of her tasks was to carry out guard and patrol duties around the Falkland Islands, and the announcement of her withdrawal in the early 1980s was one of the factors that persuaded the Argentine government that they could mount a successful invasion of the islands.

Country of origin:	Germany
Date of origin:	1956
Length:	91.4m (300ft)
Beam:	14m (46ft)
Tonnage:	3657 tonnes (3600 tons)
Machinery:	Single shaft, diesel engine
Armament:	Two 20mm (7.9in) guns
Complement:	119
Main routes:	South Atlantic and Antarctic

Erebus

Launched at Pembroke Dockyard, Wales, as a mortar vessel, *Erebus* was refitted as a polar exploration ship, presumably because of her reinforced hull. On 30 September 1839, with HMS *Terror* and under the command of James Clark Ross, she sailed on a scientific voyage, chiefly to study the Earth's magnetic field and locate the south magnetic pole. Passing through pack ice, the expedition reached the Ross Sea and eventually the great Antarctic ice shelf. After wintering at Hobart, Australia, it returned to the Antarctic, suffering many perils in ice-filled and stormy waters. It eventually returned to England on 4 September 1843. In 1844, auxiliary engines and screw propellers were fitted to *Erebus* and *Terror*, and, on 19 May 1845, under Sir John Franklin, they sailed in search of the Northwest Passage. The ships became icebound and the expedition perished.

Country of origin:	Britain
Date of origin:	1826
Length:	32m (105ft)
Beam:	8.7m (28ft 6in)
Tonnage:	378 tonnes (372 tons)
Rigging:	Three masts, square rig
Machinery:	Single screw, auxiliary steam; 20hp
Complement:	67
Main routes:	Antarctic, Arctic

Exploration

Fram

When the Norwegian explorer Fridtjof Nansen wanted a ship to take him as close as possible to the North Pole, he turned to the expatriate Briton Colin Archer to design and build her, and the resulting vessel was massively strongly built. Two balks of American elm, some 36cm (14in) square, made up her keel, and attached to them were frames of Italian oak, each grown to shape, which had been maturing in the Navy Yard at Horten for 30 years. The *Fram*, Nansen told her designer, must be 'as round and slippery as an eel', so that the ice would not grip her, but would instead tend to push her up and out as it tried to take hold. His theory worked perfectly. Although a far from handy vessel, *Fram* carried Nansen's 1893–96 expedition home safely, and then took Roald Amundsen south to conquer the Antarctic in 1911.

Country of origin:	Norway
Date of origin:	1892
Length:	39m (127ft 9in)
Beam:	10.4m (34ft)
Tonnage:	408 tonnes (402 tons)
Machinery:	Single shaft, auxiliary triple-expansion; 220hp
Rigging:	Three masts, schooner-rigged
Complement:	Not known
Main routes:	Arctic, Antarctic

Gjoa

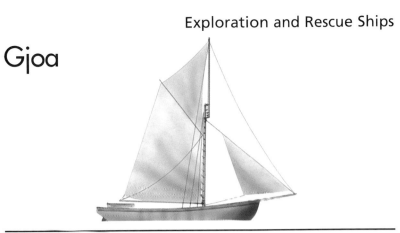

The *Gjoa* served as a fishing boat for 28 years before she was bought in 1900 by the Norwegian explorer Roald Amundsen. The *Gjoa* then became a part of history when Amundsen made the first ever northern passage between the Atlantic and Pacific oceans in her. He reinforced her hull with 76mm (3in) of oak, adding iron strapping to the stem and a small paraffin-fuelled engine. Amundsen left Oslo on 16 January 1903, arriving at the western extremity of the Northwest Passage on 26 August 1905, too late to continue that year, and reached San Francisco in October 1906. For the next 68 years, the *Gjoa* remained in San Francisco's Golden Gate Park, eventually being returned to Norway to become an exhibit in the Norsk Sjofartsmuseum. In 1913, the Panama Canal was completed, providing a fast route between Atlantic and Pacific; Amundsen was invited to inaugurate it, but declined.

Country of origin:	Norway
Date of origin:	1872
Length:	21.3m (70ft)
Beam:	6.2m (20ft 6in)
Tonnage:	68 tonnes (67 tons)
Machinery:	Single shaft, paraffin auxiliary; 13hp
Service speed:	Not known
Constructor:	Kurt Johannesson, Hardanger
Built for:	Asborn Sexe

Goliath

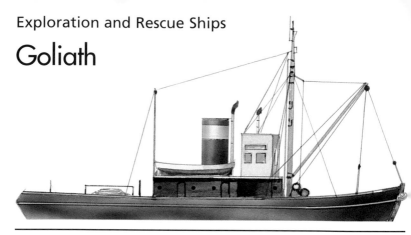

The *Goliath* was typical of harbour tugs designed in the period between the two world wars, although she was somewhat unusual in having at some stage been equipped with a forward derrick for use in salvage operations. She was in daily use in the large German port of Bremen until the 1960s, when she fell into disrepair. She was later restored to working condition, however, by an historic trust in Bremerhaven. At the end of World War II, many of the tugboats that had served in the harbours of northern Germany and escaped the intense Allied bombing were pressed into service as part of the huge rescue operation to evacuate German troops and civilian refugees from East Prussia, ahead of the advancing Soviet forces. Some, which had escaped destruction in their home ports, now fell victim to Soviet fighter-bombers.

Country of origin:	Germany
Date of origin:	1941
Length:	31.3m (102ft 7in)
Beam:	7m (23ft 1in)
Tonnage:	145 tonnes (143 tons)
Machinery:	Two shafts, diesels; 940hp
Service speed:	Not known
Constructor:	Deschimag, Bremen
Built for:	German Navy

Gronland

With the exception of Roald Amundsen's *Gjoa*, the *Gronland* was the only single-masted polar expeditionary ship. She was built in Norway on the lines of a fishing boat, although somewhat modified and strengthened, to carry the first German expedition to the Arctic in 1868. This group fell well short of its polar objective, but returned relatively unharmed, and the *Gronland* subsequently operated in the coastal trade. She was later transferred to the maritime museum in Bremerhaven, where she was preserved in something very like her original condition. In the mid-nineteenth century, very little was still known about the Arctic regions; the first tentative explorations had begun in 1819, but it was not until explorers began their search for the Northwest Passage that serious research began.

Country of origin:	Germany
Date:	1867
Length:	25.8m (84ft 8in)
Beam:	6m (19ft 8in)
Displacement:	50.8 tonnes (50 tons)
Machinery:	Single shaft, steam auxiliary
Service speed:	Not known
Constructor:	Tollef Tollefson, Matre
Built for:	German North Pole Expedition

Hansteen

The *Hansteen* is believed to be one of the oldest purpose-built sailing ships still in existence. She was constructed in Oslo in 1866 by Nylands Verksted for use as a hydrographic survey ship and provided a base for the first systematic survey of Norwegian coastal waters. She was an auxiliary schooner, with the kind of four-sided lug topsails found on the Baltic *galeas* of the period. She was later employed as a cargo carrier in the coastal trade. Late on in her career, she passed into the hands of a private owner in Oslo, who restored her to her original condition. Carrying out a full survey of the Norwegian coast proved to be a task of mammoth proportions and took several years to complete; the coastline, deeply indented with numerous fjords and fringed with an immense number of rocky islands, is 2650km (1645 miles) in length.

Country of origin:	Norway
Date of origin:	1866
Length:	30.9m (101ft 6in)
Beam:	5m (16ft 4in)
Tonnage:	116 tonnes (114 tons)
Machinery:	Single shaft, steam auxiliary; 125hp
Service speed:	Not known
Constructor:	Nylands Verksted, Oslo
Built for:	Norges Geografiske Opmaaling

India

The *India* submarine was designed for underwater salvage and rescue operations. Her hull was built for high surface speeds, enabling her to be deployed rapidly to her rescue coordinates. Two rescue submarines are carried in semi-recessed deck wells aft, and personnel can enter the mother boat through these hatches when she is submerged. The boat can also operate under ice. *India*-class submarines are believed to operate in support of Russian Spetsnaz special operations forces when not being used in their primary role, carrying two IRM amphibious reconnaissance vehicles; these are capable of travelling along the sea bed on tracks, as well as operating in the normal swimming mode. Two Indias were built, and deployed with the Northern and Pacific fleets. They have been observed going to the aid of Russian submarines involved in accidents.

Country of origin:	USSR
Date of origin:	1979
Length:	106m (347ft 9in)
Beam:	10m (32ft 10in)
Tonnage:	3251 tonnes (3200 tons) surfaced
Machinery:	Twin shafts, diesel-electric motors
Service speed:	15 knots surfaced
Armament:	Four 533mm (21in) torpedo tubes
Complement:	70

James Clark Ross

The *James Clark Ross*, as her name might suggest, was purpose-built for the British government's National Environmental Research Council to carry out oceanographic surveys in the Antarctic. To that end, she has a reinforced hull and is able to break fresh ice and navigate in broken floe ice up to 1.5m (5ft) thick and in fragmented ice up to 3m (10ft) thick. She is equipped with both special and general laboratories; if needed, other laboratories can be loaded in containerized form and located on the quarterdeck. The *James Clark Ross* is able to remain at sea for 10 months at a time, should that prove necessary. Somewhat surprisingly, she is not equipped to carry an on-board helicopter. Sir James Clark Ross, the admiral and explorer whose name the ship bears, was the first to be credited with discovering the Southern Continent, in 1841.

Country of origin:	Britain
Date:	1991
Length:	99.1m (325ft)
Beam:	10.8m (35ft 5in)
Tonnage:	5503 tonnes (5416 tons)
Machinery:	Single shaft, diesel engines
Service speed:	15.5 knots
Constructor:	Swan Hunter, Wallsend-on-Tyne
Built for:	National Environmental Research Council

JFJ de Nul

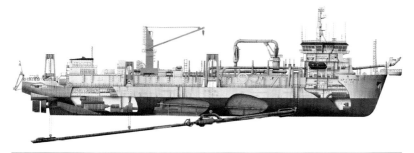

Launched in 1992, the *JFJ de Nul* is a suction hopping dredger, with the capability of recovering material from depths of up to 46m (150ft) via two 110cm (43in) pipes, or from twice that depth using a single 90cm (35in) pipe incorporating a submerged 1800kW (2414hp) pump. She can pump spoil up to 8km (5 miles) inland if necessary. The ship is air-conditioned throughout and can operate in temperatures from 50 degrees to minus 20 degrees Celsius; the bow and the hull are strengthened for ice operation. Suction dredgers are commonly used either to recover material for building or so-called 'beach nourishment', or to keep navigation lanes clear. The *JFJ de Nul* has an internal capacity of 11,750 cubic metres (414,948 cubic feet) and is one of the most modern and effective vessels of her type.

Country of origin:	The Netherlands
Date:	1992
Length:	144m (472ft 5in)
Beam:	25.5m (83ft 8in)
Tonnage:	12,177 tonnes (11,985 tons)
Machinery:	Twin shafts, diesels plus bow thruster; 15,800hp
Service speed:	15 knots
Constructor:	Merwede, Giessendam
Built for:	Ondernemingen Jan de Nul

KDD Ocean Link

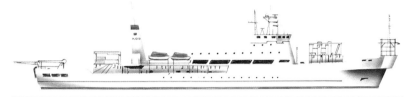

Even after the advent of reliable satellite communications at the end of the twentieth century, there was still a very large demand for submarine cables, although by that time these were almost exclusively fibre optics, rather than true cables. Built to operate in the North Pacific and to endure the most severe weather conditions, the *KDD Ocean Link* is a fourth-generation cable ship, with two full-length decks and three cable holds. The cable was laid over the stern and buried in one operation, the plough carrying both television and forward-scanning sonar. The use of underwater cable for communication can be traced back to the late eighteenth century. In 1795, a single wire cable was run across the bed of the River Medway in England, but it was insufficiently protected against the ingress of water and failed within a few hours.

Country of origin:	Japan
Date of origin:	1991
Length:	133.1m (436ft 10in)
Beam:	19.6m (133.15m)
Tonnage:	9663 tonnes (9510 tons)
Machinery:	Two shafts, diesel; 8800hp
Service speed:	15 knots
Constructor:	Mitsubishi Heavy Industries, Japan
Built for:	Kokusai Cable Ships

L'Astrolabe

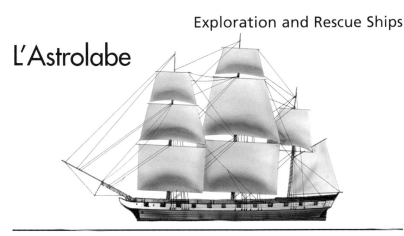

Originally named *Coquille (Shell)*, this vessel (a corvette) was renamed in 1825 in memory of the frigate *L'Astrolabe*, which was captained by the French explorer Comte de la Pérouse and lost on a voyage of exploration to the South Pacific in 1788. The most notable of the second Astrolabe's three great voyages of exploration with the scientist Jules Dumont d'Urville was that to locate the south magnetic pole in 1837-40, which took her to the Antarctic ice pack – despite the fact that she was not armoured against ice. She had already been twice to the South Seas and had brought back more data and specimens of natural history than any vessel before her. Her post-1840 history is unknown. In the course of one voyage around the world, d'Urville discovered the remains of La Pérouse's shipwreck on Vanikoro Island in the New Hebrides.

Country of origin:	France
Date of origin:	1811
Length:	Not known
Beam:	Not known
Tonnage:	386 tonnes (380 tons)
Rigging:	Three masts, square rig
Complement:	79
Main routes:	South Seas, Antarctic
Role:	Exploration vessel

L'Uranie

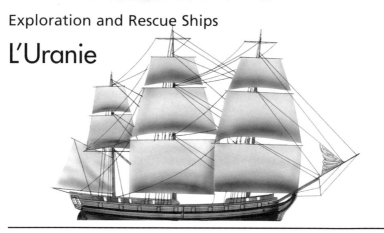

Originally launched in 1800 as *La Ciotat*, a corvette of 20 guns, this vessel was renamed in 1816 and refitted for a scientific voyage to Australia and the South Seas, leaving Toulon, France, on 17 September 1817. The voyage went successfully for more than two years, until the ship, laden with scientific specimens, ran hard aground at Berkeley Sound in the Falkland Islands on Christmas Day 1819; she had to be abandoned and left derelict. Her captain, Louis-Claude de Freycinet, had brought his wife on the cruise, initially disguised as a midshipman; they both returned safely to France. Freycinet later wrote a book entitled *Voyage around the World* about his exploits and experiences. *L'Uranie* was the first ship to carry water supplies in tin drums rather than wooden barrels; she also had metal anchor chains.

Country of origin:	France
Date of origin:	1800
Length:	Not known
Beam:	Not known
Displacement:	Not known
Rigging:	Three masts, square rig
Armament:	20 guns
Complement:	126
Main routes:	Australia and the South Seas

La Boussole

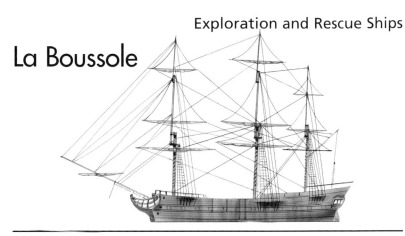

A sister ship of the original *L'Astrolabe*, *La Boussole* (the name means 'compass') was originally launched in 1781 as the fisheries store ship *Le Portefaix*, which worked the Newfoundland Grand Banks. Refitted and renamed, she subsequently became flagship of the Comte de la Pérouse's geographic–scientific expedition to the South Pacific, which left Brest on 1 August 1785. Having cruised over a vast area of the South and West Pacific, *La Boussole* and her sistership *L'Astrolabe* were wrecked on a coral reef near Ambi, New Caledonia. Items from *La Boussole* were also seen by Dumont d'Urville from the second *L'Astrolabe* in 1828; however, despite a thorough search, no trace could be found of the crew. Their fate remains just one of the mysteries to be found in the history of maritime exploration.

Country of origin:	France
Date of origin:	1781
Length:	Not known
Beam:	Not known
Tonnage:	457 tonnes (450 tons)
Rigging:	Three masts, square rig
Armament:	20 guns
Complement:	113
Main routes:	South Pacific

La Dauphine

Built in the royal dockyard of Le Havre, *La Dauphine* was named after the Dauphin, or crown prince, of France. The ship was selected to sail for North America in 1523 under the command of the Italian navigator Giovanni da Verrazzano, with the aim of finding a westward passage to China for the benefit of French trade. Landfall was made at Cape Fear, North Carolina, and Verrazzano explored the coast to the south for 362km (225 miles) before turning north and making a thorough investigation of the bays and inlets of New Jersey and 'Orumbega', later called New England. The Verrazzano Narrows of New York Bay commemorate his search. *La Dauphine* returned to Dieppe, France, on 8 July 1524; her later history is not known. On a later voyage, Verrazzano was captured and eaten by Carin Indians.

Country of origin:	France
Date of origin:	1519
Length:	24.4m (80ft)
Beam:	5.8m (19ft)
Tonnage:	101.6 tonnes (100 tons)
Rigging:	Two masts, square-rigged
Armament:	Not known
Complement:	50
Main routes:	Transatlantic

La Grande Hermine

In 1535, Jacques Cartier had already made one voyage to North America when the French king, Francois I, commissioned him to lead a flotilla to explore beyond Newfoundland. The exploration was in the hope of finding a route to China. *La Grande Hermine* was Cartier's flagship; the other vessels were the 61-tonne (60-ton) *La Petite Hermine* and the pinnace *L'Emerillon*. On 10 August 1535, St Lawrence's Day, Cartier named a small bay after the saint, then sailed up what he called '*la grande rivière*' (now the St Lawrence) and into Quebec. Cartier returned to France in early 1536, but in 1541 he sailed to Canada, again with *La Grande Hermine*, which the king had presented to him. This new expedition was intended to set up a permanent colony, but, after trouble with the Indians, Cartier returned to France with the mission unaccomplished.

Country of origin:	France
Date of origin:	c. 1534
Length:	24m (78ft 8in)
Beam:	7.6m (25ft)
Tonnage:	122 tonnes (120 tons)
Rigging:	Three masts, fore and main square-rigged; lateen mizzen; spritsail
Armament:	12 guns
Complement:	112
Main routes:	North Atlantic

La Recherche

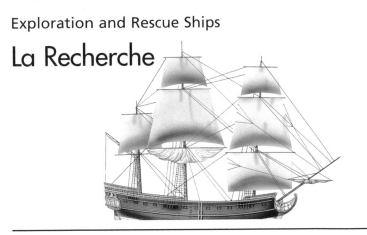

Ｉn September 1791, the Chevalier Antoine Bruni d'Entrecasteaux, governor of
Mauritius and an experienced seaman, was sent in this store ship to look for any
traces of the Comte de la Pérouse's ill-fated *La Boussole* expedition of 1785. He
failed to find anything, but made significant voyages of exploration off the coasts of
Tasmania and mainland Australia. His voyage was dogged by disputes over whether
the expeditions should sail under the white ensign of the French monarchy or the
tricolour of the Republic. D'Entrecasteaux died of scurvy in Java in July 1793.
Scurvy is the result of a deficiency of vitamin C (ascorbic acid), commonly found in
fresh vegetables and fruit. Although the causes of scurvy had been known for many
years, it was not until the close of the eighteenth century that a universal remedy
was administered, initially by the Royal Navy, in the form of lime juice.

Country of origin:	France
Date of origin:	1790
Length:	37.8m (124ft)
Beam:	9.8m (32ft)
Tonnage:	508 tonnes (500 tons)
Rigging:	Square
Armament:	26 guns
Complement:	Not known
Main routes:	South Pacific

Louis S. St Laurent

The Canadian Coast Guard's icebreaker *Louis S. St Laurent* was that organization's most important vessel. Built for service in the Arctic and the Gulf of St Lawrence, this triple-screw vessel was the most powerful non-nuclear icebreaker in the world at the time of her construction. She was fitted with a hangar, large enough to accommodate two helicopters, below the flight deck. She proved her worth in 1976 when she negotiated the Northwest Passage, in company with the oil exploration vessel *Canmar Explorer*, even though she lacked modern systems such as water flushing, waterline air injection and forward propellers. In 1988, she was re-engined with a diesel-electric power plant comprising five generator sets and three electric motors; during this refit, she also received a re-profiled bow.

Country of origin:	Canada
Date of origin:	1966
Length:	111.7m (366ft 6in)
Beam:	24.45m (80ft 3in)
Tonnage:	11,083 tonnes (10,908 tons)
Machinery:	Three shafts, turbo-electric (later diesel-electric); 27,000hp
Service speed:	16 knots
Complement:	216
Constructor:	Canadian Vickers, Montreal

Matthew

Four years after the epic voyage of Christopher Columbus to the New World, King Henry VII of England granted letters patent to another Italian to make a westward voyage to the Orient. The Italian, his name anglicised to John Cabot, planned to assemble a fleet of five ships, but could raise neither interest in nor funds for the voyage. However, on 20 May 1497, Cabot and his son Sebastian set out in the solitary *Matthew*, described at the time as '*navicula*' ('little ship'). Although the *Matthew* was even smaller than Columbus's ship *Niña*, she was an excellent ship, and her 11-week round voyage to North America remained unbeaten for another 100 years. Cabot made landfall off Newfoundland, followed the coast for some distance, then sailed back to Bristol, England, believing he had found the coast of China.

Country of origin:	England
Date of origin:	1493
Length:	22.3m (73ft)
Beam:	6.25m (20ft 6in)
Tonnage:	86.4 tonnes (85 tons)
Rigging:	Three masts; square-rigged on fore and main; lateen mizzen
Complement:	18
Armament:	Not known
Main routes:	North Atlantic, Ireland, France, Spain

Niña

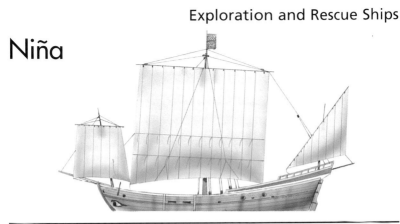

Officially named *Santa Clara*, the name *Niña* came from her owner Juan Niña de Moguer. She made at least five transatlantic voyages, including the historic first one under the command of Christopher Columbus, accompanied by the *Santa Maria* and the *Pinta*. After making the historic landfall in the Bahamas on 12 October 1492, *Niña* sailed along the Cuban coast, where she was fitted with a new mizzen mast. On 25 December, *Santa Maria* having grounded, the admiral shifted his flag to *Niña* and set sail for home. Having weathered two major storms, *Niña* was first to reach Las Palos, a few hours ahead of *Pinta*. In 1493, Columbus included *Niña* in his second fleet to America, returning to Spain in 1496. After an interlude in which she was briefly captured by Sardinian corsairs, *Niña* made a further Atlantic voyage in January 1498.

Country of origin:	Spain
Date of origin:	c. 1491
Length:	c. 18.3m (60ft)
Beam:	c. 5.5m (18ft)
Tonnage:	c. 76 tonnes (75 tons)
Rigging:	Three masts; square-rigged on fore and main; lateen mizzen
Armament:	Not known
Complement:	24
Main routes:	Spanish coast, North Atlantic

Port Fairy Lifeboat

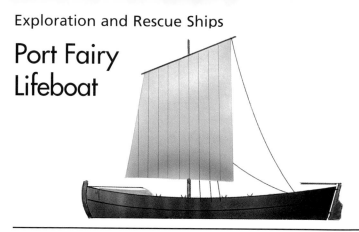

An excellent example of an early shore-based rescue craft, the *Port Fairy (Victoria) Lifeboat* stayed in continuous service from 1858 until 1941. Built of double-diagonal wooden planking on a wooden frame with an iron keel, she was generally propelled by oars (although she had a dipping lugsail for use in easier conditions). She was later preserved in the town where she was stationed, and put on display in the boathouse that had been built for her in 1861. As far as can be ascertained, the first dedicated lifeboat in the world was patented by a London coach builder, Lionel Lukin, in November 1785. In the following year, the 'Lukin lifeboat', a converted coble, was emplaced in a new lifeboat station at Bamburgh, Northumberland, England, which had been established by Archdeacon John Sharp.

Country of origin:	Australia
Date of origin:	1858
Length:	9.1m (30ft)
Beam:	2.3m (7ft 6in)
Tonnage:	4 tonnes (4 tons)
Rigging:	Single mast, dipping lugsail
Complement:	Not known
Main routes:	Coastal waters of Victoria, Australia
Built for:	Port Fairy Authority

Princess Mary

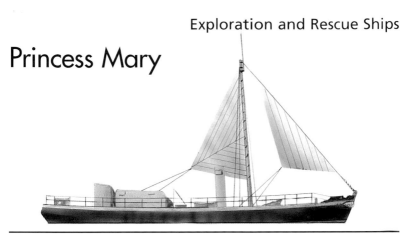

The British Lifeboat Service was founded in 1824 by Colonel Sir William Hillary and, over the years, has been responsible for saving many thousands of lives. The steam-powered *Princess Mary*, stationed in north Cornwall, was one of the best lifeboats afloat when first completed. Steam-powered lifeboats, the first of which, the *Duke of Northumberland*, went into service at Harwich, England, in 1890, represented a massive advance over earlier boats, which relied upon the crew to row out to a stricken vessel. The area around the *Princess Mary*'s engine room was packed with flotation boxes, and the hull was double-skinned for added strength. The vessel could carry up to 130 people. By the time *Princess Mary* entered service, however, motor lifeboats were beginning to replace the steam-powered craft.

Country of origin:	Britain
Date of origin:	1929
Length:	18.6m (61ft)
Beam:	4.6m (15ft)
Tonnage:	40.6 tonnes (40 tons)
Machinery:	Not known
Service speed:	9.5 knots
Constructor:	Not known
Built for:	British Lifeboat Service

Resolution

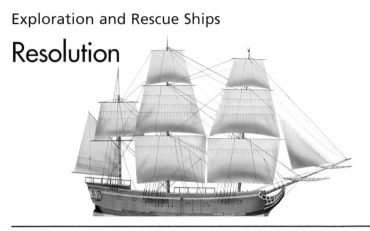

Built at Whitby, Yorkshire, as the collier brig *Drake*, then renamed *Marquis of Grandby*, this vessel's most famous name was bestowed by the Admiralty in 1772, when she was converted to a ship-rigged sloop. With her sister HMS *Adventure*, she was despatched under Captain James Cook on a voyage to ascertain the existence of a continent in the Southern Ocean. Between 13 July 1772 and 29 July 1775, she explored the stormy and empty waters between South Africa, Australia, South America and the Antarctic, twice crossing the Antarctic Circle and making the furthest voyage to the south yet achieved. A year later, *Resolution* and Cook set out on a second voyage, this time to the Pacific, and it was on this expedition that Cook was killed by Hawaiian islanders. In 1782, *Resolution* was captured by French ships in the Indian Ocean; her subsequent fate is unknown.

Country of origin:	Britain
Date:	1770
Length:	33.7m (110ft 8in)
Beam:	9.2m (30ft 5in)
Tonnage:	471 tonnes (461 tons)
Rigging:	Three masts, square rig
Complement:	110
Main routes:	Southern Ocean, North Pacific
Built for:	Not known

São Gabriel

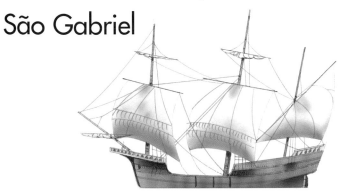

The thrust of Portuguese exploration and exploitation was down the west coast of Africa, and *São Gabriel* was built specifically to extend exploitation beyond the Cape of Good Hope. She was the flagship of the aristocrat Vasco da Gama, in a four-ship flotilla. The epic voyage lasted from 8 June 1497 until late July 1499. When *São Gabriel* docked at Lisbon, she had found the sea route to India and so instigated a major change in the pattern of East–West trading across the world. It can be reliably assumed that she was a three-masted, square-rigged ship, as this had become the standard for a long-distance voyage of exploration. At the time, Portugal was at the forefront of maritime science and technology. Vasco da Gama made a second voyage to the Indies in 1502, but the further history of the *São Gabriel* is not known.

Country of origin:	Portugal
Date:	1497
Length:	c. 21.3m (70ft)
Beam:	c. 7m (23ft)
Tonnage:	c. 101 tonnes (100 tons)
Rigging:	Three masts, square-rigged on fore and main; lateen mizzen
Complement:	90
Armament:	20 guns
Main routes:	African coast, Indian Ocean

Sea Spider

The *Sea Spider* was a specialist ship for laying cables between Sweden and Poland, and was built in only nine months by a consortium of suppliers. It was initially planned to convert an existing ship, but eventually a purpose-built vessel was constructed which was capable of laying cable down to a considerable depth and in heavy seas with waves of up 2.4m (8ft). The 5080 tonnes (5000 tons) of high voltage cable is carried on a carousel with a diameter of 24m (78ft) and on a smaller 1626-tonne (1600-ton) cable basket. There are three cable engines with pick-up arms to handle the cable over the stern via a large A-frame, which also handles the trencher. The long afterdeck of *Sea Spider* enables swift cable-laying operations to be carried out in most sea conditions. A double bottom is installed for fuel and spares.

Country of origin:	The Netherlands
Date of origin:	1999
Length:	86.9m (285ft)
Beam:	23.8m (78ft)
Tonnage:	4072 tonnes (4008 tons)
Machinery:	Controllable pitch, diesel-electric
Service speed:	9.5 knots
Main routes:	Sweden–Poland
Built for:	Communications industry

Squirrel

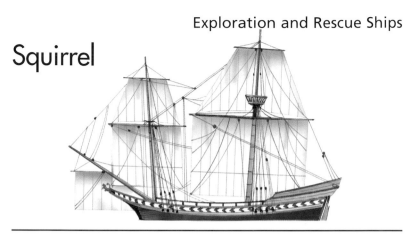

Sir Humphrey Gilbert (c. 1539–83), who was the half-brother of Sir Walter Raleigh, claimed Newfoundland for England in 1583. His expedition consisted of five ships, of which *Squirrel*, apparently his own property, was by far the smallest. On the outward journey to Newfoundland, Gilbert sailed in *Delight*, which was wrecked later in the expedition. He chose *Squirrel* for the return journey to England, but she was lost, with all hands, somewhere in the Atlantic, having last been seen by the crew of the *Golden Hind* on 9 September 1583. The small size of *Squirrel*, which was wholly unsuited to a lengthy, oceanic voyage of exploration, particularly in the treacherous conditions of the North Atlantic, was indicative of the problems faced by explorers in assembling a squadron for voyages of uncertain outcome.

Country of origin:	England
Date:	1583
Length:	12.8m (42ft)
Beam:	3.8m (12ft 6in)
Tonnage:	Not known
Rigging:	Three masts; square-rigged fore and main; lateen mizzen
Armament:	Not known
Complement:	11
Main routes:	English coast, North Atlantic

Stena Seawell

The rapid expansion of the offshore gas and oil industries led to requirements for a whole new range of purpose-built ships, one of which was the *Stena Seawell* (later called simply *Seawell*), the most sophisticated multi-role offshore support vessel in the world when she entered service in 1988. She had accommodation for 147 and was certified as a standby and rescue ship; she had saturation diving chambers, a remotely operated unmanned submarine and two diving bells, a hospital, a large helicopter platform forwards and even a conference suite for clients. Her twin cranes could lift 142 tonnes (140 tons) when operating in tandem, and she was equipped as an anchor-handler, with a dynamic positioning system. The *Stena Seawell* was a good example of a third-generation offshore support ship, at home in any maritime oilfield in the world.

Country of origin:	Britain
Date of origin:	1987
Length:	111.4m (365ft 6in)
Beam:	22.5m (73ft 10in)
Tonnage:	12,126 tonnes (11,935 tons)
Machinery:	Three shafts, diesel plus bow thruster; 12,000 plus 2000hp
Service speed:	13 knots
Constructor:	North-East Shipbuilders, Sunderland, UK
Built for:	Stena Offshore

Trieste

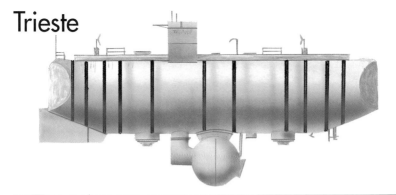

The bathyscaphe *Trieste* was designed and built by Auguste Piccard and was a vessel in two parts. The upper was simply a tank containing 106 cubic metres (3745 cubic feet) of gasoline. Being of lower specific gravity than water, this provided a sufficient measure of buoyancy to return the craft to the surface when water ballast held in two small tanks at the extremities was blown out by compressed air. The permanent ballast (initially 9.1 tonnes [nine tons], then later 16.3 tons [6 tonnes] of iron pellets) was also contained in this portion. The lower section was an alloy sphere, big enough for two, with walls 10cm (4in) thick. Piccard made his first dive in August 1953, and five years later Trieste was sold to the US Navy. In January 1960, crewed by Piccard's son Jacques and Lieutenant Don Walsh USN, *Trieste* descended to 10,912m (35,800ft) in the Challenger Deep, southwest of Guam.

Country of origin:	USA
Date of origin:	1953
Length:	18.1m (59ft 6in)
Beam:	3.5m (11ft 6in)
Tonnage:	50.8 tonnes (50 tons)
Machinery:	Two shafts, electric motors; 2hp
Service speed:	1 knot
Constructor:	Navalmeccanica, Naples
Built for:	US Navy

Victoria

A small Spanish carrack, *Victoria* was the first ship to circumnavigate the globe. She was one of five ships under the command of the Portuguese navigator Fernão de Magalhães (Magellan). The fleet sailed from Sanlucar, on the Guadalquivir River, on 20 September 1519. The mission, backed by the Emperor Charles V, was to succeed where Columbus was now known to have failed, in finding a sea route westwards to the Indies. On 28 November 1520, the fleet, by then reduced to three ships, completed the passage of the strait at the tip of South America that now bears Magellan's name. With crews beset by starvation and scurvy, the ships reached the Mariana Islands in March 1521. On 27 April, Magellan was killed in a skirmish on the Philippine island of Cebu. *Victoria* was the only ship to return home, after an absence of three years. She was later lost on an Atlantic voyage.

Country of origin:	Spain
Date of origin:	c. 1519
Length:	Not known
Beam:	Not known
Tonnage:	86 tonnes (85 tons)
Rigging:	Three masts, square-rigged on fore and main; lateen mizzen
Armament:	Not known
Complement:	60
Main routes:	Circumnavigation of the globe

X1

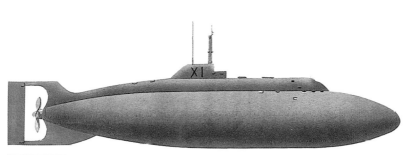

The *X1* was an experimental submarine completed in 1955. She was intended to be the prototype for a series of midget submarines that would penetrate enemy harbours, and her design was based on that of the British *X5*. She had a displacement of 31 tonnes (31 tons) and measured just 15m (49ft 3in) in length. *X1* normally carried a four-man crew, but on short missions she could accommodate six. Originally, she was fitted with a hydrogen peroxide propulsion unit, which allowed her diesel engines to be used while she was submerged. A small electric motor was fitted to allow her to 'creep' silently while under water. In 1958, an explosion of the hydrogen peroxide unit blew her into three pieces. She was repaired, but was laid up in 1960, and was later used for research purposes until 1973. *X1* was the only midget submarine ever built for the US Navy.

Country of origin:	USA
Date of origin:	1954
Length:	15m (49ft 3in)
Beam:	2m (7ft)
Tonnage:	31 tonnes (31 tons)
Machinery:	Single shaft, diesel-electric
Service speed:	15 knots surfaced, 12 knots submerged
Complement:	3–6
Built for:	US Navy

Adriatic

Built at the Novelty Works, New York, this two-funnelled paddle steamer was the largest and last vessel of the Collins Line. The company was in severe difficulty, caused by the loss of passenger confidence after the sinking of one of its other ships, the *Arctic*. *Adriatic* was laid up almost as soon as she was delivered, and was later sold to the Galway Line. After a boiler explosion in 1864, she was towed to Liverpool, England. She ended her career at Bonny, West Africa, and was broken up in 1885. It was another American company, the Black Ball Line, that inaugurated the first scheduled passenger service on 5 January 1818, when the sailing packet *James Monroe* sailed from New York's East River and reached Liverpool in England 28 days later. She carried eight passengers and was richly furnished.

Country of origin:	USA
Date of origin:	1856
Length:	105.2m (345ft)
Beam:	15.2m (50ft)
Tonnage:	5982 tonnes (5888 tons)
Rigging:	Two masts, brig rig
Machinery:	Side wheels, side lever; 1350hp
Service speed:	Not known
Constructor:	Novelty Works, New York

America

The National Line first began operations during the American Civil War, in 1863; by the 1880s, it had become established on the Liverpool – Queenstown (Cork) – New York run. By then, however, the youngest member of its fleet was a decade old, and none of its ships had ever made a record-breaking crossing. In 1884, it tried to remedy that situation, taking delivery of a new and very elegant ship, the *America*. She was to fail narrowly in her attempt to win the Blue Riband, but made a very satisfactory crossing in six days, fourteen hours and eight minutes from Sandy Hook to Queenstown, averaging 17.78 knots, on her maiden voyage. She was briefly taken up by the Admiralty in the following year, in a war scare that came to nothing, for conversion as an armed merchant cruiser. She was sold to the Italian Navy in 1887 and was scrapped in 1925.

Country of origin:	Britain
Date of origin:	1883
Length:	134.6m (441ft 9in)
Beam:	15.6m (52ft)
Tonnage:	5616 tonnes (5528 tons)
Machinery:	Single shaft, compound engines
Service speed:	17 knots
Capacity:	300 1st class, 700 steerage
Constructor:	J&G Thompson, Glasgow

Anastasis

The *Anastasis* was the largest unit in a small fleet of privately owned hospital ships. Built as the *Victoria*, a small passenger liner, for the Lloyd Triestino Line, and intended for operations on the Genoa–Hong Kong and Trieste–Beirut runs, she was later converted to the role of cruise ship. In 1978, she was acquired by Mercy Ships and, in three years, was outfitted as a hospital ship, with three operating tables, a 25-bed recovery ward, laboratories, radiology facilities, a large pharmacy and a dental surgery. Funded by charitable organizations, *Anastasis* has operated in many parts of the world, providing medical assistance to UN personnel engaged in relief operations. *Anastasis* was built as one of two small passenger ships; her sister vessel, the *Asia*, became a livestock carrier.

Country of origin:	Malta
Date of origin:	1953
Length:	159m (521ft 6in)
Beam:	20.7m (67ft 10in)
Tonnage:	11,882 tonnes (11,695 tons)
Machinery:	Two shafts, diesels; 16,100hp
Service speed:	19.5 knots
Capacity:	286 1st, 181 tr
Constructor:	Cantieri Riuniti dell'Adriatico, Trieste

AP.1-88

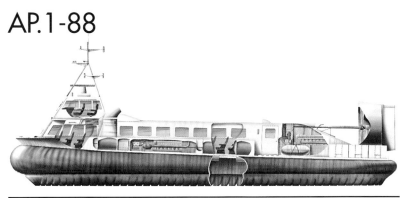

In its original form, the commercial hovercraft was powered by very expensive gas turbine engines. By the 1980s, however, advances in diesel engine technology enabled this much cheaper power plant to be substituted, a fact which went a long way towards making the small hovercraft commercially viable. The Type A.1-88 was the first diesel-powered air cushion vehicle to appear on the market, and it made a considerable impact, both as a freight carrier and a passenger ferry. A militarized version, armed with 30mm (1.18in) Rarden cannon and surface-to-air missiles, was also made available. The first hovercraft was developed by Christopher Cockerell (later Sir Christopher), an electronics engineer and spare-time boat builder of Somerleyton, Suffolk, who patented the idea on 12 December 1955.

Country of origin:	Britain
Date of origin:	1982
Length:	24.5m (80ft 4in)
Beam:	11m (36ft)
Tonnage:	40.6 tonnes (40 tons)
Machinery:	Four diesel engines; 1800hp
Service speed:	40 knots
Capacity:	101 passengers, 12.2 tonnes (12 tons) freight
Constructor:	British Hovercraft Corporation

Aquitania

The Cunard Line's *Aquitania* was thought by many to be the most beautiful of all the liners that plied the North Atlantic route. It was also considered to be the finest example of the 'four-stackers', the profiles of which had become so famous in the years before World War I. Her lines, superstructure and four massive raked funnels were all in perfect proportion. Constructed to operate in concert with the *Lusitania* and *Mauretania*, she served in both world wars as a troopship and spent most of the rest of the time navigating the North Atlantic, with occasional Mediterranean cruises. She ended her days carrying war brides, returning service-men, displaced persons and immigrants to the United States. Refused a certificate in 1950, she was sold for scrap, and her passing marked the end of an era in the story of passenger liners.

Country of origin:	Britain
Date of origin:	1913
Length:	274.6m (901ft)
Beam:	29.6m (97ft)
Tonnage:	46,380 tonnes (45,547 tons)
Machinery:	Four shafts, geared turbines
Service speed:	23 knots
Capacity:	618 1st class, 614 2nd class, 1998 3rd class
Constructor:	John Brown & Co Ltd, Glasgow

Arabia

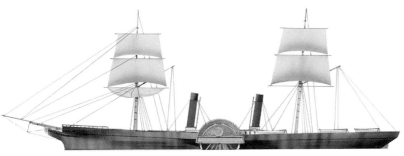

The *Arabia* was a two-funnelled paddle steamer belonging to Samuel Cunard's British and North American Royal Mail Steam Packet Company. She was built in Govan, on the River Clyde, Scotland, and was the last wooden-hulled Cunard liner. She was subsequently succeeded by the iron-hulled *Persia* in the development of this premier Atlantic fleet. In 1855, *Arabia* was converted to carry 203 horses for service in the Crimean War ; in 1856, she resumed the company's transatlantic sailings, which had begun in 1840. In 1858, she was damaged in a collision with another ship. She was sold for conversion to a sailing vessel in 1864 and was eventually broken up. As a passenger liner, *Arabia* boasted steam central heating, a cupola over the saloon to give increased height and two well-stocked libraries.

Country of origin:	Britain
Date of origin:	1851
Length:	86.6m (284ft)
Beam:	12.5m (41ft)
Tonnage:	2440 tonnes (4202 tons)
Machinery:	Side wheels, steam
Rigging:	Two masts, square rig
Service speed:	Not known
Capacity:	Not known

Arabia Maru

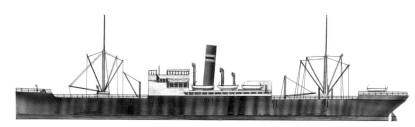

Among the world's shipbuilding nations, Japan was a latecomer, her expansion into maritime technology only coming about in the last years of the nineteenth century. During World War I, under a wartime agreement with the United States, Japan was supplied with steel in order to build a fleet of new merchant ships. One of the largest vessels built for Japan's expanding mercantile fleet was the *Arabia Maru*. She had three continuous decks with accommodation for 356 passengers, and could uplift 11,685 tonnes (11,500 tons) of cargo. Her bunker capacity was 2743 tonnes (2700 tons) of coal, and she burnt 86 tonnes (85 tons) per day. *Arabia Maru* was sunk east of Manila by a United States submarine in October 1944, a fate that overtook most of Japan's merchant fleet as its ships came under increasing attack.

Country of origin:	Japan
Date of origin:	1918
Length:	144.8m (475ft)
Beam:	18.6m (61ft)
Tonnage:	9652 tonnes (9500 tons)
Machinery:	Two shafts, triple-expansion engines; 8153hp
Service speed:	16.2 knots
Capacity:	42 1st class, 314 3rd class
Constructor:	Mitsubishi Zosen Kaisha

Arctic

The *Arctic* was one of a group of four wooden-hulled paddle-wheel steamers built in New York for the E.K. Collins Line; at the time of their entry into service, they were well in advance of any other vessels then serving on the North Atlantic run. On 21 September 1854, *Arctic* left Liverpool, bound for New York, with 246 passengers and 135 crew. On the 27th, while steaming in thick fog in the vicinity of Cape Race, she collided with the iron-hulled French steamer *Vesta*. *Arctic* was holed in three places and sank with the loss of 322 people drowned; the dead included Collins's wife and children. There was no rescue drill, and there were insufficient lifeboats for the number of passengers and crew on board. The tragedy led to much-needed reforms in maritime safety arrangements, including lifeboat provision and the establishment of Atlantic 'sea lanes'.

Country of origin:	USA
Date of origin:	1850
Length:	86m (282ft)
Beam:	13.7m (45ft)
Tonnage:	2896 tonnes (2850 tons)
Machinery:	Side wheels, side lever
Rigging:	Two masts, square-rigged on foremast
Service speed:	12.5 knots
Capacity:	250 passengers, 135 crew

Ferries and Liners

Arizona

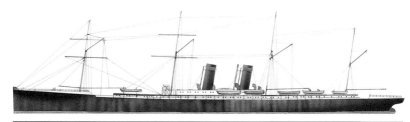

The Guion Line had no really fast ship until it took delivery of the *Arizona* from the Glasgow shipbuilder John Elders in 1879. On her second voyage eastbound, she beat *Britannic*'s best average speed by 0.02 knots with a passage of seven days, eight hours and eleven minutes to capture the Blue Riband. In November 1879, on her fifth voyage back to Liverpool, she hit an iceberg at full speed in dense fog off Newfoundland, but the forward bulkhead held and she was able to make St John's for repairs under her own steam. The *Arizona* was re-engined in 1898 and operated between San Francisco and China. She was bought by the US Navy in 1903 and renamed *Hancock*, and was used as a supply ship and troop transport. The first US ship to bear the name *Hancock* was a frigate of the Continental Navy in 1776.

Country of origin:	Britain
Date of origin:	1879
Length:	137m (450ft)
Beam:	13.7m (40ft)
Tonnage:	5247 tonnes (5164 tons)
Machinery:	Single shaft, compound (later three triple-expansion)
Service speed:	15 knots
Capacity:	140 1st class, 70 2nd class, 140 3rd class, 1000 steerage
Constructor:	John Elder & Co, Glasgow

Augusta Victoria

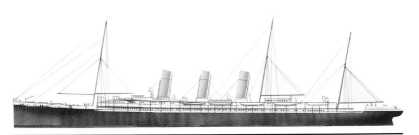

In 1887, the German Hamburg-Amerika Line decided to start an express liner service between Hamburg and New York, and commissioned the *Augusta Victoria* from AG Vulcan shipbuilders of Stettin. At the time of her completion in 1899, she was the largest ship ever built in Germany. Her maiden voyage in the same year was a record-breaking Atlantic crossing, taking just seven days and two-and-a-half hours. From 1894, she spent some of her time cruising, her winter European terminus being Genoa. In 1896–97, she was lengthened by 17.7m (58ft) by Harland & Wolff, which increased her displacement to 8615 tonnes (8479 tons). In 1904, she was sold to the Imperial Russian Navy and went into service as the auxiliary cruiser *Kuban*. After serving briefly in the Far East during the Russo-Japanese war, she returned to Russia and was scrapped in 1907.

Country of origin:	Germany
Date of origin:	1889
Length:	140m (459ft)
Beam:	17m (56ft)
Tonnage:	7783 tonnes (7661 tons)
Machinery:	Two shafts, vertical triple-expansion
Service speed:	18 knots
Capacity:	400 1st class, 120 2nd class, 580 3rd class
Constructor:	AG Vulcan, Stettin

Balmoral Castle

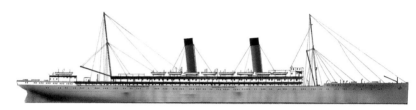

The Union and Castle Lines were fierce rivals over the lucrative United Kingdom – South Africa route; when they merged, they enjoyed a virtual monopoly. In 1909, Union-Castle took delivery of two new passenger liners for service on this route, the *Balmoral Castle* and the *Edinburgh Castle*; both were equipped with quadruple expansion engines, giving them an impressive service speed of 17 knots. Quadruple expansion engines were developed at the same time as turbines and were soon superseded by them, both in merchant vessels and warships. *Balmoral Castle* was the first Cape liner to be fitted with wireless. In 1910, she was transformed into a royal yacht for the celebrations to mark the creation of the Union of South Africa. She served as a troopship during World War I and was sold for scrap in 1939.

Country of origin:	Britain
Date of origin:	1909
Length:	180m (590ft 6in)
Beam:	19.6m (64ft 4in)
Tonnage:	13,574 tonnes (13,360 tons)
Machinery:	Two shafts, quadruple-expansion engines
Service speed:	17 knots
Capacity:	317 1st class, 220 2nd class, 268 3rd class
Constructor:	Harland & Wolff, Belfast

Baloeran

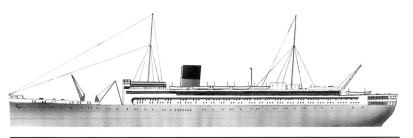

The passenger liner *Baloeran* was built for service between Holland and the Dutch East Indies and was one of the earliest liners to use electric cranes for cargo handling. In May 1940, she was seized by the Germans after they overran the Low Countries, together with many other vessels. She was renamed *Strassburg* and pressed into service as a hospital ship. She subsequently served in the Mediterranean theatre of war, evacuating wounded German and Italian troops from North Africa to hospitals in Italy and, after November 1942, southern France. She played a prominent part in supporting the Axis forces in Tunisia, where they were trapped by the British and American pincer movement early in 1943, but fell accidental victim to a British torpedo shortly before the last enemy troops surrendered in May.

Country of origin:	The Netherlands
Date of origin:	1929
Length:	175m (574ft)
Beam:	21.3m (70ft)
Tonnage:	21,336 tonnes (21,000 tons)
Machinery:	Two shafts, diesel engines
Service speed:	18.5 knots
Capacity:	252 1st class, 280 2nd class, 118 3rd class
Constructor:	Not known

Barbara

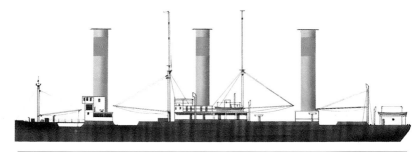

The *Barbara* was the only merchant ship purpose-built to harness the Magnus effect, discovered in 1852. In broad terms, this holds that a sphere or a cylinder rotating in an air stream generates a force at right angles to the direction of its flow. In 1920, German physicist Anton Flettner attempted to prove that the Magnus effect had applications in marine engineering. He constructed twin rotor cylinders, 16.8m (55ft) high by 2.7m (9ft) in diameter, which he mounted aboard a stripped-down steel barquentine named the *Buckau*, driving them by means of 45hp motors. He tested her against a conventionally rigged sister ship and proved his point. The Hamburg-Amerika line ordered ten ships fitted with Flettner rotors to supplement their diesel engines, but only one, the *Barbara*, was ever built, and her cylinders were removed after only a few voyages.

Country of origin:	Germany
Date of origin:	1926
Length:	90m (295ft 3in)
Beam:	13m (42ft 8in)
Tonnage:	2183 tonnes (2075 tons)
Machinery:	Single shaft, diesel engines plus Flettner cylinders
Service speed:	13 knots (6 knots with cylinders only)
Capacity:	Not known
Constructor:	Vulcan AG, Stettin

Bremen

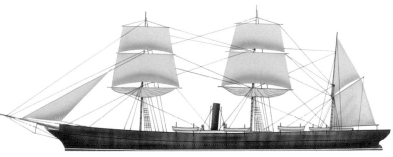

Built at Greenock on the River Clyde for Norddeutscher Lloyd, *Bremen* was iron-hulled with a single funnel and could make a speed of 13.1 knots. She and her sister ship *New York* were the first German transatlantic liners, with *Bremen* opening the North Atlantic route on behalf of her company in June 1858. She carried 22 cabin and 93 steerage passengers, as well as 155 tonnes (152 tons) of cargo. She reached New York in just over 12 days, a performance that helped establish the company's reputation. In 1874, *Bremen* was sold to a British company. Her engines were removed and she served as a sailing ship until she was wrecked in 1882. At this time, steamships had scarcely more superstructure – funnel apart – than sailing vessels, mainly because they were still fully sparred with the consequent lack of clearance for construction on deck.

Country of origin:	Germany
Date of origin:	1858
Length:	97m (318ft)
Beam:	12.5m (41ft)
Tonnage:	2717 tonnes (2674 tons)
Rigging:	Three masts, barque rig
Machinery:	Single screw, compound engine
Service speed:	10 knots
Capacity:	Not known

Britannia

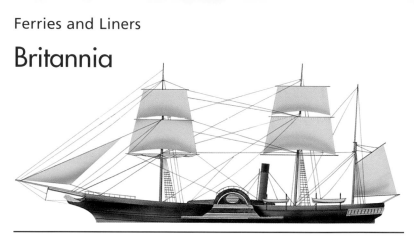

One of the first ships built for the Cunard Line, *Britannia* was launched on the Clyde in 1840. She was the first steamer to carry mail from Britain to the United States, making her first crossing in 12 days and 10 hours. In 1849, she was sold to the North German Confederation Navy, fitted with nine heavy 68-pounder guns and renamed *Barbarossa*. In 1852, she was transferred to the new Prussian Navy for use as a floating barracks and guardship. Her final role was as a target ship, with engine removed. In 1880, she was sunk at Kiel during a practice shoot, but was later salvaged for scrap. Cunard's early disposal of *Britannia* reflects the speed of steamer development in the rapidly expanding transatlantic passenger and mail business; vessels were becoming obsolete almost as soon as they were put into service.

Country of origin:	Britain
Date of origin:	1840
Length:	70m (228ft)
Beam:	17m (56ft)
Tonnage:	2083 tonnes (2050 tons)
Rigging:	Three masts, barque rig
Machinery:	Side wheels, steam
Service speed:	8.5 knots
Capacity:	Not known

Britannic

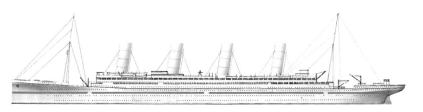

The *Britannic* was the largest of three big liners ordered by the White Star Line from Harland & Wolff, but she was destined never to sail, as intended, on the Southampton–New York route. Instead, she was requisitioned by the British Admiralty, which ordered her to be completed as a hospital ship. In this role, *Britannic* could accommodate over 3000 patients. She was commissioned in November 1915 and assigned to serve in the Mediterranean. On 21 November 1916, after she had made five successful voyages to the Eastern Mediterranean and returned with a total of 15,000 British and Empire servicemen, she struck a mine in the Aegean and capsized and sank within an hour, with the loss of 21 of her crew. The *Britannic* was an improved version of the ill-fated *Titanic*; she was one of five White Star liners lost during World War I.

Country of origin:	Britain
Date of origin:	1914
Length:	275.2m (903ft)
Beam:	28.7m (94ft)
Tonnage:	48,928 tonnes (48,158 tons)
Machinery:	Three shafts, two triple-expansion reciprocating engines
Service speed:	21 knots
Capacity:	3109 patients, 489 medical staff
Constructor:	Harland & Wolff, Belfast

Caledonia

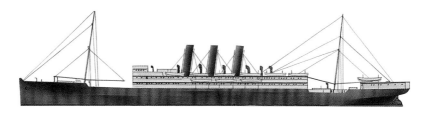

The *Caledonia* was a large turbine steamer built for the Anchor Line for use on its New York to London service. She was built with five decks and had her lifeboats double-banked above the top deck. She worked on the North Atlantic route regularly until World War II put a stop to passenger services. In September 1939, she was requisitioned by the Admiralty, who pressed her into service as a hastily converted auxiliary cruiser. She was given eight obsolete 152mm (6in) guns, plus two 76mm (3in) guns for anti-aircraft defence, and in this new configuration she was renamed *Scotstoun*. Like others of her kind assigned to protect Atlantic convoys, *Scotstoun*'s main weakness was a complete lack of protection; on 13 June 1940, she was torpedoed and sunk by the German submarine *U-25*.

Country of origin:	Britain
Date of origin:	1925
Length:	168m (552ft)
Beam:	22m (72ft)
Tonnage:	17,319 tonnes (17,046 tons)
Machinery:	Two shafts, geared turbines
Service speed:	16 knots
Capacity:	205 1st class, 403 2nd class, 800 3rd class
Constructor:	Alexander Stephen & Sons, Glasgow

Californian

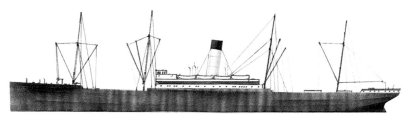

The *Californian* was a mixed cargo and passenger liner. She had four masts, each equipped with several derricks for handling her large cargo capacity. Passenger accommodation was amidships. In 1912, *Californian* became embroiled in the *Titanic* controversy when she was named as the mystery ship that failed to respond to calls for help from the sinking liner. The British Court of Enquiry deemed that *Californian* had only been 19km (10 miles) away from the doomed vessel, but later evidence suggests that this was not the case. The discovery of the *Titanic*'s final resting place off Newfoundland suggests that the *Californian* would not have been within sight of any distress signals from the liner, and it is quite possible that other vessels were in a better position to render assistance. There is always likely to be controversy over the matter, however.

Country of origin:	Britain
Date of origin:	1901
Length:	146.3m (480ft)
Beam:	14m (46ft)
Tonnage:	6322 tonnes (6223 tons)
Machinery:	Single shaft, reciprocating engines
Service speed:	13 knots
Capacity:	Not known
Constructor:	Not known

Campania

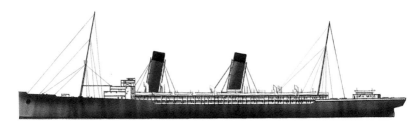

The *Campania* and her sister ship *Laconia* were built for the Cunard Line's Liverpool–New York service; they were the first new construction for eight years and were an immediate success. In 1893, on her maiden voyage, *Campania* took the eastbound Blue Riband and repeated the feat westbound in the following year. The two ships dominated the Europe–New York route until 1897, when *Kaiser Wilhelm der Grosse* entered service. In 1914, by which time she was largely worn out as well as obsolescent, the *Campania* was transferred to the Anchor Line, making two voyages from Liverpool and one from Glasgow in place of the *Aquitania*. She was later purchased by the Admiralty for conversion to an aircraft carrier, being fitted with a flight deck, hangars and workshops. In November 1918, she sank after colliding with the battleship HMS *Revenge* in the Firth of Forth, Scotland.

Country of origin:	Britain
Date of origin:	1892
Length:	189m (620ft)
Beam:	19.9m (65ft 3in)
Tonnage:	18,288 tonnes (18,000 tons)
Machinery:	Two shafts, two vertical triple-expansion engines, 28,000hp
Service speed:	21 knots
Capacity:	600 1st class, 400 2nd class, 1000 3rd class
Constructor:	Fairfield Co. Ltd, Glasgow

Canberra

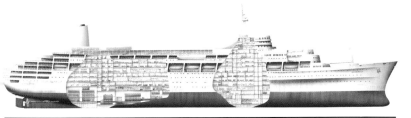

The *Canberra*, instantly recognizable then by her futuristic lines, was constructed in 1960 as a passenger liner to operate on the newly merged P&O-Orient Line's United Kingdom–Australia service alongside the *Oriana*. Within ten years, however, air fares had dropped to a level with which she could not compete, and, in 1973, she began year-round cruises. *Canberra* had just completed one in April 1982 when she was requisitioned by the British government to act as a troopship in support of the operation to retake the Falkland Islands from Argentina. *Canberra* had been secretly surveyed for this task by naval experts in Gibraltar as she neared the end of her latest cruise. She sailed for the Falklands with three battalions of Royal Marine Commandos; although she came under threat on a number of occasions, she survived the campaign without damage, later returning to the cruise trade.

Country of origin:	Britain
Date of origin:	1961
Length:	249m (817ft)
Beam:	31m (101ft 8in)
Tonnage:	45,524 tonnes (44,807 tons)
Machinery:	Two shafts, turbo-electric; 88,000hp
Service speed:	27.5 knots
Capacity:	2186 passengers, 938 crew; 1700 troops
Constructor:	Harland & Wolff, Belfast

Cap Trafalgar

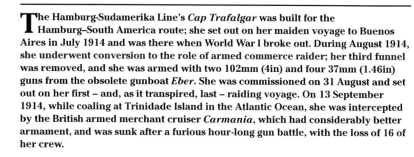

The Hamburg-Sudamerika Line's *Cap Trafalgar* was built for the Hamburg–South America route; she set out on her maiden voyage to Buenos Aires in July 1914 and was there when World War I broke out. During August 1914, she underwent conversion to the role of armed commerce raider; her third funnel was removed, and she was armed with two 102mm (4in) and four 37mm (1.46in) guns from the obsolete gunboat *Eber*. She was commissioned on 31 August and set out on her first – and, as it transpired, last – raiding voyage. On 13 September 1914, while coaling at Trinidade Island in the Atlantic Ocean, she was intercepted by the British armed merchant cruiser *Carmania*, which had considerably better armament, and was sunk after a furious hour-long gun battle, with the loss of 16 of her crew.

Country of origin:	Germany
Date of origin:	1913
Length:	186m (610ft 3in)
Beam:	21.9m (71ft 10in)
Tonnage:	19,106 tonnes (18,805 tons)
Machinery:	Not known
Service speed:	17 knots
Capacity:	400 1st class, 275 2nd class, 900 3rd class
Constructor:	AG Vulcan, Hamburg

Carmania

The *Carmania* was built for the Cunard Line's Liverpool–New York service. She was the company's first turbine-powered ship (and, indeed, one of the first major merchant vessels to be fitted with turbines) and she operated alongside a reciprocating-engined sister vessel, the *Caronia*, for purposes of comparison. *Carmania* worked the North Atlantic route from 1905. In 1913, she made headlines when she assisted in the dramatic rescue of 600 America-bound immigrants from the burning merchant ship *Volturno*. In 1914, she was taken up by the British Admiralty as an armed merchant cruiser, with eight 119mm (4.7in) guns. On her first voyage, she sank the German raider *Cap Trafalgar* in a fierce action, taking many hits herself. She later served as a troopship before being returned to Cunard. She was scrapped in 1932.

Country of origin:	Britain
Date of origin:	1905
Length:	205.7m (674ft 10in)
Beam:	22m (72ft 2in)
Tonnage:	19,836 tonnes (19,524 tons)
Machinery:	Three shafts, direct-acting turbines; 32,000hp
Service speed:	18 knots
Capacity:	300 1st class, 350 2nd class, 900 3rd class, 1100 steerage
Constructor:	John Brown & Co, Glasgow

Carpathia

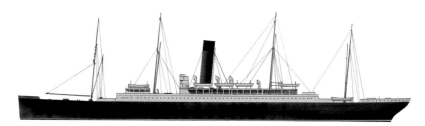

The *Carpathia*, constructed to operate on the Cunard Line's mixed passenger/ cargo service between Trieste and New York, with only second- and third-class accommodation, was typical of the second-rate liners of the period. Many of *Carpathia*'s passengers were Italian emigrants, fleeing the poverty of the Old World in anticipation of a better existence in the New. *Carpathia* briefly entered the limelight when, bound from North America for the Mediterranean, she was the first ship on the scene of the sinking of the *Titanic* in April 1912, rescuing 706 survivors. She herself was sunk late in World War I, on 17 July 1918, when she was torpedoed about 195km (120 nautical miles) west of Queenstown, Cork, by the German submarine *U-55*, with the loss of five lives. The *U-55* survived the war and was surrendered to Japan in its aftermath, being scrapped at Sasebo in 1922.

Country of origin:	Britain
Date of origin:	1903
Length:	170m (558ft)
Beam:	19.6m (64ft 4in)
Tonnage:	13,781 tonnes (13,564 tons)
Machinery:	Two shafts, quadruple-expansion engines
Service speed:	14 knots
Capacity:	204 2nd class, 1500 3rd class
Constructor:	Swan, Hunter and Wigham Richardson, Wallsend

Castalia

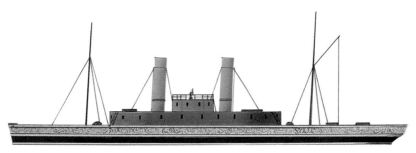

The *Castalia* was the world's first catamaran ferry and briefly operated on the London, Chatham and Dover Railway's cross-channel service between the United Kingdom and France during the mid-1870s. She was the brainchild of a Captain Dicey in the employ of the East India Company, who had encountered small double-hulled craft in the Far East. The *Castalia* consisted of two identical hulls, joined at deck level by a simple platform that carried the bridge and upperworks. The Paris Exhibition of 1867 had increased cross-channel trade, but the voyage was dreaded by travellers as standard vessels were uncomfortable in often stormy weather. Although the catamaran form greatly improved stability and comfort, *Castalia* was slow, and the paddle floats had to be repaired after each trip. She served as a ferry for only two summer seasons and was then used as a hospital ship.

Country of origin:	Britain
Date of origin:	1874
Length:	88.3m (290ft)
Beam:	15.25m (50ft)
Tonnage:	1533 tonnes (1508 tons)
Machinery:	Sidewheels, side-lever
Service speed:	6 knots
Capacity:	Not known
Constructor:	Not known

City of New York

By 1886, even though it was still second only to the White Star Line in the number of passengers it carried on the North Atlantic route, the Inman Line was in grave danger of falling behind its competitors. Its newest ships were 11 years old and unable to come within two days of the average crossing times of Cunard's ships. The line was insolvent by the end of the year and was taken over by American interests. Extra capital allowed new construction; in 1887, the *City of New York* was laid down, followed the next year by her sister ship, the *City of Paris*. They were the company's first twin-screw ships, and both were destined to be record-breakers, taking the coveted Blue Riband. In 1893, *City of New York* passed to the American Line, carrying mail. She twice served with the US Navy, as an armed cruiser in 1898 and as a transport in 1918. She was scrapped in 1923.

Country of origin:	USA
Date of origin:	1888
Length:	160.8m (527ft 6in)
Beam:	19.3m (63ft 2in)
Tonnage:	10,667 tonnes (10,499 tons)
Machinery:	Two shafts, vertical triple-expansion
Service speed:	20 knots
Capacity:	540 1st class, 200 2nd class, 1000 3rd class
Constructor:	J&G Thomson, Glasgow

City of Rome

The *City of Rome* was the first ship the Inman Line had built outside Scotland. The original intention was to construct her of steel, but sufficient supplies were not available, and she was constructed of iron instead. She was widely held to be the most beautifully proportioned and graceful vessel of her day, with a pronounced clipper bow and stern, and equal angles of rake to her three funnels and four masts. The *City of Rome* was ordered to meet competition from the Guion Line and specifically to rival the *Arizona* and the *Alaska*, but she never came even close to doing so, with a maiden crossing of over nine-and-a-half days, and was eventually handed back to her builders as unsatisfactory. She was transferred to the Anchor Line in 1882 and remained in service for 20 more years, before being scrapped in 1902.

Country of origin:	Britain
Date of origin:	1881
Length:	170.7m (560ft 2in)
Beam:	15.9m (52ft 3in)
Tonnage:	8550 tonnes (8415 tons)
Machinery:	Single shaft, three-cylinder compound
Service speed:	16 knots
Capacity:	271 1st class, 250 2nd class, 810 3rd class
Constructor:	Barrow Shipbuilding Co.

Club Med I

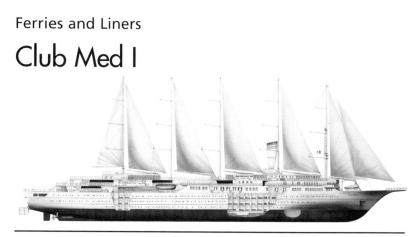

The auxiliary five-masted staysail schooner *Club Med I* was one of the first of a new generation of sailing cruise ships. Constructed by Ateliers et Chantiers du Havre, she entered service in 1990 with a month-long cruise the length of the Mediterranean from Cannes on the Côte d'Azur to Egypt and back, and then sailed across the Atlantic. Sail handling was motorized and under computer control, although the auxiliary diesel engine could be brought into operation when required. After ten years' service with her original owners, she was sold to Winstar Cruises and renamed *Wind Surf*, but continued to operate as before. For ease of handling, the schooner carried only staysails, except on the no. 5 spanker mast, where she also carried a conventional Bermuda course. Club Med I represented a remarkable marriage of modern technology and traditional grace.

Country of origin:	France
Date of origin:	1989
Length:	187m (613ft 6in)
Beam:	20m (65ft 6in)
Tonnage:	1625 tonnes (1600 tons)
Machinery:	Two shafts, auxiliary diesel-electric
Service speed:	12 knots
Capacity:	410
Constructor:	Ateliers et Chantiers de Havre, Le Havre

Condor Express

The *Condor Express* is one of a pair of catamaran vehicle and passenger ferries linking Poole, Dorset, on the south coast of England, with St Malo in Brittany via the Channel Islands. In optimum conditions, the journey takes just four hours at speeds of up to 40 knots; the vessels can carry up to 776 passengers and 200 cars. Like the majority of catamaran ferries in service at the end of the twentieth century, they were built by International Catamarans (Incat) in Hobart, Australia, and feature the very latest water-jet propulsion technology. During trials, *Condor Express* achieved a top speed of 48.7 knots over a five-minute period and maintained over 45 knots at full displacement. The first catamaran in the British Isles was the *Experiment*, built in 1662 for Sir William Petty, a founder member of the Royal Society.

Country of origin:	Britain
Date of origin:	1997
Length:	86.2m (282ft 10in)
Beam:	26m (85ft 3in)
Tonnage:	386 tonnes (380 tons)
Machinery:	Four water jets, four diesels; 37,950hp
Service speed:	40 knots
Capacity:	776 passengers, 200 vehicles
Constructor:	Incat, Hobart, Australia

Conte di Savoia

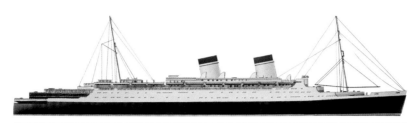

Britain, France and Germany all produced large luxury ocean liners within the space of a few years, and Italy was not slow to follow. *Conte di Savoia* and her near-sister *Rex* both began operations on the Atlantic route in 1932. While *Rex* was built for speed, with the Blue Riband in mind, the *Conte di Savoia* was built for style and grace. At the start of their service, both vessels were the largest merchant ships built in Italy. *Conte di Savoia* was the first ship to be fitted with a gyroscopic stabilizing system, although it was only a partial success. After seven years on the Genoa–New York route, she was laid up in 1939 and was sunk by Allied air attack in September 1943. She was salvaged in 1946 and serious consideration was given to restoring her to operational condition, but the plan was abandoned and she was broken up in 1950.

Country of origin:	Italy
Date of origin:	1931
Length:	248.3m (814ft 8in)
Beam:	29.3m (96ft 2in)
Tonnage:	49,280 tonnes (48,502 tons)
Machinery:	Four shafts, geared turbines
Service speed:	27 knots
Capacity:	500 1st class, 366 2nd class, 922 3rd class
Constructor:	Cantieri Riuniti dell'Adriatico, Trieste

Conte Verde

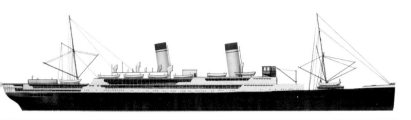

In 1921, the Lloyd Sabaudo Line ordered a 19,305-tonne (19,000-ton) twin-screw turbine ship, the *Conte Verde*, from Beardmore in Glasgow, Scotland, to operate its service to the east coast of South America. Her maiden voyage was between Genoa and Buenos Aires, after which she operated for a time on the New York route. In 1926, she transferred back to the South American run, and, in 1931, she was sent to the Far East to operate on routes out of Shanghai. She was laid up in that port from June 1940, when Italy entered World War II, until 1942, when she made a few voyages between China and Japan as a prisoner-of-war exchange ship on charter to the Japanese. Scuttled by her crew in September 1943, she was raised by the Japanese and used as a troopship before being wrecked in an air raid in 1944.

Country of origin:	Italy
Date of origin:	1922
Length:	170.5mm (559ft 5in)
Beam:	22.6m (74ft 2in)
Tonnage:	19,065 tonnes (18,765 tons)
Machinery:	Two shafts, geared turbines
Service speed:	18.5 knots
Capacity:	230 1st class, 290 2nd class, 1880 3rd class
Constructor:	Wm Beardmore & Co., Glasgow

Deutschland

When she was launched, the *Deutschland* of the Hamburg-Amerika Line was the largest and finest liner in the world, and was built specifically to be the fastest ship across the Atlantic in order to capture the Blue Riband from rival Norddeutscher Lloyd Line's *Kaiser Wilhelm der Grosse*. This she accomplished on her maiden voyage to New York, with an average speed of 22.4 knots. She held the record for six years. In 1910, she underwent conversion to a cruise liner and, in this new guise, was renamed *Victoria Luise*. In 1914, she was fitted out as an auxiliary cruiser, but her boilers were in such poor condition that she never saw operational service. After World War I, Germany was permitted to keep her, making her the largest ship in the German merchant fleet. She was scrapped in 1925.

Country of origin:	Germany
Date of origin:	1900
Length:	208.5m (684ft)
Beam:	20.4m (67ft)
Tonnage:	16,766 tonnes (16,502 tons)
Machinery:	Two shafts, quadruple-expansion engines; 37,800hp
Service speed:	22 knots
Capacity:	450 1st class, 300 2nd class, 350 3rd class
Constructor:	AG Vulcan, Stettin

Doric

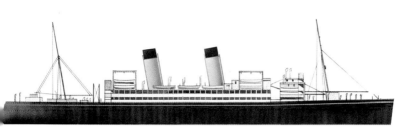

The White Star Line's *Doric* was essentially a sister ship of the *Regina*, built some six years earlier for the Dominion Line, but with single-reduction turbines in place of the twin triple-expansion/low-pressure turbine system which Harland & Wolff employed for many years. She was initially employed on the Liverpool–Canada service, operating between Liverpool and the St Lawrence River for nearly 10 years before becoming a cruise liner in May 1932. Doric could accommodate a total of 2300 passengers. In September 1935, she was involved in a collision with the French freighter *Formigny* off the Spanish coast. She was patched up in Vigo and made seaworthy enough to see her home, but she was never properly repaired and was scrapped a month later. The *Doric* was the only turbine-powered liner to be built for the White Star Line.

Country of origin:	Britain
Date of origin:	1923
Length:	183m (600ft 6in)
Beam:	20.6m (67ft 6in)
Tonnage:	28,935 tonnes (28,480 tons)
Machinery:	Two shafts, single-reduction turbines
Service speed:	15 knots
Capacity:	600 cabin, 1700 3rd class
Constructor:	Harland & Wolff, Belfast

Duilio

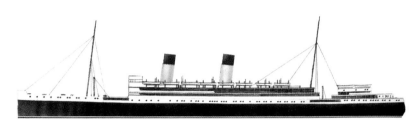

In 1914, Ansaldo laid down what was to be the biggest ship yet built in Italy, the 24,385-tonne (24,000-ton) *Duilio*, for Navigazione Generale Italiana. As very little work was carried out during World War I, with priority being given to the production of warships, the *Duilio* was not completed until 1923, when she was put into service on the New York run. Later, her destination was changed to Buenos Aires and then, in Italia Line colours, to Durban, South Africa. Transferred to the Lloyd Triestino Line in 1937, she was laid up in 1940. Briefly chartered to the International Red Cross in 1942, she was sunk by Allied bombers in 1944. *Duilio* was named after Gaius Duilius (200 BC), a Roman general who did a great deal to establish a Roman fleet. The name had earlier been carried by a warship that was stricken in 1909.

Country of origin:	Italy
Date of origin:	1916
Length:	193.5m (634ft 10in)
Beam:	23.2m (76ft)
Tonnage:	24,670 tonnes (24,281 tons)
Machinery:	Four shafts, single-reduction turbines
Service speed:	15 knots
Capacity:	280 1st class, 670 2nd class, 600 3rd class
Constructor:	Ansaldo, Sestri Ponenti

Empire Windrush

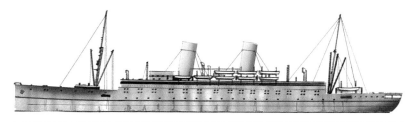

The *Empire Windrush* was formerly the German ship *Monte Rosa*, built for the Hamburg–South America Line. From the outbreak of World War II, she was used as a troop transport, being mostly employed in ferrying troops and equipment between German-occupied Denmark and Norway. When the German battleship *Tirpitz* put to sea early in 1942, however, the then *Monte Rosa* joined the small fleet of vessels assigned to support the warship, being employed as a floating workshop. In 1944, she struck a mine and, after repair, was assigned to the Baltic, where she became a hospital ship. After World War II, she was taken over by the British and renamed *Empire Windrush*, under the management of the New Zealand Line. In March 1954, an explosion in the engine room set the liner on fire, and she sank.

Country of origin:	Germany
Date of origin:	1930
Length:	160m (524ft)
Beam:	20.1m (66ft)
Tonnage:	14,104 tonnes (13,882 tons)
Machinery:	Two shafts, geared diesels
Service speed:	15 knots
Capacity:	Not known
Constructor:	AG Vulcan, Stettin

Empress of Britain

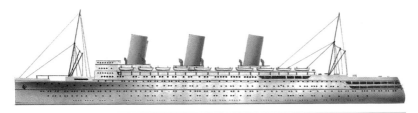

The Canadian Pacific Line had two ships named *Empress of Britain*. The first, launched in 1905, operated on the Liverpool–St Lawrence River route and had a considerable amount of third-class accommodation to meet the needs of the poor immigrants who were flocking to North America in the early years of the twentieth century. She served as a troopship throughout World War I, returned to Canadian Pacific service in 1919, underwent a refit in 1924 and was then renamed *Montroyal*, sailing from Antwerp. She was replaced by a second vessel of the same name, illustrated here, which went into service in 1931 on the Southampton–Quebec route. Taken up as a troopship during World War II, she was attacked and left disabled by a German long-range Focke-Wulf Kondor bomber southwest of Ireland on 26 October 1940, to be sunk by the submarine *U-32* two days later.

Country of origin:	Britain
Date of origin:	1930
Length:	231.8m (760ft 6in)
Beam:	29.7m (97ft 5in)
Tonnage:	43,025 tonnes (42,348 tons)
Machinery:	Not known
Service speed:	25.5 knots
Capacity:	465 1st class, 260 2nd class, 470 3rd class
Constructor:	John Brown & Co.

Eridan

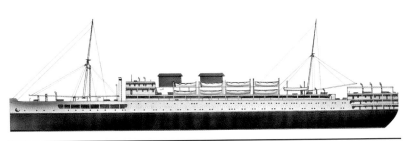

When she was launched, *Eridan* was the biggest motor ship built in France. She had somewhat unusual styling, with the lifeboats double-tiered above the promenade deck. She was built for Messageries Maritime, to operate between Marseille and New Caledonia via the Panama Canal. She was in the hands of the Vichy French government until November 1942, when she was captured by the Allies. She was returned to her owners in 1946; after a major refit in the following year, she served on the Indian Ocean route from Marseille. In the course of a second refit in 1951, she was given a large, oval funnel and revised passenger accommodation. On several occasions, she was used as a troopship to French Indo-China (Vietnam), having accommodation for 900 troops. She was sold for scrap in 1956.

Country of origin:	France
Date:	1928
Length:	142.6m (468ft 7in)
Beam:	18.5m (61ft)
Tonnage:	14,361 tonnes (14,135 tons)
Machinery:	two shafts, diesels
Service speed:	15 knots
Capacity:	60 1st class, 91 2nd class, 468 steerage
Constructor:	La Ciotat

Erinpura

Launched in 1911, *Erinpura* was built for the the British East India Company's Far Eastern routes. During World War I, she served as a hospital ship, and, in 1919, shortly before she was due to be returned to trade, she ran aground in a sandstorm off the Arabian peninsula. She remained stranded and derelict for over a year, before it was decided to salvage at least part of her. She was cut in half and her stern section was towed to Bombay, India, where a new forward section was fitted. In 1923, she returned to normal service in the Indian Ocean; after Italy's entry into World War II, she carried stores to British garrisons on the Red Sea, North Africa and Malta. In May 1942, she was part of a convoy attempting to run supplies to the besieged island of Malta when she came under heavy air attack and was sunk.

Country of origin:	Britain
Date of origin:	1911
Length:	125m (411ft)
Beam:	16m (52ft 6in)
Tonnage:	5224 tonnes (5142 tons)
Machinery:	Three shafts, triple-expansion engines
Service speed:	15 knots
Capacity:	Not known
Constructor:	Not known

Etruria

The Cunard Line's *Etruria* was the last North Atlantic express liner to be powered by compound engines and the last single-screw Cunarder. She was the second of a pair of ships, similar in character to the *Oregon* from the same builders, but built in steel rather than iron. She soon proved herself to be a superior ship, taking the westbound Blue Riband on her second voyage, at an average speed of 18.87 knots, and breaking records again in 1887 and 1888. Both she and her sister ship, the *Umbria*, became noticeably faster with age, an unusual but by no means unique occurrence. In company with her sister ship and the *Campania* and *Lucania*, she continued to operate on the prestigious Liverpool–New York route, but her days were numbered when she lost her propeller in mid-Atlantic in 1902. She made her last crossing in 1908 and was scrapped the following year.

Country of origin:	Britain
Date of origin:	1884
Length:	153m (502ft)
Beam:	17.4m (57ft)
Tonnage:	7841 tonnes (7718 tons)
Machinery:	Single shaft, compound
Service speed:	19 knots
Capacity:	550 1st class, 160 2nd class, 800 3rd class
Constructor:	John Elder & Co., Glasgow

Europa

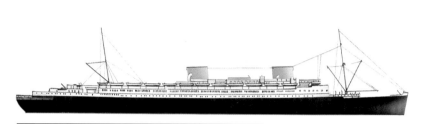

The Norddeutscher Lloyd Line's *Europa* and her sister ship, the *Bremen*, were launched on consecutive days, *Europa* first, on 15 August 1928. She was to be many months late in completion, however, because of a serious fire. *Europa* took the westbound Blue Riband with an average speed of 27.91 knots in 1930, but the *Bremen* was always marginally the faster of the two. *Europa* spent World War II laid up in Germany, having been in port when war broke out. Allied air forces made a number of attempts to bomb her, but caused no more than light damage. She was seized by the Allies in 1945 and made three voyages to New York, carrying a total of almost 19,000 returning servicemen. Awarded to France, she sank in harbour in 1946, but, after being rebuilt, was put into service between Le Havre and New York as the *Liberté*. She was scrapped in 1962.

Country of origin:	Germany
Date of origin:	1928
Length:	285.5m (936ft 10in)
Beam:	31.1m (102ft 2in)
Tonnage:	50,542 tonnes (49,746 tons)
Machinery:	Four shafts, single-reduction turbines
Service speed:	27 knots
Capacity:	723 1st class, 500 2nd class, 600 3rd class
Constructor:	Blohm & Voss, Hamburg

Europa

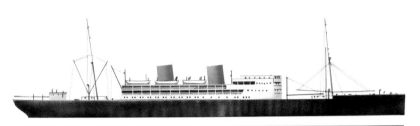

The *Europa* was one of two motor ships built for the East Asiatic Company's service between Copenhagen and North America. During the 1920s and 1930s, the motor ship was popular with small companies because it was economical to run, requiring fewer engine room staff. The single-class system and good-quality service made *Europa* popular with passengers, of whom she carried 640. When the Germans occupied Denmark in 1940, *Europa* transferred to the British flag. On 3 May 1941, she was burnt out at Liverpool, England, during a German air raid, this being the period of the so-called 'Liverpool Blitz'. Her sister ship *Amerika* was also lost during World War II, torpedoed and sunk in the North Atlantic by the German submarine *U 306*. The latter was herself sunk by British warships north of the Azores in October 1943.

Country of origin:	Denmark
Date of origin:	1931
Length:	147.6m (484ft 3in)
Beam:	19m (62ft 4in)
Tonnage:	10.387 tonnes (10,224 tons)
Machinery:	Single shaft, diesel
Service speed:	17.2 knots
Capacity:	640
Constructor:	Burmeister & Wain, Copenhagen

Europa

Built for Hapag-Lllloyd, the *Europa* is a distinctly unusual vessel. She was designed from the outset with passenger comfort very firmly in mind. In that respect, she is by no means unique, but, in her case, the constructors went so far as to mount the propulsion stage of her diesel-electric machinery in orientable outboard pods, in order to reduce noise and vibration aboard. A secondary effect is that this arrangement improves the ship's manoeuvrability. They also fitted tractor rather than pusher propellers which, coupled with a very refined hull form, makes her markedly more efficient than other ships with similar power-to-weight ratios. Aimed at the luxury end of the market, there is space for only 410 passengers, with most cabins having a private balcony; there is more space per person than aboard any other contemporary cruise liner.

Country of origin:	Germany
Date of origin:	1999
Length:	196.4m (644ft 6in)
Beam:	23.8m (78ft)
Tonnage:	28,698 tonnes (28,400 tons)
Machinery:	Two shafts, diesel-electric
Service speed:	21 knots
Capacity:	410
Constructor:	Kavaerner-Masa, Helsinki

Ferdinando Palasciano

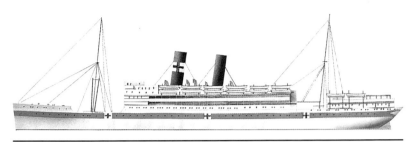

*F*erdinando Palasciano** was built for the German Norddeutscher Lloyd Line, and was orignally named *König Albert*. She had the capacity to carry 257 first class, 119 second class and 1799 steerage passengers. She was manned by a crew numbering 230 men. The vessel was interned in Italy at the start of World War I; she was then taken over by the Italians, who renamed her *Ferdinando Palasciano* and converted her for use as a hospital ship. After the war, she was bought by the Navigazione Generale Italiana of Genoa, who, after restoring her to civilian use, set her on a regular passenger service between Genoa and New York. In 1923, *Ferdinando Palasciano* was renamed Italia, and she became a troop transport. After a useful and versatile career, like so many other passenger liners of her period, *Italia* was scrapped in 1926.

Country of origin:	Italy
Date of origin:	1899
Length:	152m (499ft 3in)
Beam:	18.3m (60ft 2in)
Tonnage:	10,651 tonnes, (10,484 tons)
Machinery:	Twin screw, quadruple expansion engines
Service speed:	15.3 knots
Capacity:	257 1st class, 119 2nd class, 1799 steerage
Constructor:	Not known

Ferry Lavender

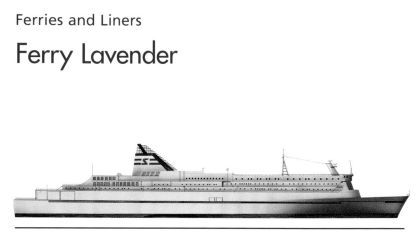

The *Ferry Lavender*, operated by Shin Nohonkai Ferry Co. in Japan and put into service in 1991, is typical of the third generation of fast ferries, able to carry around 800 passengers and up to 300 light vehicles. The stern ramp gives access to the two-storey car deck, wide enough to allow 'U-turn' drive-through loading and unloading, which simplifies docking procedures considerably. Despite the growing number of submarine tunnels, by the end of the twentieth century, many fast, short-route passenger and vehicle ferries were still being built every year. The first roll-on, roll-off freight transport service was introduced on 20 May 1948 between Preston in Lancashire, England, and Larne, Northern Ireland. A roll-on, roll-off service was inaugurated between Tilbury, London, and Antwerp, Belgium, in March 1957.

Country of origin:	Japan
Date of origin:	1991
Length:	193.5m (632ft)
Beam:	29.4m (96ft 6in)
Tonnage:	20,224 tonnes (19,905 tons)
Machinery:	Two shafts, diesel; 23,600hp
Service speed:	21 knots
Capacity:	880 passengers, 300 vehicles
Constructor:	IHI

Flandria

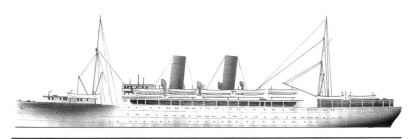

The *Flandria* was completed in September 1922 for service on Royal Holland Lloyd's Amsterdam–South America route, with accommodation for 215 first-class, 110 second-class and 1000 third-class passengers. In appearance and general configuration, she was a typical passenger liner of the post–World War I period. After 14 years on the South American run, the liner was sold to the French Cie Transatlantique. She was renamed *Bretagne*, and her accommodation was refitted to take 440 cabin-class passengers from French ports to the West Indies, a route she took over in 1937. On 14 October 1939, *Bretagne* was torpedoed and sunk by the German submarine *U-45* when only 570km (300 miles) from the English Channel. Shortly after this attack, the *U-45* (Lieutenant-Commander Gelhaar) was herself sunk by Allied escort vessels.

Country of origin:	The Netherlands
Date of origin:	1922
Length:	143.9m (472ft)
Beam:	18m (59ft)
Tonnage:	10,334 tonnes (10,171 tons)
Machinery:	Two shafts, turbines
Service speed:	14.5 knots
Capacity:	215 1st class, 110 2nd class, 1000 3rd class
Constructor:	Barclay, Curle & Co., England

France

The Compagnie Général Transatlantique's second ship to bear the name *France* was originally to have been called *La Picardie*. She made her maiden voyage from Le Havre to New York in 1912. At that time, she was the fastest liner in service except for the Cunard Line's twins *Lusitania* and *Mauretania*. She served as a troopship and then a hospital ship from 1914 to 1919, and then returned to service on the North Atlantic route. She was so popular that passengers had to bid for their cabins. In 1923–24, she was converted to oil fuel in the course of a major refit. She remained in service for a further eight years and was eventually scrapped in 1935. Although *France*'s nominal capacity was 2025 passengers, on 16 January 1921, the ship arrived in New York with no fewer than 2591 people aboard, the most ever carried by a CGT liner on a single trip.

Country of origin:	France
Date of origin:	1910
Length:	217.2m (712ft 7in)
Beam:	23m (75ft 6in)
Tonnage:	27,188 tonnes (26,760 tons)
Machinery:	Four shafts, direct-acting turbines
Service speed:	24 knots
Capacity:	535 1st class, 440 2nd class, 250 3rd class, 800 steerage
Constructor:	Chantiers et Ateliers de St-Nazaire, France

France

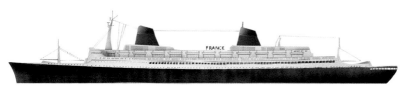

The third *France* was, by design, the longest passenger ship in the world when she was launched. She was also the last of the true North Atlantic express liners, the later *Queen Elizabeth II* having been designed with cruising in mind (although the *France* was also given over to cruising at a later date). Her first circumnavigation of the globe in 1972 took her round Cape Horn, as she was marginally too broad in the beam to transit the Panama Canal. In 1974, the heavy government subsidy that had kept her in service was stopped, and she was withdrawn from service. In 1979, however, she was sold to the Norwegian Caribbean Line and refitted as a cruise ship, being renamed *Norway*. The refit which transformed *France* into *Norway* cost $80 million; two of her turbine sets were removed in the course of it, making her much more economical to run.

Country of origin:	France
Date of origin:	1961
Length:	315.5m (1035ft)
Beam:	33.5m (110ft)
Tonnage:	67,406 tonnes (66,344 tons)
Machinery:	Four (later two) shafts, double-reduction turbines
Service speed:	30 (later 16) knots
Capacity:	2181
Constructor:	Chantiers de l'Atlantique, St-Nazaire, France

Franconia

The *Franconia* and the *Laconia* were built primarily for the Cunard Line's Liverpool–Boston service, although both occasionally sailed to New York instead. At that time, the company operated four different North Atlantic routes. However, the vessels were clearly also constructed with an eye to Mediterranean cruising in the slack winter months, their first- and second-class accommodation being particularly well appointed. Neither ship, however, was destined to survive World War I. On 4 October 1916, *Franconia* was torpedoed without warning (at that time it was usual for submarines to give merchant ships a warning) by a U-boat to the east of Malta, with the loss of 12 lives. In February of the following year, the *Laconia* met a similar fate northwest of Fastnet, with 12 lives also being lost on that occasion.

Country of origin:	Britain
Date of origin:	1910
Length:	190.5m (625ft)
Beam:	21.6m (71ft)
Tonnage:	18,440 tonnes (18,150 tons)
Machinery:	Two shafts, quadruple-expansion engines
Service speed:	17 knots
Capacity:	300 1st class, 350 2nd class, 2200 3rd class
Constructor:	Swan, Hunter and Wigham Richardson, Wallsend, England

Frans Suell

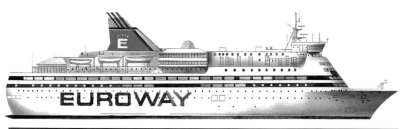

The *Frans Suell* is a super car ferry built in Split, Croatia, and operated in the Baltic by Sea Link Shipping of Sweden. The basic hull design is the same as that used on two large ferries built for the Viking Line in the late 1980s. She was launched in January 1991, and displaces 35,850 tonnes (35,285 tons). From the lowest part of the vessel to the top of the wheelhouse, there are 12 decks, two of which are used for road vehicles. Accommodation is provided for 2300 passengers, with some cabins having balconies. The design of such superb vessels has come a long way since the first car ferry, a motor vessel called the *Artificer*, began a regular service from Dover to Calais in 1928. The first purpose-built car ferry, the *Autocarrier*, entered service on the cross-Channel route in 1930; it was owned and operated by the Southern Railway company.

Country of origin:	Sweden
Date of origin:	1991
Length:	169.4m (556ft)
Beam:	27.6m (90ft 6in)
Tonnage:	35,850 tonnes (35,285 tons)
Machinery:	Two shafts, diesel engines
Service speed:	21 knots
Capacity:	2300
Constructor:	Not known

Furnessia

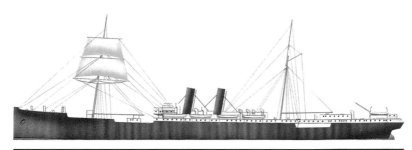

For a period of just nine months, *Furnessia*, launched in 1880, was the largest Atlantic liner in service. Her passenger accommodation was of a high standard when she made her maiden voyage from Glasgow to New York in January 1881. She underwent a major rebuild in 1891, when the passenger accommodation was revised. By 1909, she was taking second- and third-class passengers only, as she had long since been superseded by newer and faster liners. *Furnessia* was eventually scrapped in 1912, having given 30 years of almost continuous service on the Atlantic route until the previous year. *Furnessia* and others like her were a lasting tribute to the skill of British shipbuilders, whose expertise was sought by emerging maritime nations the world over during the latter part of the nineteenth century.

Country of origin:	Britain
Date of origin:	1880
Length:	135.6m (445ft)
Beam:	13.7m (45ft)
Tonnage:	5583 tonnes (5495 tons)
Machinery:	Single shaft, compound engines
Service speed:	14 knots
Capacity:	Not known
Constructor:	Not known

Gallia

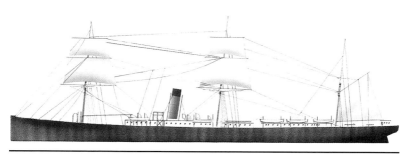

In the late 1870s, the Cunard Line, which in its early years had held the monopoly on steamship travel across the Atlantic, was struggling to improve its position as a major player on the North Atlantic routes. Sir Samuel Cunard, a Canadian-born Englishman had founded his company in 1840. In 1878, the company received a fresh injection of capital which allowed a major shipbuilding programme to go ahead. The first ship to enter service with the new Cunard Steam Ship Company was the *Gallia*, built for service on the Liverpool–New York route. She was switched to Boston in 1886, when the *Umbria* and *Etruria* – both newer, bigger and faster ships – joined the fleet. She changed ownership three times during her career, mostly sailing between Liverpool and the St Lawrence River in Canada, before going aground near Quebec. She was broken up in situ.

Country of origin:	Britain
Date of origin:	1878
Length:	131.1m (430ft 1in)
Beam:	13.6m (44ft 6in)
Tonnage:	4886 tonnes (4809 tons)
Machinery:	Single shaft, compound engines
Service speed:	13 knots
Capacity:	300 1st class, 1200 3rd class
Constructor:	J & G Thomson, Glasgow

Grampian

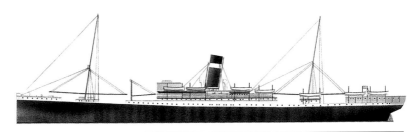

The *Grampian* and her sister ship the *Hesperian*, both mixed passenger and cargo vessels, were built for the Allen Line's Glasgow–Canada service, operating to St John or Halifax in winter and into the St Lawrence River in the summer months, when the waterway was free from ice. The *Grampian* remained in fairly regular service throughout World War I. She made a number of voyages on charter to the Canadian Pacific Line before passing into that company's ownership, together with the Allan Line itself, in 1917; at the time of the takeover, the Allan Line owned 20 vessels. She later operated out of London, Liverpool and occasionally Antwerp, as well as her old home port of Glasgow, mostly carrying emigrants. She was gutted by a fire during a refit in 1921 and subsequently scrapped in 1926.

Country of origin:	Britain
Date of origin:	1907
Length:	148m (486ft)
Beam:	18m (60ft)
Tonnage:	11,130 tonnes (10,955 tons)
Machinery:	Two shafts, triple-expansion engines
Service speed:	15 knots
Capacity:	210 1st class, 250 2nd class, 1000 3rd class
Constructor:	Alexander Stephen & Sons, Glasgow

Great Britain

L ike all Brunel's ships, *Great Britain* was an epoch-making vessel. Built by
William Patterson of Bristol, she was the biggest iron ship yet built; the first to
be intended for deep-sea voyaging, the first to be driven by a screw propeller and
the first screw steamer to cross the Atlantic. She set out on her maiden voyage from
Liverpool on 26 July 1845, arriving at New York 14 days and 21 hours later. In
September 1846, she ran aground near Belfast Lough and remained there for nine
months without suffering much damage, a vindication of the iron hull. She was laid
up for three years, before being sold by her owners, the Great Western Steamship
Co. In 1877, her engines were removed and she worked as a sail bulk carrier
between Britain and San Francisco. In 1970, she was retrieved from the Falkland
Islands, where she had been a storage hulk, and restored as a museum ship.

Country of origin:	Britain
Date:	1843
Length:	88m (289ft)
Beam:	15.2m (50ft)
Tonnage:	3322 tonnes (3270 tons)
Machinery:	Single shaft, compound engine
Rigging:	Six masts, one square-rigged, others fore-and-aft rigged
Service speed:	9 knots
Capacity:	350 passengers, 300 crew

Great Eastern

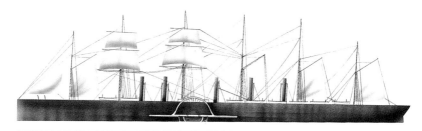

Brunel's ship the *Great Eastern* was almost five times larger than any other ship in the world at the time of her launch in January 1858. Far ahead of her time, she proved a commercial failure. She was underpowered and, despite her size, she had a tendency to roll. Few harbours could accommodate her, and she was too big for tugboats to handle. She made 10 return voyages across the Atlantic before being withdrawn. Her greatest value was as a cable layer. She went on to lay five cables across the Atlantic, plus a trans-oceanic cable between Suez, Aden and Bombay. Sold to a French company for passenger work again, she made a single voyage between France and New York before being laid up at Milford Haven, Wales, between 1875 and 1886. Used for two years as a floating exhibition site at Liverpool, she was broken up in 1888.

Country of origin:	Britain
Date of origin:	1858
Length:	210m (689ft)
Beam:	25.3m (83ft)
Tonnage:	19,217 tonnes (18,915 tons)
Machinery:	Side paddle wheels
Rigging:	Six masts, two square-rigged, remainder fore-and-aft rigged
Service speed:	13.5 knots
Capacity:	4000 passengers, 6096 tonnes (6000 tons) of cargo

Great Western

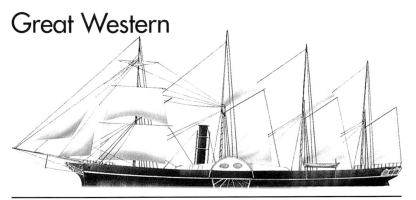

It is said that in 1833, at a board meeting of Isambard Kingdom Brunel, who had recently been appointed engineer of the projected Great Western Railway, it was suggested that its line should be extended to Bristol, where it would link up with a passenger liner that would sail on to New York. The ship, naturally, would be called the *Great Western*. Brunel's directors took the idea seriously and designed the vessel. The first of Brunel's trio of liners, *Great Western* was a wooden-hulled vessel. After her launch at Bristol, she was towed to London to have her machinery fitted. She was much the largest steamer that had ever been built and indeed was the first purpose-built passenger liner. After a poor start – the lagging of her boilers caught fire on her first commercial sailing – she went on to make 64 round trips across the Atlantic before being broken up in 1856.

Country of origin:	Britain
Date of origin:	1837
Length:	72m (236ft)
Beam:	18m (58ft 3in)
Tonnage:	1341 tonnes (1320 tons)
Machinery:	Paddle wheels, side lever engines
Rigging:	Four masts; foremast square-rigged, rest fore-and-aft rigged
Service speed:	9 knots
Capacity:	50 passengers

Grosser Kurfürst

The *Grosser Kurfürst* was constructed for the Norddeutscher Lloyd Line's second-class North Atlantic service. In addition, between 1900 and 1912, she made nine return voyages between Germany and Australia. She was interned in New York in August 1914, at the outbreak of World War I, and, in 1917, when the United States entered the war, she was seized by the US government. Until the end of the war, she was employed by the US Navy as a transport, under the name *Aeolus*. In 1922, she was transferred to the Los Angeles Steam Ship Company and renamed *City of Los Angeles*. Refitted and re-engined with turbines, she operated as a cruise ship until 1933 and was scrapped four years later. While the *Grosser Kurfürst* was only marginally smaller than her livery companion, the record-breaking *Kaiser Wilhelm der Grosse*, her service speed was some six knots slower.

Country of origin:	Germany
Date of origin:	1899
Length:	177m (581ft)
Beam:	19m (62ft 4in)
Tonnage:	13,392 tonnes (13,182 tons)
Machinery:	Two shafts, quadruple-expansion engines
Service speed:	16 knots
Capacity:	424 1st class, 176 2nd class, 1211 3rd class
Constructor:	F Schichau, Danzig

Highland Chieftain

The *Highland Chieftain* was the fourth of a class of five ships built for the Nelson Line, and she passed to the Royal Mail Line, Nelson's majority owners, in 1932. She was built to operate between London and Buenos Aires, and stayed on the South American route until she was sold in 1959 and converted to the whaling trade under the name *Calpean Star*. On 1 June 1960, as she left Montevideo for London, a seacock failed and flooded the engine room, forcing her to be run ashore and abandoned. She was assessed as a total constructive loss and abandoned. The development of the motor ship reached a new peak with the laying down of the *Highland Chieftain* and her sisters in the 1920s; although not fast, they were economical to operate and required only 10,000hp to drive them at a steady 15 knots.

Country of origin:	Britain
Date of origin:	1928
Length:	166m (544ft 6in)
Beam:	21m (69ft)
Tonnage:	14,357 tonnes (14,131 tons)
Machinery:	Two shafts, diesel; 10,000hp
Service speed:	15 knots
Capacity:	150 1st class, 70 2nd class, 500 3rd class
Constructor:	Harland & Wolff, Belfast

Imperator

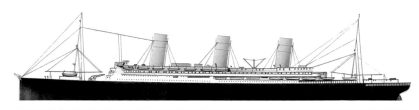

When completed in April 1913, *Imperator* was the world's largest ship. She was built for the Hamburg-Amerika Line as an answer to the giant White Star liner *Olympic*, sister ship to the ill-fated *Titanic*. *Imperator* made her maiden voyage to New York in June 1914; on her return to Germany, she was laid up in Hamburg for the duration of World War I. (Every German merchant vessel that could not make a home port was ordered to head for a neutral harbour, for fear of being intercepted by the Royal Navy.) In 1919, she saw a brief period of service as a transport vessel in the employ of the US Army, repatriating American troops from Europe. In 1921, she was sold to Cunard and renamed *Berengaria* (Berengaria was the queen of Richard the Lionheart). The ship was damaged by fire at New York in 1938, but was not broken up until 1946.

Country of origin:	Germany
Date of origin:	1912
Length:	277.1m (909ft 2in)
Beam:	29.9m (98ft)
Tonnage:	52,951 tonnes (52,117 tons)
Machinery:	Four shafts, turbines
Service speed:	24 knots
Capacity:	Not known
Constructor:	Not known

Infanta Beatriz

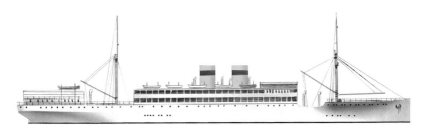

The *Infanta Beatriz* was the first motor passenger ship built for the Spanish mercantile marine. She was built by Krupp of Kiel, the design closely following that of two successful motor ships constructed for a large German shipping firm. *Infanta Beatriz* was a major addition to the fleet of her owner, Cia Transmediterranea, which consisted of 60 vessels, all of them older and smaller. Passenger accommodation was of a high standard, with an unusually large number of single cabins. Cargo holds were fitted out for the banana trade, since she was intended for service between Spain and the Canary Islands. While moored at Barcelona in January 1939, during the Spanish Civil War, the vessel – now renamed *Ciudad de Sevilla* – was bombed and sunk. She was later raised and repaired, and served until the 1960s.

Country of origin:	Spain
Date of origin:	1928
Length:	125m (410ft)
Beam:	15.8m (52ft)
Tonnage:	6380 tonnes (6279 tons)
Machinery:	Two shafts, diesels, 4340hp
Service speed:	14 knots
Capacity:	134 1st class, 38 2nd class, 60 3rd class; 5283 tonnes (5200 tons) cargo
Constructor:	Krupp AG (Germaniawerft), Kiel

Ishikari

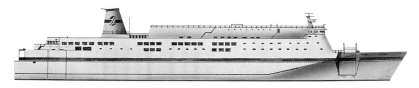

Launched in November 1990, *Ishikari* was one of the first of a new series of luxury, high-speed ferries to enter Japanese service. She is able to carry 850 passengers, 151 cars and 165 lorries. Her hull is designed for high speed and economy, and she burns 76 tonnes (75 tons) of fuel oil a day in regular service. The box-shaped upper part of the hull houses nine separate decks, the top three being devoted to passengers. The large internal decks are allocated to vehicles. Passenger areas are fully air-conditioned, with cabins arranged in classes in a choice of Japanese or Western style. *Ishikari* also has shops, restaurants and an observation lounge, and features a central staircase surrounding a tall living tree. More than 500 car ferries are used on more than 260 routes between the Japanese islands.

Country of origin:	Japan
Date of origin:	1990
Length:	192.5m (631ft 6in)
Beam:	27m (88ft 7in)
Tonnage:	7050 tonnes (6938 tons)
Machinery:	Two shafts, diesel engines
Service speed:	21.5 knots
Capacity:	850 passengers, 315 vehicles
Constructor:	Mitsubishi Heavy Industries, Japan

Jervis Bay

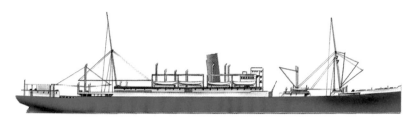

Launched in 1922, the *Jervis Bay* was built for the Australian emigrant trade. As originally completed, she carried 732 third-class passengers in two-, four- and six-berth cabins. Only 12 first-class passengers were carried, and these were usually government officials. By the early 1930s, the ship had been taken over by the P&O Line, and tourist class replaced third class. In 1939, *Jervis Bay* was fitted out as an armed merchant cruiser and provided with an armament of eight 152mm (6in) guns. In November 1939, the convoy of 38 ships she was escorting was attacked by the German battleship *Admiral Scheer*. Captain Fegen of the *Jervis Bay* at once gave the convoy the order to scatter under cover of a smokescreen and then attacked the *Scheer*, which sank the British ship with heavy loss of life. Thirty-two merchant vessels managed to escape.

Country of origin:	Britain
Date of origin:	1922
Length:	167.3m (549ft)
Beam:	20.7m (68ft)
Tonnage:	23,601 tonnes (23,230 tons)
Machinery:	Twin screws, steam turbines
Service speed:	15 knots
Capacity:	12 1st class, 732 3rd class
Constructor:	Vickers-Armstrong, Barrow

John Bell

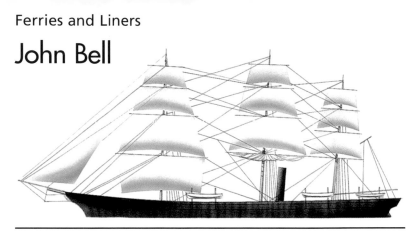

The *John Bell* started life as a sailing ship, but in 1856 she was chartered by the anchor line and fitted with engines. The following year she was put into service on the Glasgow–Canada route. During the Indian Mutiny, the vessel saw brief service as a troop transport, but was back in service on the Glasgow–Quebec–Montreal run by July 1859. She was purchased outright by the Anchor Line in 1862 and her name changed to *Saint Patrick*. She continued to serve until 1875, when her engines were removed. She later became *Diamant*. The layout of the vessel was typical of the period, with a large saloon cabin, first-class passenger cabins forward, plus steerage. The engine room was aft with the boiler room just in front of the mizzen mast. With slender, graceful lines, the *John Bell* was without doubt one of the most attractive vessels afloat in the mid-nineteenth century.

Country of origin:	Britain
Date of origin:	1854
Length:	70.4m (231ft)
Beam:	10.1m (33ft)
Tonnage:	1118 tonnes (1101 tons)
Machinery:	Single screw, compound engines
Rigging:	Three masts, square-rigged
Service speed:	12 knots
Capacity:	Not known

Kaiser Franz Josef I

For a period until the end of World War I, Austria had an outlet to the world's oceans via the Adriatic and Mediterranean, and possessed a minor shipping line, the Unione Austriaca, founded by the Cosiluch brothers in 1903. Its most important vessel by far was the *Kaiser Franz Josef I*, which was built primarily to carry emigrants to the United States. She had the capacity for over 1900 passengers, the vast majority of them in third class accommodation. She made a number of round trips to North America (and one to South America) before the outbreak of World War I, when she was laid up at Trieste. She was awarded to Italy in 1919 and handed to the Cosiluch Line, which operated her as the *Presidente Wilson*. She was later transferred to Lloyd Triestino as the *Gange* and then to Adriatica as the *Marco Polo*, and was eventually scuttled at La Spezia in 1944.

Country of origin:	Austria
Date of origin:	1911
Length:	152.4m (500ft)
Beam:	18.9m (62ft)
Tonnage:	17,170 tonnes (16,900 tons)
Machinery:	Two shafts, quadruple-expansion; 12,500hp
Service speed:	17 knots
Capacity:	125 1st class, 550 2nd class, 1230 3rd class
Constructor:	Cantiere Navale Triestino, Monfalcone

Kaiser Wilhelm der Grosse

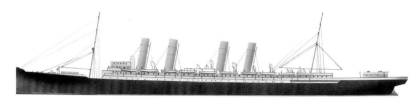

By the 1890s, Germany's merchant marine had reached a position where it was eager to challenge the British domination of the steamship routes between Europe and North America. To do so, the Norddeutscher Lloyd Line ordered the largest and most powerful ship ever built up to that time, the *Kaiser Wilhelm der Grosse*. She was to achieve everything expected of her and more, for she was truly the first 'superliner'. She took the eastbound Blue Riband in September 1897 and added the westbound in the following March. She narrowly escaped destruction in June 1900, when fire broke out at the company's piers in New York; five years later, she was rammed by the British freighter *Orinoco*. Armed as a merchant cruiser at the outbreak of World War I, she was scuttled to avoid capture by the British cruiser HMS *Highflyer* on 21 August 1914.

Country of origin:	Germany
Date of origin:	1897
Length:	191.1m (627ft)
Beam:	20.1m (66ft)
Tonnage:	14,578 tonnes (14,349 tons)
Machinery:	Two shafts, triple-expansion; 14,000hp
Service speed:	22 knots
Capacity:	332 1st class, 343 2nd class, 1074 3rd class
Constructor:	AG Vulcan, Stettin

Lake Champlain

Built for Elder Dempster's Beaver Line and launched in 1900, the passenger liner *Lake Champlain* had a long and varied career. In May 1901, she commenced service on the Europe–Canada run, carrying the first useful wireless to be fitted to a North Atlantic liner. Earlier, less effective radio sets had been used only to announce a ship's impending arrival. In 1913, she was transferred to Austria and operated from Trieste and then London as the *Ruthenia*. During World War I, she acted as a decoy, being disguised as the battleship *King George V* in an attempt to conceal the true whereabouts of the British battle fleet; she later became a store ship, then an oiler. She was sent to Singapore as an oil hulk in 1929; in 1942, she was captured by the invading Japanese and renamed *Choran Maru*. Retaken in 1945, she was scrapped in 1949.

Country of origin:	Britain
Date of origin:	1900
Length:	140.2m (460ft)
Beam:	15.8m (52ft)
Tonnage:	7510 tonnes (7392 tons)
Machinery:	Two shafts, triple-expansion
Service speed:	13 knots
Capacity:	100 1st class, 80 2nd class, 500 3rd class
Constructor:	Barclay, Curle & Co., Glasgow

Lusitania

During October 1907, the Cunard Line's 32,000-tonne (31,500-ton) *Lusitania*, the biggest ship in the world at that time and the most luxuriously appointed, held both eastbound and westbound Blue Ribands simultaneously; she eventually achieved an average speed, westbound, of 25.65 knots over 5352km (2890 nautical miles). Her achievements, however, have tended to be overshadowed by the manner of her demise. On 7 May 1915, she was sunk without warning by a torpedo from the German submarine *U-20* off the Old Head of Kinsale on the south coast of Ireland, with the loss of 1198 (some reports say 1201) men, women and children. About 228 were US citizens, and it was long held that their deaths were a factor that eventually persuaded the United States to join the Allies in World War I. A factor in her loss was her master's inexplicable failure to zig-zag at maximum speed.

Country of origin:	Britain
Date of origin:	1930
Length:	232m (761ft)
Beam:	26.8m (88ft)
Tonnage:	32,954 tonnes (31,550 tons)
Machinery:	Four shafts, direct drive turbines; 68,000hp
Service speed:	24 knots
Capacity:	563 1st class, 464 2nd class, 1138 3rd class
Constructor:	John Brown & Co., Glasgow

Magdalena

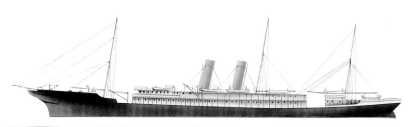

The *Magdalena* was the second of a quartet of small ships constructed for the Royal Mail's east coast of South America service. The vessels were somewhat anachronistic in appearance, having clipper bows and bowsprits, but were otherwise quite modern, with triple-expansion machinery. *Magdalena*'s first public appearance came at the annual naval revue at Spithead in August 1889, after which she embarked on her routine operations to South America. Together with two other ships, the *Thames* and the *Clyde*, she operated a regular service terminating at Buenos Aires, her sister ship, *Atrato*, having been switched over to the West Indies. She proved to be a popular ship with her passengers; first-class accommodation was in a sumptuous two-tier deckhouse, one of her design innovations. She was scrapped in 1921.

Country of origin:	Britain
Date of origin:	1889
Length:	128.3m (421ft)
Beam:	15.2m (50ft)
Tonnage:	5459 tonnes (5373 tons)
Machinery:	Single shaft, triple-expansion
Service speed:	15 knots
Capacity:	174 1st class, 44 2nd class, 330 3rd class
Constructor:	R. Napier & Sons, Glasgow

Majesty of the Seas

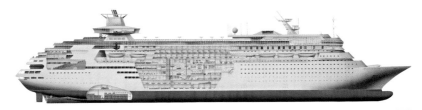

The *Majesty of the Seas* was the third of a trio of almost identical gigantic cruise ships constructed in France for Norway's Royal Caribbean Cruise Lines. They were purpose-built for Caribbean cruises of one week duration, so the emphasis was on public recreational areas, the passengers (up to 2350 in number) being accommodated in small double staterooms. She displaces 75,128 tonnes (73,941 tons) and measures 266.4m (874ft) in length. The concept of the one-week cruise has proved very successful; at the height of the season, *Majesty of the Seas* generates more than $3 million in revenue per voyage. Expenses can be high if unexpected snags are encountered, however; when *Majesty of the Seas*'s sister ship *Monarch of the Seas* hit a shoal off the island of St Maarten in December 1998 and had to be beached, the repair bill was $41 million.

Country of origin:	Norway
Date of origin:	1992
Length:	266.4m (874ft)
Beam:	32.3m (106ft)
Tonnage:	75,128 tonnes (73,941 tons)
Machinery:	Single shaft, diesel; 27,840hp
Service speed:	21 knots
Capacity:	2350 standard class
Constructor:	Chantiers de l'Atlantique, France

Mary Murray

The *Mary Murray* was one of the famous passenger and vehicle ferries which linked Staten Island with Manhattan. Constructed by United Shipyards on Staten Island, these were some of the simplest ships, with a large unencumbered vehicle deck surmounted by open-sided passenger accommodation, on top of which sat a pilot house giving an all-round view – a very necessary attribute in what was one of the world's busiest waterways. She was retired from service in the 1960s, and there were plans to turn her into a floating restaurant, but these never came to fruition. The Staten Island ferries take between 20 and 30 minutes to make the 10km (6.2-mile) trip between St George's Terminal and the Whitehall terminal in Manhattan. All the Staten Island ferries were built for, and owned by, the City of New York.

Country of origin:	USA
Date of origin:	1938
Length:	77m (252ft 6in)
Beam:	14.6m (47ft 9in)
Tonnage:	2160 tonnes (2126 tons)
Machinery:	Two shafts, compound engines; 4000hp
Service speed:	8 knots
Capacity:	Not known
Constructor:	United Shipyards, Staten Island, New York

Mauretania

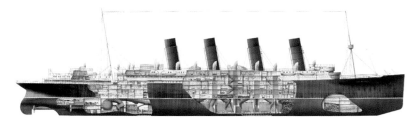

The Cunard liner *Mauretania* had few rivals for sheer variety and length of service, which began in 1907 on the Liverpool–New York run and ended in a Scottish breakers' yard in 1935. She was sister vessel to the *Lusitania*, both vessels being launched in 1906. They were the first British express liners to be designed in the twentieth century, and the British engineers exploited their advantages to the full. They were the world's largest ships; the first turbine-powered, high-speed, four-screw steam ships; and the first liners to offer a service speed of 25 knots from their unprecedentedly powerful engines. *Mauretania* won the Blue Riband in September 1909. She served as a troopship during World War I and returned to the Atlantic run after the war, being repaired and refitted after a serious fire in 1921. She was scrapped at Rosyth in 1935.

Country of origin:	Britain
Date of origin:	1906
Length:	240.8m (790ft)
Beam:	26.8m (88ft)
Tonnage:	32,450 tonnes (31,938 tons)
Machinery:	Four shafts, turbines; 76,000hp
Service speed:	25 knots
Capacity:	563 1st class, 464 2nd class, 1138 3rd class; 4000 troops
Constructor:	Swan, Hunter & Wigham Richardson, Newcastle

Monumental City

The nineteenth-century discovery of gold in Australia attracted thousands of prospectors from America, who travelled across the Pacific in sailing ships to seek their fortune from this new source. Seeing a good opportunity to open up a new and lucrative line, an enterprising man called Peter Stroebed purchased the steamer *Monumental City*. She left San Francisco on 17 February 1853, arriving at Sydney on 23 April. She proved a successful ship and was placed on the Melbourne–Sydney trade list on 15 May 1853. Unfortunately, *Monumental City* – the first steamship to cross the Pacific – had a sad end; during a routine trip, she ran aground and was wrecked on a small rocky island, becoming a total loss. Not only the dreams of her owner, Peter Stroebed, died with her; he was on board at the time and was drowned.

Country of origin:	USA
Date of origin:	1853
Length:	71.6m (235ft)
Beam:	11.6m (38ft)
Tonnage:	780 tonnes (768 tons)
Machinery:	Not known
Service speed:	Not known
Capacity:	Not known
Constructor:	Not known

Mount Clinton

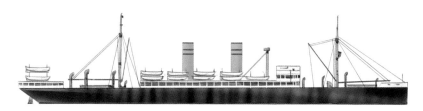

At the end of World War I, thanks to large-scale construction that had taken place in the last two years of the conflict, there was a large surplus of merchant shipping, and it was some years before further new building recommenced. *Mount Clinton* and her sister ship, *Mount Carol*, were the first to be laid down for private owners in the United States and were not launched until 1921. To meet the changing needs of the times, both vessels were converted to carry a large number of emigrants, up to 1500 per trip. As the emigrant trade was from Europe to the United States, the cabins, on two upper decks, were designed for quick assembly and removal, so that on the return trip to Europe the space could be used for cargo. *Mount Clinton* was sold to the Matson Line in 1925; she was sold on twice more before being scrapped in 1954.

Country of origin:	USA
Date of origin:	1921
Length:	139.3m (457ft)
Beam:	17.4m (57ft)
Tonnage:	15,240 tonnes (15,000 tons)
Machinery:	Single shaft, turbine; 4200hp
Service speed:	13 knots
Capacity:	1500 (later 585) standard
Constructor:	Merchant Shipbuilding Corporation

Nieuw Amsterdam

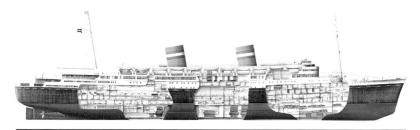

The *Nieuw Amsterdam* was the second vessel to bear the name; like her predecessor, she operated on the Rotterdam–New York service, and was built for the Holland America Line. She was designed and constructed with economy, rather than record-breaking speed, in mind. As a result – apart from an interruption during World War II – she enjoyed a long and useful career. She made her last pre-war Atlantic crossing in September 1939 and then operated out of New York as a cruise liner for some time before being converted to a troopship in 1941. She returned to mercantile service in October 1947 after a refit, having sailed more than 800,000km (500,000 miles) in her role of troopship, transporting US servicemen to the European theatre of operations. She was used for cruising from 1971 and was scrapped in 1974.

Country of origin:	The Netherlands
Date of origin:	1937
Length:	231.2m (758ft 6in)
Beam:	26.9m (88ft 4in)
Tonnage:	36,869 tonnes (36,287 tons)
Machinery:	Two shafts, geared turbines
Service speed:	20.5 knots
Capacity:	556 cabin, 455 tourist, 209 3rd class
Constructor:	Rotterdamsche Droogdok Mij, Rotterdam

Norman

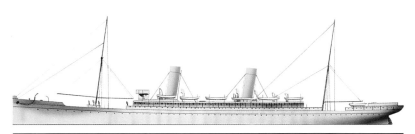

When the Union Line and the Castle Packet Co. merged in 1900, the former company's liner *Norman* was the new undertaking's most important ship and had already made nearly 50 voyages between Southampton in England and South Africa. She had luxurious accommodation for up to 250 in first class and also had limited third-class accommodation for emigrants. The *Norman* was representative of the mail steamers of the period. In 1899, at the outbreak of the Boer War, she was taken up for service as a troopship and continued in that role for the duration of this unhappy conflict. After her release, she underwent a major refit in 1904 and was placed on the reserve in 1910. During World War I, she again saw service as a troopship, having briefly resumed her South African service just before the start of hostilities. She was laid up in 1925 and scrapped in the following year.

Country of origin:	Britain
Date of origin:	1894
Length:	154.5m (507ft)
Beam:	16.2m (53ft 2in)
Tonnage:	13,615 tonnes (13,400 tons)
Machinery:	Two shafts, triple-expansion
Service speed:	15 knots
Capacity:	250 1st class, 100 3rd class
Constructor:	Not known

Normandie

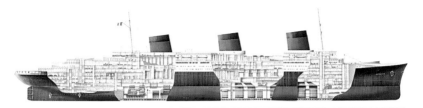

The *Normandie* was the biggest liner of her day; in fact, a new dock had to be built for her at St-Nazaire, France, at enormous cost. She was also the most powerful and the fastest, taking both westbound and eastbound Blue Ribands on her maiden voyage. She was to lose the record to the new Cunarder, the *Queen Mary*, and, although she won it back again in March 1937, she lost it for good in August 1938. Laid up in New York in August 1939 and taken over by the US Navy as the USS *Lafayette* in December 1941, she was destroyed just days before she was due to enter service in February 1943, by a fire started in stored bedding by a careless welder. She capsized in New York harbour as a result of all the water pumped into her in an attempt to extinguish the blaze. She was eventually sold for scrap for just $160,000 dollars.

Country of origin:	France
Date of origin:	1935
Length:	313.6m (1029ft)
Beam:	35.7m (117ft 10in)
Tonnage:	80,552 tonnes (79,280 tons)
Machinery:	Four shafts, turbo-electric; 165,000hp
Service speed:	29 knots
Capacity:	848 1st class, 670 tourist, 454 3rd class
Constructor:	Chantiers et Ateliers de l'Atlantique, St-Nazaire, France

Oceanic

The *Oceanic* was one of most popular liners in service with the White Star Line in the early years of the twentieth century – the reason for this was not hard to find. The company had made the decision to sacrifice speed in exchange for the extra weight penalty imposed by providing luxurious accommodation for all classes of passenger, including the 1000 third-class customers who would normally have travelled in more spartan conditions. She set the standard for other White Star liners, with particular regard to comfort and stability. *Oceanic* went into service on the Liverpool–New York run in 1899, moved to Southampton in 1907 and, in 1914, was requisitioned as an auxiliary cruiser. Her career in this role was destined to be brief; commissioned on 31 August 1914, she was wrecked off the Shetland Islands on 8 August.

Country of origin:	Britain
Date of origin:	1899
Length:	209m (686ft)
Beam:	20.7m (68ft)
Tonnage:	17,550 tonnes (17,274 tons)
Machinery:	Two shafts, triple-expansion engines
Service speed:	19.5 knots
Capacity:	410 1st class, 300 2nd class, 1000 3rd class
Route:	North Atlantic

Parisian

The Allan Line's single-screw steamer *Parisian* was the first steel liner on the North Atlantic route and, temporarily at least, the largest. She was also the first to have bilge keels. In 1882, she made the passage from Rimouski, on the St Lawrence River, to Moville, the port of Londonderry, in six days and 14 hours. In 1899, by which time she had made more than 150 round-trip crossings, she was re-engined with triple-expansion machinery, her second funnel was removed and her sailing rig was reduced to pole masts. Until 1905, she operated out of Liverpool, to Quebec and Montreal in the summer months, when the St Lawrence was ice-free, and to Halifax and St John, New Brunswick, with occasional extensions to Boston, in the winter. She was later relegated to the second-class service from Glasgow and was scrapped in 1914.

Country of origin:	Britain
Date of origin:	1880
Length:	134.3m (440ft 9in)
Beam:	14.1m (46ft 2in)
Tonnage:	5444 tonnes (5359 tons)
Machinery:	Single shaft, compound (later triple-expansion)
Service speed:	14 knots
Capacity:	150 1st class, 100 2nd class, 1000 3rd class
Constructor:	R. Napier & Sons, Glasgow

Princesse Elisabeth

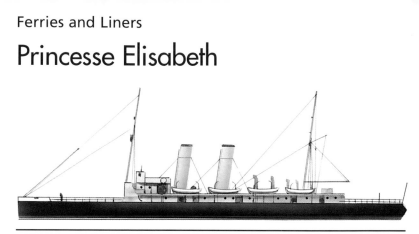

In the service between Ostend and Dover, the changeover from paddle wheels to turbine came in 1904 with the introduction of the *Princesse Elisabeth*. Although she had a design speed of 24 knots, during her trials off Greenock, Scotland, she achieved 26.25 knots, making her the fastest merchant ship afloat. As a result of her success, two more ships of similar design were built, entering service in 1910, with two more slightly smaller versions following on shortly afterwards. However, none of these vessels was as successful as the *Princesse Elisabeth*, and it was not until 1922 that a ship added to this service could match her performance. In fact, *Princesse Elisabeth* set a trend for fast ferry travel across the North Sea and could carry a sizeable payload of 900 passengers in reasonable comfort. This illustration shows her as she looked in 1904.

Country of origin:	Belgium
Date of origin:	1904
Length:	91.4m (300ft)
Beam:	11m (36ft)
Tonnage:	1795 tonnes (1767 tons)
Machinery:	Three shafts, turbines; 12,000hp
Service speed:	24 knots
Capacity:	900
Constructor:	John Cockerill, Hoboken

Queen Elizabeth II

The last Cunarder built for the transatlantic passenger service, the *QEII*, as she was popularly known from the outset, was an anachronism even before she was launched on 20 November 1967, airline travel having surpassed the seaborne trade. Her maiden voyage was delayed by five months because of mechanical trouble, which continued to plague her at intervals throughout her career. In 1974, she was left adrift off Bermuda after an engine failure; in 1975, she hit a coral reef off the Bahamas; and, in 1976, she was partially crippled by an engine-room fire while in the eastern Atlantic, forcing her return to Southampton. In 1982, she played a key role as a troopship in the Falklands war, and later, after a refit, she had an active career as a cruise liner. In 2000, she was still making occasional scheduled voyages between Southampton and New York.

Country of origin:	Britain
Date of origin:	1967
Length:	293.5m (963ft)
Beam:	32.1m (105ft)
Tonnage:	66,893 tonnes (65,836 tons)
Machinery:	Two shafts, geared turbines; later diesel-electric; 118,000hp
Service speed:	29 knots
Capacity:	564 1st class, 1441 tourist, 1820 standard
Constructor:	John Brown & Co., Glasgow

Queen Mary

The *Queen Mary* was built to take the Blue Riband and was to hold the record, both ways, until 1952. She was by no means an austere ship; in fact, she was a fitting successor to the *Aquitania*, with which she operated prior to World War II. Wartime service as a troopship was marred by a collision in October 1942 with the cruiser HMS *Curacoa*, which sank with the loss of most of her crew (there were only 26 survivors). Because of the danger from lurking U-boats, the *Queen Mary* was forbidden to stop in order to render assistance. During her career in mercantile service, the *Queen Mary* completed 1001 Atlantic crossings. In 1967, she was sold to the City of Long Beach, California, as a museum and hotel. To reach her new home, she had to round Cape Horn, being too wide by just one metre (39in) to pass through the Panama Canal.

Country of origin:	Britain
Date of origin:	1934
Length:	310.7m (1019ft 6in)
Beam:	36.1m (118ft 7in)
Tonnage:	82,040 tonnes (80,744 tons)
Machinery:	Four shafts, geared turbines; 160,000hp
Service speed:	29 knots
Capacity:	776 cabin, 784 tourist, 579 3rd class; 15,000 troops
Constructor:	John Brown & Co., Glasgow

Radisson Diamond

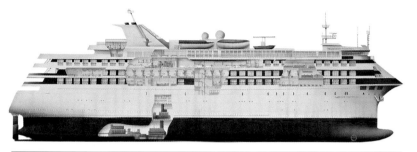

By the end of the twentieth century, cruise ships were little more than enormous floating luxury hotels, but the *Radisson Diamond* was slightly different. Much smaller than most, she was based on a catamaran hull form and had a length to beam ratio of little more than 4:1, which both maximized the deck area and improved her seakeeping and manoeuvrability. Her machinery was located low down in each hull and thus was removed from the passenger areas, which made her a very quiet craft indeed. She cruises in the Mediterranean, Caribbean and Baltic. Among the *Radisson Diamond*'s more unusual attractions were a 270m (295yard) jogging track and a hydraulic platform which could be lowered to the waterline between the hulls after to act as a boat dock. *Radisson Diamond* is a good example of the excellent and futuristic craft produced by Finnish shipyards.

Country of origin:	Finland
Date of origin:	1991
Length:	131m (423ft)
Beam:	32m (105ft)
Tonnage:	18,695 tonnes (18,400 tons)
Machinery:	Two shafts, diesels, bow thrusters; 15,200/2650hp
Service speed:	29 knots
Capacity:	354 standard
Constructor:	Finnyards OY, Rauma

Rex

In 1927, Navigazione Generale Italiana ordered what was to be the biggest passenger liner ever built in Italy, to supplement the *Roma* and *Augusta* on its Genoa–Côte d'Azur–New York service. From the outset, the *Rex* was meant to win the Blue Riband, until then the preserve of British and latterly German ships. She was thwarted by engine trouble on her maiden voyage, limping into New York to await the arrival of spares, and it was a year before she captured the record. Despite this, she never became popular among the wealthy passenger class; most of those she carried were westbound emigrants. *Rex* was laid up in the spring of 1940, just before Italy entered the war, first at Bari and then at Trieste. In September 1944, she fell victim to RAF air attack and sank in the Gulf of Muggia. Salvage proved economically unviable and scrapping began in 1947.

Country of origin:	Italy
Date of origin:	1931
Length:	268m (879ft)
Beam:	29.3m (96ft)
Tonnage:	51,882 tonnes (51,062 tons)
Machinery:	Four shafts, geared turbines; 136,000hp
Service speed:	28 knots
Capacity:	604 1st class, 378 2nd class, 410 tourist, 866 3rd class
Constructor:	Ansaldo, Genoa

St Louis

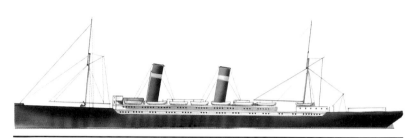

The *St Louis* and her sister ship the *St Paul* were the first American-built passenger liners with screw propulsion. The ships were constructed for the American Line's service between New York and Southampton, the passengers being accommodated in the usual three classes. In 1898, the *St Louis* was briefly taken up by the US Navy and employed as an armed merchant cruiser during the Spanish-American war. She resumed service in October that year. In 1903, she was reboilered and had her two funnels raised in height. Just prior to the outbreak of World War I, she was refitted with second- and third-class passenger accommodation only and was switched to the Liverpool service. She operated as a troopship from late 1918 to 1920, under the name *Louisville*. Damaged by fire during a refit, she was scrapped in 1924.

Country of origin:	USA
Date of origin:	1894
Length:	163.2m (535ft 6in)
Beam:	19.2m (63ft)
Tonnage:	11,816 tonnes (11,629 tons)
Machinery:	Two shafts, triple-expansion
Service speed:	19 knots
Capacity:	350 1st class, 220 2nd class, 800 3rd class
Constructor:	W Cramp & Co., Philadelphia

Savannah

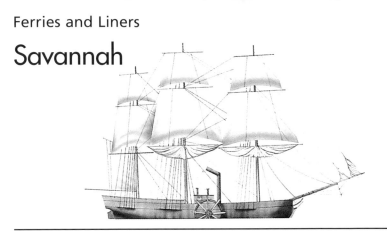

The *Savannah* was the first steam-powered vessel to cross the Atlantic. She was originally intended as a sailing packet for service to France. Before her completion, however, she was purchased by the Savannah Steam Ship Company, who had her adapted for auxiliary steam propulsion with collapsible paddle wheels that could be stored on deck. The engine and boilers occupied most of the hold between the fore and main masts, leaving little room for cargo. *Savannah* sailed from New York for Liverpool in May 1819, making the journey in 27 days and 11 hours. On this trip, she also visited the Baltic, sailing to Kronstadt on a sales trip that came to nothing. Upon her return to the United States, her engine was removed, and she served as a sailing ship until she ran aground during a storm off Long Island in 1821, becoming a total wreck.

Country of origin:	USA
Date of origin:	1818
Length:	33.5m (110ft)
Beam:	7.8m (25ft 8in)
Tonnage:	325 tonnes (320 tons)
Machinery:	Paddle wheels, single-cylinder engine
Service speed:	6 knots
Capacity:	32
Constructor:	Francis Fickett, New York

Silja Serenade

In the early 1990s, the Swedish Silja Line introduced a pair of ships onto its Stockholm–Helsinki service, describing them as 'cruise ferries'. The *Serenade* and the *Symphony* have accommodation for more than 2500 people and 450 cars, and has a service speed of 21 knots. They feature a ballroom big enough to hold 650 guests, a five-storey atrium running three-quarters the length of the ship, swimming pools and a 'show lounge', as well as the normal run of restaurants, discotheques and shops. These Baltic cruise ferries are some of the biggest and best appointed in the world, finished up to the best cruise ship standards. As is the case with the *Radisson Diamond*, vessels such as the *Silja Serenade* and *Symphony* are a testimony to the high and forward-looking standards of Finnish designers and shipyards.

Country of origin:	Sweden
Date of origin:	1991
Length:	203m (666ft 1in)
Beam:	31.9m (104ft 9in)
Tonnage:	59,313 tonnes (58,376 tons)
Machinery:	Two shafts, diesel; 44,300hp
Service speed:	21 knots
Capacity:	2656 passengers, 450 vehicles
Constructor:	Kvaerner Masa, Finland

Sirius

This Scottish-built paddle steamship, launched at Leith, was the first to cross the Atlantic under sustained steam power. Her engines had Samuel Hall's patent condensers fitted, preventing the boilers from caking up with sea salt, although these were only partially successful through lack of suitable lubrication. Although intended for work between Cork and London, she was chartered by a rival company to snatch the honour of making the first all-steam crossing from Brunel's *Great Western*. *Sirius* left Cork on 4 April 1838 and made New York in 18 days and 10 hours, a day ahead of *Great Western*, which had left three days after her. *Sirius* made one more transatlantic round voyage in July 1838 before returning to her short-sea routes. She was wrecked in Ballycotton Bay, off the south coast of Ireland, on 29 January 1847, while on the way from Glasgow to Cork.

Country of origin:	Britain
Date of origin:	1837
Length:	54.3m (178ft)
Beam:	7.6m (25ft)
Tonnage:	714 tonnes (713 tons)
Machinery:	Side wheels, sidelever engines
Service speed:	8 knots
Capacity:	19 cabin, 21 steerage
Constructor:	Not known

Society Adventurer

The *Society Adventurer* is a new-style luxury cruise expedition ship able to operate for up to eight weeks at a time without needing to take on extra fuel or provisions; she has a range of 16,150km (8500 miles). She was specifically designed for cruises to areas of special interest such as Antarctica, the Arctic, the South Pacific and the Amazon River. She can accommodate 188 passengers in well-appointed twin cabins fitted with closed-circuit televisions so that passengers can watch transmissions from specialist diving teams. There is an observation lounge on top of the bridge. There is a growing demand for the scientific expeditionary type of cruise such as that offered by *Society Adventurer*, which affords passengers the chance to visit exotic areas of the globe whilst remaining in comfort – representing the luxury end of the eco-tourism market.

Country of origin:	Bahamas
Date of origin:	1991
Length:	122.7m (402ft 8in)
Beam:	18m (59ft)
Tonnage:	8512 tonnes (8378 tons)
Machinery:	Two shafts, diesel engines
Service speed:	21 knots
Capacity:	188
Routes:	Arctic, Antarctic, South America, South Pacific

Suwa Maru

The *Suwa Maru* and her sister ship *Fushimi Maru* were the largest Japanese merchant ships of the time to operate from Japan to European waters. During World War I, the route to European ports was transferred from the Suez Canal to the long route round Africa. There was accommodation for 170 passengers, plus more than 300 steerage, but the latter were usually carried only on the ship's eastern routes. There were six holds, two continuous decks and a third partial deck, with three of the holds having partial decks. Bunker capacity was 4064 tonnes (4000 tons), and the vessel burned about 132 tonnes (130 tons) per day. *Suwa Maru* was sunk near Wake Island in March 1943. Nine US submarines were operating in the Central Pacific area at this time; the boat that torpedoed *Suwa Maru* was most probably the USS *Seadragon* (Lieutenant-Commander Rutter).

Country of origin:	Japan
Date of origin:	1914
Length:	157.3m (516ft)
Beam:	19m (62ft 6in)
Tonnage:	21,357 tonnes (21,020 tons)
Machinery:	Two-shaft, triple expansion engines
Service speed:	15.5 knots
Capacity:	170 1st/2nd class, 300 steerage
Constructor:	Not known

Teutonic

The White Star liner *Teutonic* and her sister ship, the *Majestic*, represented a milestone for their owners. Built, like all the White Star ships, by Harland & Wolff of Belfast, they were the first White Star passenger liners to have triple-expansion machinery. They were also the first in the world to dispense entirely with a sailing rig and the first to be built to incorporate Admiralty requirements to allow them to be transformed into armed merchant cruisers in time of war. *Teutonic* appeared for the first time at the 1889 Spithead Naval Review and, seven days later, made her maiden voyage from Liverpool to New York. In August 1891, she captured the Blue Riband. In 1914, after 25 years of mercantile service, she was taken up and armed, later operating as a troopship. She was sold for scrap in 1921.

Country of origin:	Britain
Date of origin:	1889
Length:	172.4m (565ft 9in)
Beam:	17.6m (57ft 9in)
Tonnage:	10,144 tonnes (9984 tons)
Machinery:	Two shafts, triple-expansion
Service speed:	19 knots
Capacity:	300 1st class, 190 2nd class, 1000 3rd class
Constructor:	Harland & Wolff, Belfast

Titanic

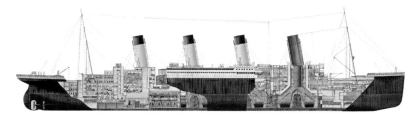

The White Star liner RMS *Titanic* left Southampton on her maiden voyage, bound for New York via Cherbourg and Queenstown (Cork) on 10 April 1912. By the afternoon of 14 April, the *Titanic* was some 1100km (600 nautical miles) east of Newfoundland. Her wireless operators received warnings of ice in her path, but her captain, Edward Smith, chose to ignore them and the ship continued at an undiminished 22 knots. At 23:40 hours, a lookout reported ice ahead. The First Officer gave orders to leave it to starboard, but the ship grazed an underwater spur, buckling her port side hull plates along the riveted seams. She sank, with the loss of 1503 of the 2223 people aboard, in less than two-and-a-half hours. Much of the resulting scandal centred on the disproportionate number of lives lost (75 per cent) among the third-class passengers.

Country of origin:	Britain
Date of origin:	1911
Length:	259.8m (852ft 6in)
Beam:	28.2m (92ft 6in)
Tonnage:	47,072 tonnes (46,328 tons)
Machinery:	Three shafts, triple-expansion; 50,000hp
Service speed:	21 knots
Capacity:	1034 1st class, 510 2nd class, 1022 3rd class
Constructor:	Harland & Wolff, Belfast

Tycho Brahe

The train and vehicle ferry *Tycho Brahe* was named after the Danish astronomer who was certainly the greatest observer of pre-telescope times – even though he remained convinced, until his death in 1601, that the Earth was at the centre of the solar system. She was built for Dansk Statsbaner to operate across the 5-km (2.7-mile) straits separating Helsingor in Denmark and Helsingborg in Sweden. She is the largest double-ended ferry in the world, with room for 260 trucks, 240 cars and nine railway passenger carriages. This double-ended construction ensures the fastest possible turnaround on what is one of the world's shortest international ferry routes. One of *Tycho Brahe*'s most important features is her ability to accelerate and decelerate to and from her 14-knot service speed over a very short distance.

Country of origin:	Denmark
Date of origin:	1991
Length:	111m (364ft)
Beam:	28.2m (92ft 6in)
Tonnage:	12,193 tonnes (12,000 tons)
Machinery:	Four shafts, diesel; 3350hp
Service speed:	14 knots
Capacity:	1250 passengers, 500 vehicles, six carriages
Constructor:	Langsten, Tomresfjord

United States

The SS *United States* was the most advanced passenger ship ever built when she entered service in 1952 and certainly the most powerful, being equipped with four 60,000hp turbines. These were originally intended for a cancelled aircraft carrier and gave her a top speed of more than 38 knots on trials. She had no trouble in taking both eastbound and westbound Blue Ribands – held for the past 14 years by the *Queen Mary* – on her maiden voyage and did not lose them until the mid-1990s, when they fell to a specially designed speedboat carrying just two 'paying passengers'. The *United States* was laid up in 1969 after just 17 years' service. Plans by a Turkish consortium to refurbish her came to nothing after she had been towed to the eastern Mediterranean and a great deal of money spent, and she was returned to the United States in 1996 to become a static exhibit in Philadelphia.

Country of origin:	USA
Date of origin:	1952
Length:	301.8m (990ft)
Beam:	31m (101ft 7in)
Tonnage:	54,185 tonnes (53,329 tons)
Machinery:	Four shafts, geared turbines; 240,000hp
Service speed:	34 knots
Capacity:	913 1st class, 558 cabin, 537 tourist
Constructor:	Newport News Shipbuilding & Dry Dock Co.

Vanderbilt

When first completed for the North Atlantic Mail Steamship Line, the *Vanderbilt* was one of the fastest, largest and most luxurious liners on the route. She had a top speed of 14 knots. In March 1862, she was taken over by the Union Navy and sent on a year-long patrol in search of the elusive Confederate frigate *Alabama*, which was wreaking havoc with the Union's commerce. After an overhaul, she was sent out again, sometimes missing *Alabama* by only a few hours. (The *Alabama* was eventually cornered and sunk by the Union ironclad frigate *Kearsarge* in the English Channel in 1864.) *Vanderbilt* was retained in the US Navy until 1873, then sold to a shipping company. Her machinery was removed and she was given a full rig. Renamed *Three Brothers*, she then spent most of her career in the grain trade. She was scrapped in 1899.

Country of origin:	USA
Date of origin:	1857
Length:	100.9m (331ft)
Beam:	14.5m (47ft 6in)
Tonnage:	3413 tonnes (3360 tons)
Machinery:	Paddle wheels, single-beam engine
Rigging:	Two masts, square-rigged
Service speed:	14 knots
Owner:	North Atlantic Mail Steamship Line

Voyager of the Seas

At the close of the twentieth century, Royal Caribbean Cruise's *Voyager of the Seas* was the world's biggest passenger ship. She is equipped with facilities which would not disgrace any land-based holiday resort. They include an ice rink big enough for hockey games, a putting course and driving range, a 1500 square metre (16,150 square foot) fitness centre, a climbing wall and even a wedding chapel, not to mention six restaurants and five bars. She has 2221 guest and crew staterooms and enormous public recreational areas on a total of 14 decks, with three others given over to the ship's services. All of this was completed in just 57 weeks by a workforce numbering 10,000. The ship has a crew of 1180 to look after the needs of her 3880 passengers, each of whom expects the voyage of a lifetime during a week spent cruising the Caribbean out of Florida.

Country of origin:	Norway
Date of origin:	1999
Length:	310.9m (1020ft)
Beam:	38.7m (127ft)
Tonnage:	139,504 tonnes (137,300 tons)
Machinery:	Three shafts, diesel-electric; 101,340hp
Service speed:	22 knots
Capacity:	3880 standard class
Constructor:	Kvaerner, Helsinki

Washington

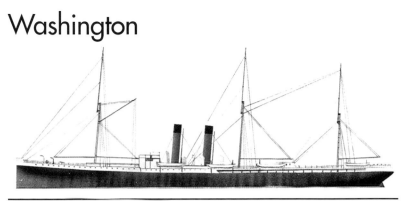

The first liner built for the Compagnie Général Transatlantique, the *Washington* was the forerunner of such famous liners as the *Normandie* of 1936. She had luxurious accommodation for 128 first-class and 54 second-class passengers, and she also carried 29 third-class passengers in steerage. In 1868, the *Washington* was converted to a twin-screw vessel with single-expansion engines. She was scrapped in 1900. By this time, the Atlantic crossing was firmly established as the 'voyage of voyages'. Money was in it and so therefore were the best and fastest ships in the world. The shipping companies played down the fact that the Atlantic is the roughest and hardest of oceans, especially in winter; even in summer, even for the steadiest of liners, the Atlantic was never the pond that it was sometimes depicted as being on the advertising posters.

Country of origin:	France
Date of origin:	1847
Length:	105.2m (345ft)
Beam:	13.4m (44ft)
Tonnage:	3462 tonnes (3408 tons)
Machinery:	Paddle wheels, sidelever engines
Service speed:	9 knots
Capacity:	128 1st class, 54 2nd class, 29 3rd class
Constructor:	Not known

British Skill

BP Oil's medium-capacity crude oil-carrying tanker *British Skill* was one of the most efficient ships afloat when she entered service in the early 1990s – although she was by no means one of the biggest; many contemporaries had well over twice her 130,054-tonne (128,000-ton) carrying capacity. Nevertheless, she is very representative of the smaller crude oil carriers that were a familiar sight on the world's oceans in the 1990s. Much of the running of the ship is entrusted to a computerized automatic pilot, and only when entering and leaving an anchorage is it necessary for the captain and pilots to assume manual control. *British Skill* shows the distinctive silhouette of a modern tanker, with the dominant superstructure housing the navigating bridge, living quarters and other facilities mounted near the stern.

Country of origin:	Britain
Date of origin:	1990
Length:	261m (856ft 3in)
Beam:	40m (131ft 3in)
Tonnage:	67,090 tonnes (66,034 tons)
Machinery:	Single shaft, diesel; 16,250hp
Service speed:	13.5 knots
Capacity:	130,054 tonnes (128,000 tons)
Constructor:	Harland & Wolff, Belfast

Dalmazia

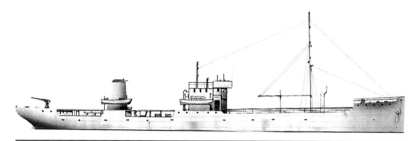

The *Dalmazia* was built by the Quarnaro shipyard, Fiume, and launched in 1922. She served the Italian Navy as a water carrier for many years. Unlike most of the Italian fleet, she survived World War II and was taken over by the Allies when the Italians concluded an armistice in September 1943. After refurbishment, she was re-allocated to the postwar Italian Navy and was reclassified as an oil carrier in 1958. In 1959, *Dalmazia* was joined by a second oiler, the *Sterope*; this vessel was a former US T2 type oiler and was refitted at La Spezia. *Dalmazia*'s engines developed 1450hp at full speed; she had a cargo capacity of 1829 tonnes (1800 tons). For her wartime service she was fitted with a modest armament: as well as carrying a 120mm (4.7in) gun, she was armed with two 20mm (0.79in) anti-aircraft weapons. She served until the late 1970s.

Country of origin:	Italy
Date of origin:	1922
Length:	80m (260ft)
Beam:	10m (32ft 6in)
Tonnage:	5080 tonnes (5000 tons)
Machinery:	Two shafts, triple-expansion engines
Service speed:	10 knots
Capacity:	1829 tonnes (1800 tons)
Constructor:	Quarnaro shipyard, Fiume

Esso Manchester

The *Esso Manchester* was one of the very successful T2-SE-A1 tankers, a standard design evolved in the United States in 1942. Production totalled 481 units, all built in four yards. The T2s were widely held to have been one of the most successful merchant ship designs of the period, and many were to stay in service long after World War II was over, often with new midsections and renewed engines. They performed a wide variety of roles, including that of floating power station. The *Esso Manchester*, formerly the *Santiago*, had a long career, but remained substantially unmodified when the Esso Company sold her for scrap in Scotland in 1963. Note the bridge structure, which in the typical tanker design fashion of the 1940s is situated amidships, with the after superstructure being placed over the engine room.

Country of origin:	USA
Date of origin:	1944
Length:	159.6m (523ft 6in)
Beam:	20.75m (68ft)
Tonnage:	10,616 tonnes (10,448 tons)
Machinery:	single shaft, turbo-electric; 6000hp
Service speed:	14.5 knots
Capacity:	Not known
Constructor:	Sun Shipbuilding & Drydock Co, Chester, Pennsylvania

Front Driver

The *Front Driver* was characteristic of a new breed of dual-purpose oil and bulk ore (OBO) carriers first introduced in the 1970s, with cargo space that amounted to about a quarter of a million cubic metres (327,000 cubic yards). *Front Driver* was designed with nine separate holds with large oil- and gas-tight covers, all of which could accommodate either oil or ore, as well as wing tanks for oil products. The OBO carriers were built in an attempt to reduce the time that ships of this type spent in ballast by allowing them to carry a different cargo in each direction, at least for part of the way. *Front Driver*, which entered service in April 1991, has a double-bottom hull which comprises 52 per cent high-tensile steel to provide extra strength. Although promising in concept, the demand for OBO carriers has been small.

Country of origin:	Sweden
Date of origin:	1991
Length:	285m (935ft)
Beam:	45m (147ft 8in)
Tonnage:	90,433 tonnes (89,004 tons)
Machinery:	Single shaft, diesel; 21,964hp
Service speed:	15 knots
Capacity:	171,860 tonnes (169,146 tons)
Constructor:	Hyundai Heavy Industries

Futura

The environmental impact of the grounding of a supertanker is so devastating, and the public outcry so loud, that oil companies have been forced to go to considerable lengths to improve the chances of an oil or petroleum products tanker surviving such an incident without releasing its cargo into the sea. The Dutch-owned *Futura* is a development of the standard bulk cargo or oil carrier. She was one of the first of a series to enter service that include improved safety features such as a double hull, the space between the two hulls being empty except for pumping equipment and gas venting pipes. Pumping facilities within the double hull eliminate the need for separate spaces to house this equipment in the cargo-carrying area. Tanks can be vented selectively, as required, by means of an extensive layout of ballast pipes.

Country of origin:	Finland
Date of origin:	1992
Length:	241m (790ft 8in)
Beam:	40m (131ft 3in)
Tonnage:	51,724 tonnes (50,907 tons)
Machinery:	Single shaft, diesel; 12,000hp
Service speed:	14 knots
Capacity:	97,540 tonnes (96,000 tons)
Constructor:	Wärtsilä

Halla

The carriage of cement in bulk has always been complicated by problems in discharging the cargo, which tends to compact in transit. Modern purpose-built cement carriers such as the *Halla* incorporate a pneumatic system, which blows air under pressure into the cargo from the floor of the hold, so that it can be picked up by a bucket chain conveyor and carried to the machinery room. There the cement is transferred to a bucket elevator and lifted to the overside discharge room, which is suspended from the lattice tower some 22m (72ft) above the main deck. To load the cargo, cement passes from the shore facility into a distribution tank on deck; it is then piped by four air slides into both holds. By the end of the twentieth century, there were hundreds of vessels afloat carrying Portland cement: some were converted bulk carriers, able to load almost 100,000 tonnes (984,000 tons).

Country of origin:	Korea
Date of origin:	1991
Length:	111.9m (367ft)
Beam:	17.8m (58ft 5in)
Tonnage:	10,594 tonnes (10,427 tons)
Machinery:	Single shaft, diesel; 10,000hp
Service speed:	12 knots
Loading capacity:	1000 tonnes (984 tons) per hour
Constructor:	Not known

Helice

The Norwegian-owned *Helice* is a typical example of a late twentieth-century mixed cargo tanker. Her hull is divided into four holds, each of which contains freestanding prismatic tanks fabricated from corrosion-resistant carbo-manganese steel and each positioned so that it is clearly separated from all the others. She can thus carry a variety of different liquid cargoes at one time. Each hold is equipped with two large-capacity cooling fans, those in the largest hold being capable of changing the air in it every eight minutes. This venting and purging system is necessary for the transportation of liquified petroleum gas. *Helice*'s engine room is fully automated to permit unmanned operation, which is common in modern-day vessels of her kind. Full automation has enabled crew numbers to be greatly reduced, thereby saving a good deal of cost to the operator.

Country of origin:	Norway
Date of origin:	1990
Length:	205m (672ft 7in)
Beam:	32m (105ft)
Tonnage:	50,292 tonnes (49,500 tons)
Machinery:	Single shaft, diesel; 15,000hp
Service speed:	16 knots
Capacity:	57,000 cubic metres (2 million cubic feet)
Constructor:	Kvaerner, Govan

Inverlago

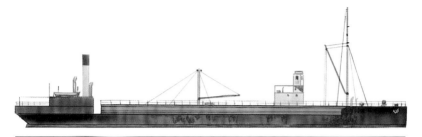

The *Inverlago* was the first of a small fleet of crude oil carriers constructed for use on Venezuela's Lake Maracaibo, an important oilfield, but one where local conditions were unique. On a draught of only just over 4m (13ft), she was able to carry 3200 tonnes (3150 tons) of cargo. As the channel into the lake was progressively deepened, larger ships came into service, and the need for these shallow-draught vessels had disappeared by 1953. Before *Inverlago* came into service, Royal Dutch Shell solved the problem of navigating the shallow waters of Lake Maracaibo by converting a number of former Royal Navy coastal monitors as tankers. These vessels, designed to approach close inshore in order to bombard land targets at relatively close range, proved reasonably effective, but their capacity was limited.

Country of origin:	The Netherlands
Date of origin:	1925
Length:	93m (305ft)
Beam:	11.6m (38ft)
Tonnage:	2642 tonnes (2600 tons)
Machinery:	Single shaft, triple-expansion; 1400hp
Service speed:	10 knots
Capacity:	3206 tonnes (3156 tons)
Constructor:	Harland & Wolff, Belfast

Isomeria

The *Isomeria* is a liquid gas and petroleum tanker, the gas being transported at a temperature of minus 162 degrees Celsius. Built by Harland & Wolff of Belfast, she is powered by two Burmeister and Wain diesel engines. These develop 18,600hp, which at 110 revolutions per minute consume 64 tonnes (63 tons) of fuel per day at 85 per cent power. The propeller has a surface area of 34.5 square metres (371 square feet); each of its four blades is 6.6m (21ft 7in) at its maximum width. The vessel is equipped with five electrically powered pumps, each of which can handle 450 cubic metres (15,892 cubic feet) of propane or butane gas per minute. *Isomeria*'s refrigeration tanks are produced by Kvaerner Kulde/Howdens. Like other vessels of her type, *Isomeria* is fully automated, reducing the number of crew members required to operate her.

Country of origin:	Britain
Date of origin:	1982
Length:	210m (688ft 10in)
Beam:	31.4m (102ft 11in)
Tonnage:	47,593 tonnes (48,357 tons)
Machinery:	Single shaft, diesel; 18,600hp
Service speed:	16.5 knots
Capacity:	Not known
Constructor:	Harland & Wolff, Belfast

Jakob Maersk

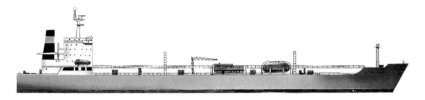

The Dutch-owned *Jakob Maersk* is one of a class of small (by the standards of the time) multi-cargo tankers, constructed with independent freestanding tanks in her four holds, lined with polyurethane to a thickness of 120mm (4.75in) to minimize damage in the event of an accident. She is equipped with an inert-gas generator and has forced-air systems incorporating dryers in each hold. Eight multi-stage centrifugal pumps are fitted for cargo handling, and the ship is equipped with a bow thruster to improve her manoeuvrability, a feature unique in tanker design. Like most ships of her type, the *Jakob Maersk* is highly automated and requires a crew of only 23 to operate her. Each crew member has the benefit of an individual cabin. The *Jakob Maersk* is an updated and enlarged version of an already proven and successful design.

Country of origin:	The Netherlands
Date of origin:	1991
Length:	185m (670ft)
Beam:	27.4m (90ft)
Tonnage:	43,205 tonnes (42,523 tons)
Machinery:	Single shaft, diesel
Service speed:	17 knots
Capacity:	Not known
Constructor:	Not known

Oilers and Tankers

Jo Alder

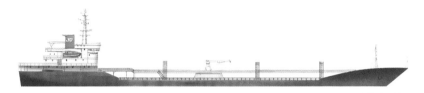

The multipurpose products tanker *Jo Alder* was constructed specifically to carry a variety of bulk liquids, including food products, in 25 stainless steel tanks constructed in her holds. Each tank has its own entirely self-contained pump and pipeline system, so in theory as many different cargoes as there were tanks could be carried at any one time without the risk of cross-contamination. All cargo management operations are computer controlled, and the engine room is designed for unmanned operation, the systems being monitored from the navigation bridge. The ship is double-hulled throughout, and the double bottom features toughened longitudinal transverse bulkheads, which also form the outer casings of the cargo tanks. The *Jo Alder* is typical of a new design of very versatile bulk liquid products carrier that first made its appearance in the 1980s.

Country of origin:	Italy
Date of origin:	1991
Length:	139m (456ft)
Beam:	21.3m (69ft 9in)
Tonnage:	12,801 tonnes (12,600 tons)
Machinery:	Single shaft, diesel; 16,400hp
Service speed:	14 knots
Capacity:	14,250 cubic metres (503,234 cubic feet)
Constructor:	Societa Esercizio Cantieri, Viareggio

Landsort

With a deadweight capacity of almost 152,400 tonnes (150,000 tons), the Swedish tanker *Landsort* was by no means the biggest crude oil and oil products carrier of her day. She was, however, the first built to conform to new International Maritime Organisation rules laid down after the grounding of the *Exxon Valdez* off Alaska, which caused huge devastation to local ecosystems. She was double-hulled throughout, with wing tanks filled with water ballast. The new layout was intended to reduce the risk of cargo loss should the vessel take the ground. Her cargo space was divided into nine self-contained tanks, each one with its own discharge pump capable of delivering 1500 cubic metres (53,000 cubic feet) per hour. At the time of her entry into service, *Landsort* had the largest rudder in the world, with an overall area of 58 square metres (624 square feet).

Country of origin:	Sweden
Date of origin:	1991
Length:	274m (899ft)
Beam:	48m (157ft 6in)
Tonnage:	165,646 tonnes (163,038 tons)
Machinery:	Single shaft, diesel; 19,200hp
Service speed:	14 knots
Capacity:	166,747 cubic metres (5,888,620 cubic feet)
Constructor:	Daewoo Shipbuilding & Heavy Machinery Co.

Marinor

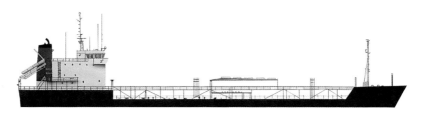

One of the late twentieth-century vessels that were built for a very specific purpose, *Marinor* is an unusual tanker in that she can transport a cargo mix of china clay and chemicals. She was designed for a specific charter centred on the east coast of North America and the Caribbean, which involved carrying china clay liquid for the paper industry alongside chemicals such as sulphuric acid. Twelve tanks are formed along the centreline bulkhead, and these are all lined with stainless steel to resist the corrosive effect of strong chemicals. The steel also helps to strengthen the ship's structure and contributes towards a saving in weight. The tanks are connected in pairs, six being for clay and six, plus a small bow tank, for chemicals. All the tanks have deck-mounted heaters which are connected to the main boilers.

Country of origin:	Britain
Date of origin:	1993
Length:	112.2m (368ft)
Beam:	18m (59ft)
Tonnage:	10,842 tonnes (10,672 tons)
Machinery:	Single shaft, diesel; 6120hp
Service speed:	14 knots
Capacity:	8500 cubic metres (300,175 cubic feet)
Constructor:	Welgelegen, The Netherlands

Mayon Spirit

The *Mayon Spirit* was one of the greatly improved tanker designs that made their appearance in the early 1980s, featuring the now mandatory double hull that provides effective protection against cargo spillage and its consequent polluting effect on the environment in the event of an accident. Such pollution can sometimes take an ecosystem years to recover from. Provision was made for a 2m (6ft 6in) space between the two hulls in the double bottom and a greater space in the wing tanks. Within this double-skin arrangement, there is only one central cargo tank in a midships position, plus small side tanks. Three pumps monitored from the control room handle cargo. Automation makes the ship simple to manage, so that the total complement is only 38. Even so, this is large by the standards of later tankers of this size, which nowadays can be managed by a crew of just 24.

Country of origin:	Liberia
Date of origin:	1981
Length:	253m (830ft 2in)
Beam:	41.2m (135ft 2in)
Tonnage:	100,000 tonnes (98,507 tons)
Machinery:	Single shaft, diesel engine
Service speed:	14 knots
Capacity:	120,043 cubic metres (4,239,285 cubic feet)
Constructor:	Not known

Northwest Sanderling

The *Northwest Sanderling*, which entered service in 1995, was designed specifically to carry natural gas in liquid form. She is the first of eight units in the Northwest class, ordered by an Anglo-Australian-Japanese consortium. The principal source of the natural gas carried by *Northwest Sanderling* is Withnell Bay, on the Burrup Peninsula in Western Australia. Gas is pumped to a shore station and is subjected to a temperature of minus 160 degrees Celsius, at which point it becomes liquid and its volume reduces to one six-hundredth of the original. This occurs because the cooling process lowers the speed of the gas molecules to the point where the forces of attraction overcome the velocity of the molecules, enabling them to bind together. At its destination, the cargo is brought back to its original state for normal consumption.

Country of origin:	Japan
Date of origin:	1995
Length:	271.9m (892ft)
Beam:	47.2m (154ft 9in)
Tonnage:	93,000 tonnes (91,530 tons)
Machinery:	Single shaft, turbine
Service speed:	18.5 knots
Capacity:	125,000 cubic metres (4,413,750 cubic feet)
Constructor:	Mitsubishi Heavy Industries, Nagasaki

Theodora

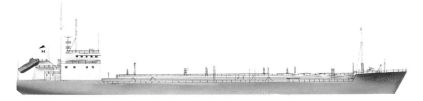

The Netherlands-registered *Theodora* is one of a relatively small number of specialist chemical products tankers designed to carry high-temperature cargoes (in other words, materials such as asphalt, bituminous coal, boiler oil creosote and antracene oil) which solidify on cooling and therefore become impossible to unload. Cargoes are carried in three separate steel tanks which rest on flexible foundations welded to the ship's hull, thereby allowing for expansion or contraction of the material. The temperature of the tanks is controlled by pumps and heat exchangers. *Theodora* has a double hull with 13 ballast tanks, these being completely separate from the cargo system. Like most chemical product carriers, Theodora operated to a schedule which was prepared months in advance and so she had no need for powerful machinery.

Country of origin:	The Netherlands
Date of origin:	1991
Length:	110.6m (362ft 10in)
Beam:	17m (55ft 9in)
Tonnage:	5080 tonnes (5000 tons)
Machinery:	Single shaft, diesel; 3570hp
Service speed:	14 knots
Capacity:	5155 cubic metres (182,050 cubic feet)
Constructor:	Meuwede, Giessendam

Alma Doepel

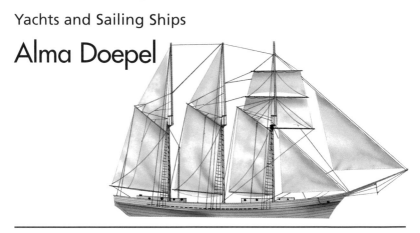

The topsail schooner *Alma Doepel* was constructed on the Bellinger River in New South Wales, to trade between there, Sydney and Hobart, a task she carried out for 56 years. During that time, she crossed the notorious Bass Strait – the waterway that separates the Australian mainland from Tasmania, where Hobart is situated – 578 times. After a period spent laid up, followed by 14 years as a motorized barge, with her masts and rigging removed, she was restored to her original condition for use as a sail training vessel at a cost of AUD$3 million. The restoration work was very extensive and took 12 years to complete, but the schooner subsequently became a great attraction in the waters around Melbourne. She epitomized the fascination for sailing ships that still exists everywhere. She is now owned and operated by Sail & Adventure Ltd.

Country of origin:	Australia
Date of origin:	1903
Length:	35.4m (116ft 2in)
Beam:	8.1m (26ft 6in)
Tonnage:	152.4 tonnes (151 tons)
Rigging:	Schooner-rigged
Complement:	Not known
Construction:	Wood
Built for:	Frederick Doepel, Bellinger

America

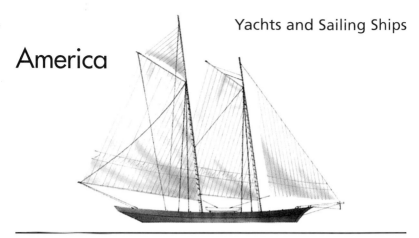

Her name perpetuated in the America's Cup, this schooner yacht had a varied career over more than 90 years. She was designed to be the fastest racing schooner of the day and specifically to win honours from British yachts in British waters. This she triumphantly did by winning the Royal Yacht Squadron's Cup at Cowes, Isle of Wight, on 22 August 1851. Between 1853 and 1861, *America* had several owners. The first renamed her *Camilla* and took her on a cruise to the Mediterranean; on her return in 1861, she was sold to the Confederate government, who used her as a blockade runner. Scuttled during the Civil War, she was later raised and used as a training ship by the US Navy. She continued to race for more than 30 years before being laid up. She was presented to the US Naval Academy, but her condition deteriorated and she was broken up in 1945.

Country of origin:	USA
Date of origin:	1851
Length:	33.8m (110ft 11in)
Beam:	7.6m (25ft)
Tonnage:	103.6 tonnes (102 tons)
Rigging:	Two masts, schooner rig
Complement:	25
Construction:	Wood
Built for:	Six members of the New York Yacht Club

Amerigo Vespucci

The Italian Navy's principal sail training ship during much of the second half of the twentieth century was the *Amerigo Vespucci*. She was purpose-built for the task from a design by Engineer Francesco Rotundi at the beginning of the 1930s, with accommodation for a large crew in addition to 170 cadets. Unlike other contemporary sail training ships, she was built to resemble a fourth- or fifth-rate ship of the line of an earlier period, with scuttles replacing gunports. However, the subterfuge was not complete; she had a modern rig and a clipper bow. She is one of the largest sailing ships in the world today. Somewhat unusually for a sail training ship, she also had a fairly sophisticated diesel-electric power plant. *Amerigo Vespucci* had a near-identical sister, the *Cristofero Colombo*, which was ceded to the Soviet Union after World War II.

Country of origin:	Italy
Date of origin:	1930
Length:	82m (269ft)
Beam:	15.5m (50ft 9in)
Tonnage:	3602 tonnes (3545 tons)
Rigging:	Three masts, square-rigged
Complement:	228 crew, 170 cadets
Construction:	Steel
Built for:	Italian Navy

Arethusa

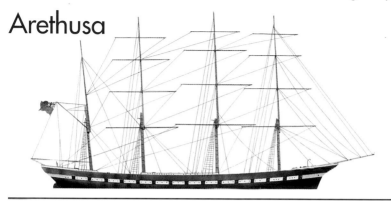

The four-masted barque *Arethusa* was originally named *Peking*. She was built for the German Flying 'P' Line to carry nitrates from Chile to Europe via Cape Horn. The *Peking* was captured by the British as she was running for home during World War I. She was laid up until 1932, when she was acquired by a British charity, the Shaftesbury Homes for Poor Boys, and converted into a school ship as the *Arethusa*. She took over from a former Royal Navy frigate of the same name (which had gained the distinction of being the last RN warship to go into battle under sail alone). *Arethusa* was well equipped, with three decks giving plenty of space for accommodation and drill. In more recent years, she was bought by New York's South Street Seaport Museum and, since 1975, has been open to the public with whom she is a popular exhibit to explore.

Country of origin:	Germany
Date of origin:	1911
Length:	97.5m (320ft)
Beam:	13.5m (4ft 3in)
Tonnage:	3242 tonnes (3191 tons)
Rigging:	Four masts, barque-rigged
Complement:	Not known
Construction:	Steel
Built for:	Reederei Ferdinand Laeisz

Atlantic

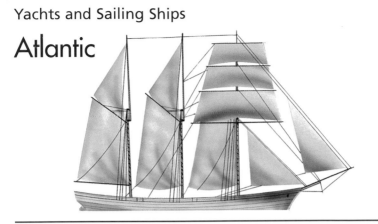

C onstructed by Townsend & Downey of Shooters Island, New York, the three-masted topsail schooner *Atlantic* was one of 12 vessels which competed for the 1905 Emperor's Cup, a prize put up by Germany's Kaiser Wilhelm for a race between New York and the Lizard (the extreme tip of Cornwall). *Atlantic* won the cup by achieving a time of 12 days and 4 hours; in one 24-hour period, she ran 645km (348 nautical miles). She was taken up by the US Navy in both world wars and was eventually acquired by the US Coast Guard Academy. Although the *Atlantic* was built as a racing craft, she had stateroom accommodation for seven people. The fastest sailing ship ever to cross the North Atlantic was the four-masted barque *Lancing*, which in 1916 made the voyage from New York to Cape Wrath, Scotland, in an astonishing 6 days and 18 hours.

Country of origin:	USA
Date of origin:	1903
Length:	56.4m (185ft)
Beam:	9m (29ft 6in)
Tonnage:	307.8 tonnes (303 tons)
Rigging:	Three masts, schooner-rigged
Complement:	Not known
Construction:	Steel
Built for:	Wilson Marshall

Bluenose

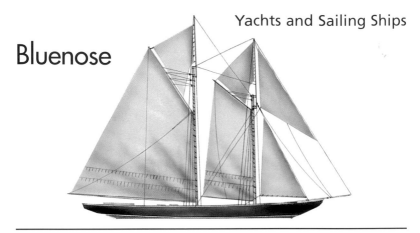

Constructed by Smith & Rhuland of Lunenburg in Nova Scotia, the Grand Banks fishing schooner *Bluenose* had a dual personality. When the fishing season was over, in October, she raced for the International Trophy, put up by the *Halifax Herald* as a rival to the America's Cup. She was built specially for the competition and won it easily at her first attempt in 1921, again in 1922, in 1930 and in 1937, its final year. Sold to the West Indies Trading Company in 1942, she was wrecked off Haiti in 1946. In 1963, the government of Nova Scotia commissioned the two-masted gaff topsail schooner *Bluenose II*, an exact replica of the original ship. The name 'Bluenose' was traditionally applied to the hardy Nova Scotians who fished for cod in the waters of the Grand Banks; it was a dangerous area, with notoriously unpredictable weather.

Country of origin:	Canada
Date of origin:	1921
Length:	43.6m (143ft)
Beam:	8.2m (27ft)
Tonnage:	289.5 tonnes (285 tons)
Rigging:	Two masts, gaff topsail rig
Complement:	Not known
Construction:	Wood
Built for:	International Trophy Race

Britannia

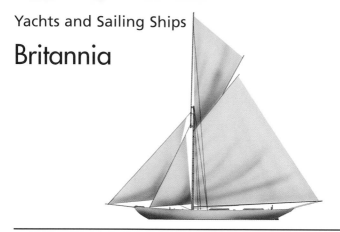

By the end of the 1880s, the United States had produced a number of successful yachts for competition in the America's Cup. The hull design was of a cutter, and stability was achieved by using a thin metal plate fin, as well as concentrating the ballast as low as possible. This class of yacht gained great favour in Britain as well as in the United States, and, in 1892, *Britannia*, a cutter-rigged yacht based on the American design, was ordered for the Prince of Wales, later to be Edward VII. Upon his death, the yacht was handed over to his son, George V, who successfully took part in some 624 regattas, winning 360 prizes with her. In the 1920s, the rig was altered to resemble a J-class yacht. *Britannia* was sunk off Cowes upon the death of George V in 1936. During her career, she took 231 first places and 129 second or third places.

Country of origin:	Britain
Date of origin:	1893
Length:	36.5m (120ft)
Beam:	7m (24ft)
Tonnage:	264 tonnes (260 tons)
Rigging:	Cutter rig
Complement:	24
Construction:	Composite, wood on iron
Built for:	HRH Prince of Wales

Calypso

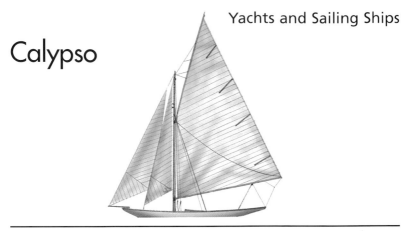

Lac Leman, which sits astride the Franco-Swiss border with the major cities of Geneva and Lausanne on its banks, was home to many racing yachts, among them the classic shallow-draught Godinet cutters, with their extreme straight-leech gunter rig. *Calypso* was a superb example of the type, and is now owned by the French Musée de la Marine and displayed at Dives-sur-Mer in Normandy, having been restored to her original condition. She was originally constructed by Chantiers Guedon at Lormont. No one knows for certain when yacht racing began in this land-locked area – the sport's history is much better documented in other places. The first recorded yachts, for example, were six sailing vessels that took part in a water festival held at Amsterdam in honour of Prince William of Orange on 17 March 1580. This rapidly became an annual event.

Country of origin:	France
Date of origin:	1911
Length:	12.6m (41ft 3in)
Beam:	2.4m (7ft 10in)
Tonnage:	3 tonnes (3 tons)
Rigging:	Gunter rig
Complement:	Two
Construction:	Wood
Built for:	Pictet de Rochement

Dar Pomorza

It was not until the introduction of the triple-expansion engine that sail power gave way completely to steam, and, as late as the 1880s, many steamships still carried auxiliary sails. Accordingly, a great many sailing vessels continued to be built after 1900 and were often fitted with small auxiliary motors to assist passage in times of calm. *Dar Pomorza* was one such vessel. Built by Blohm und Voss, Hamburg, to the order of the German Training Ship Association, she was launched as the *Prinzess Eitel Friedrich*. She was handed over to France after World War I, but was acquired by the Polish Merchant Navy Academy in 1929, becoming the *Dar Pomorza,* and in the next 50 years she trained 13,000 cadets and sailed 800,000km (500,000 miles). She was a member of the Tall Ships fleet from 1972, when she won the race, until she was retired to become a static museum exhibit at Gdynia in 1981.

Country of origin:	Germany
Date of origin:	1909
Length:	72.8m (239ft)
Beam:	12.5m (41ft)
Tonnage:	1646 tonnes (1620 tons)
Rigging:	Three masts, square-rigged
Complement:	290 (including 200 cadets)
Construction:	Steel
Built for:	German Training Ship Association

Eagle

Originally constructed by Blohm und Voss for the Kriegsmarine (German Navy) as the *Horst Wessel*, the *Eagle* was renamed when she was commissioned into the US Coast Guard after being awarded to the United States as a war reparation in 1946. A sister ship to the original *Gorch Fock*, which was later acquired by the Soviet Union and renamed *Tovarishch*, and the Portuguese Navy's *Sagres II* (originally the *Albert Leo Schlageter*), *Eagle* was easily recognizable in her standard US Coast Guard livery of white hull with a broad diagonal red stripe forward. During her wartime service with the German Navy as the *Horst Wessel*, the ship was in the Baltic as part of the Fleet Training Squadron, together with the *Schlageter*. The ships were named after 'martyred' henchmen of Adolf Hitler from the early days of the Nazi Party.

Country of origin:	Germany
Date of origin:	1936
Length:	81.1m (266ft)
Beam:	11.9m (39ft)
Tonnage:	1660 tonnes (1634 tons)
Rigging:	Three masts, square-rigged
Complement:	289 (including 200 cadets)
Construction:	Steel
Built for:	Kriegsmarine

Esmeralda

The *Esmeralda* was a purpose-built sail training ship completed in 1952. She was completed at Cadiz for the Spanish Navy and was originally to have been named *Don Juan de Austria*. However, on 12 May 1953, the new vessel was transferred to the Chilean Navy and renamed *Esmeraldo*. She served as a training ship for cadets and also took part in several tall ships races. Her total complement was 271, which included 190 cadets. Her single Fiat diesel engine developed 1400hp and range under engine p l ower alone was 15,200km (8000 miles). Her four-masted schooner rig carried 2392 square metres (26,910 square feet) of canvas. She proved a useful asset to the Chilean Navy, which since its foundation had always maintained high standards of efficiency and had often proved its superiority over the navies of neighbouring nations.

Country of origin:	Spain
Date of origin:	1951
Length:	94m (308ft 6in)
Beam:	13m (43ft)
Tonnage:	3731 tonnes (3673 tons)
Rigging:	Four masts, schooner rig
Complement:	271 (including 90 cadets)
Construction:	Steel
Built for:	Spanish Navy

Shamrock V

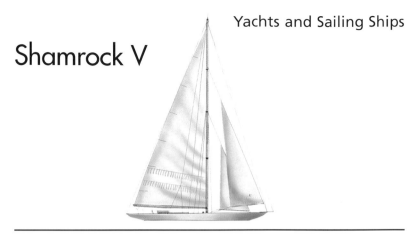

The cutter-rigged *Shamrock V*, like all her predecessors, was built for Sir Thomas Lipton to challenge for the America's Cup. She was built by Camper and Nicholson to J-class rules and lost out to the American *Resolute*. She was then sold to Tommy (later Sir Thomas) Sopwith (the celebrated World War I aircraft designer, who was responsible for the Sopwith Camel and other notable types), who used her as a trials boat for his two cup attempts. The *Shamrock V* later passed into Italian hands and was re-rigged as a cruising ketch. In the 1980s, she was acquired by the Museum of Yachting at Newport, Rhode Island, and restored. Only a handful of yachts were built to the J-class, or 'universal' rules, which permitted waterline length to vary between 22.86m (75ft) and 26.5m (87ft). Such vessels required a crew of 24.

Country of origin:	Britain
Date of origin:	1930
Length:	36.5m (119ft 9in)
Beam:	6.8m (19ft 8in)
Tonnage:	105.6 tonnes (104 tons)
Rigging:	Ketch rig
Complement:	24
Construction:	Composite, wood on steel
Built for:	Sir Thomas Lipton

Yeng He

Now located in the grounds of Beijing's Summer Palace, this iron-hulled paddlewheel steam yacht was presented by the Japanese Emperor to the last Manchu Emperor of China on his accession in 1909. Its earlier history is obscure, but it was probably built in Britain in the mid-nineteenth century, shipped out in parts and assembled in Japan. Since the Chinese Empire came to an end in 1911, it was scarcely used. The hull remains intact. The Summer Palace grounds also feature a stone-built pavilion designed to resemble a sidewheel river steamer. At the time the *Yeng He* was built, Japan had no shipbuilding industry of her own and relied entirely on foreign yards for any craft other than her native junks. It was not until about 1875 that Japanese shipyards began construction of their own. Today, Japan is one of the world's most prolific shipbuilding countries.

Country of origin:	Japan
Date of origin:	c. 1850
Length:	20m (65ft 7in)
Beam:	3.6m (11ft 10in)
Tonnage:	Not known
Rigging:	Not applicable
Complement:	Not known
Construction:	Iron
Built for:	Emperor of Japan

Index

Note: Page numbers in **bold** refer to main entries.